FAKES &
FORGERIES

FAKES & FORGERIES

THE TRUE CRIME STORIES of HISTORY'S GREATEST DECEPTIONS
The Criminals, the Scams, and the Victims

BRIAN INNES

Reader's Digest

The Reader's Digest Association, Inc.
Pleasantville, New York/Montreal/Sydney

A READER'S DIGEST BOOK

This edition published by The Reader's Digest Association, Inc., by arrangement with Amber Books Ltd

Copyright © 2005 Amber Books Ltd

Editorial and design by
Amber Books Ltd
Bradley's Close
74–77 White Lion Street
London N1 9PF
United Kingdom
www.amberbooks.co.uk

FOR AMBER BOOKS
Project Editor: James Bennett
Design: Jerry Williams
Picture Research: Natasha Jones

Jacket Design: George Berrian

FOR READER'S DIGEST
U.S. Project Editor: Marilyn J. Knowlton
Canadian Project Editor: Pamela Johnson
Project Designer: Jennifer R. Tokarski
Senior Designer: George McKeon
Executive Editor, Trade Publishing: Dolores York
President & Publisher, Books & Music: Harold Clarke

Library of Congress Cataloging in Publication Data:

Innes, Brian
    Fakes and forgeries: the true crime stories of history's greatest deceptions : the criminals, the scams, and
    the victims / Brian Innes.

        p. cm.
    Includes index.
    ISBN 0-7621-0625-5
    1. Forgery--History. 2. Swindlers and swindling--History. 3. Fraud--History. I. Title.

HV6675.I55 2005
364.16'3--dc22

                                                                    2005046462

Address any comments about *Fakes & Forgeries* to:
        The Reader's Digest Association, Inc.
        Adult Trade Publishing
        Reader's Digest Road
        Pleasantville, NY 10570-7000

For more Reader's Digest products and information, visit our websites:
        www.rd.com (in the United States)
        www.readersdigest.ca (in Canada)
        www.readersdigest.com.au (in Australia)

Printed in Singapore

1 3 5 7 9 10 8 6 4 2

CONTENTS

INTRODUCTION

This book explores "the tangled web we weave, when first we practice to deceive." Here deception takes the form of the "three Fs"—fake, forgery, and fraud activities that represent three steps on the way to crime.

A **fake** is a copy of something genuine that already exists or is recorded as having previously existed. This may be a document of any kind—an item of currency, a letter, a manuscript or a book—or a work of art. It can also involve the assumption of a false identity or that of another person, living or dead.

A **forgery** is the attribution of a fake to the originator of the item that has been copied. This might mean adding that person's name to the false copy. It can be a false signature added to a document or a work of art or the provision of supporting evidence that could identify the originator. Up to this point, in general, no crime has been committed. After all, many amateur artists make copies of paintings by Van Gogh or Matisse, for example, and some—though only for fun—even add the painter's signature.

However, if the forger then intends to profit from the forgery whether by offering the forged item for sale in some way or by using it as some other means of gaining money—this is known as **fraud**, and it is a criminal act.

By law, someone who copies an item of currency, for example, even without attempting to put it into circulation, is deemed guilty of forgery or, more accurately, counterfeiting. And a person who adopts another's name with criminal intent or who represents himself, or herself, as something other than his or her true self is moving directly from simply faking to committing an act of fraud.

As we will see in this book, almost anything, at one time or another, has been faked or forged. And it has not just been famous works of art, banknotes, and other fiscal items, wills, identity documents, furniture, jewels or pottery. Over the years, unscrupulous forgers have poured all their skill and concentration into producing fake bottles of whiskey, for example, and all sorts of merchandise, including everything from designer jeans to cans of beans.

A negative image of the Shroud of Turin, long believed to be the cloth in which Jesus was wrapped after the crucifixion. Carbon dating suggests the cloth is only around 700 years old.

CHAPTER 1
FUNNY MONEY

For many years the British criminal classes have referred to counterfeit currency as "funny money." In fact, the serious history of forging goes back nearly 25 centuries.

The concept of trading one kind of goods for another developed very early in human history. People adopted the idea of using tokens, such as beads or seashells, in exchange for practical products like food or weapons. This eventually became formalized in the minting of coins. The earliest state-sponsored production of coinage probably took place in Asia Minor in the seventh century B.C.E. Greek traders throughout the eastern Mediterranean soon followed this example, and in the fourth century B.C.E. the practice spread to the newly established state of Rome. Around the same time, the Chinese also began minting coins, which found their way to Japan, Korea and India. Most of the coins found in the West were made of silver or gold, and counterfeiters soon began to copy them.

Opposite: The £5 banknote is the lowest denomination presently issued by the Bank of England, but it has nevertheless attracted the activity of counterfeiters.

Left: Even the one-euro coin, with a value around only U.S. $1, has been forged by enterprising criminals.

It was relatively easy to detect the counterfeit coins, however, because they were lighter in weight than authentic coins. Gold was the heaviest metal known at the time; it was even heavier than lead covered with a thin coating of gold foil. A handful of forged gold coins might have seemed genuine at first glance, but weighing them quickly proved they were false. On the other hand, soldering silver foil onto a copper base made a plausible imitation of a silver coin, and forged silver coins dating from as far back as 400 B.C.E. have been discovered.

FOOLING THE COLLECTORS

The hobby of collecting coins is actually a fairly old one. In Europe, people began collecting antique coins as long ago as the seventeenth century, and their collections quickly acquired a market value far greater than their metal content. Forgers, naturally attracted by the possibility of making money, sold fakes to collectors, and many collections have been found to contain blatant forgeries.

HOW IT'S DONE

Genuine coins are usually "struck" from molten metal under pressure between two engraved dies. Early forgers (and many more recent ones) did not have the technology for this. They made casts in terra-cotta or plaster from genuine coins in order to form their molten metal. As a result, counterfeit coins usually do not have such a sharp image, and their edges are less well defined.

FAKING ANTIQUE COINS

Carl Wilhelm Becker (1772–1830) was born in Speyer, Germany, the son of a wine

The coins on the left are eighteenth-century forgeries of Roman coins by Carl Wilhelm Becker. The originals are on the right.

FORGER'S FILE
THE EUREKA MOMENT

Many are familiar with the story of Archimedes running naked through the streets yelling "Eureka!" But how many know that Archimedes was in fact an early "fake-buster"? Archimedes (c.287–212 B.C.E.) was a Greek mathematician and inventor who was born in Syracuse, Sicily. He is most famous for a discovery known as the Archimedes Principle.

Hieron II, king of Syracuse, had asked Archimedes if he could determine whether a crown that had been made for him was pure gold, as he had been told, or an inferior mixture of gold and silver. Weighing it would prove nothing, because there was no way of knowing how much the crown should weigh if it were solid gold. According to legend, Archimedes was puzzling over this problem one day while making use of the public baths—then a popular pastime in Syracuse. As he stepped into the bath, he noticed that his body made the water overflow.

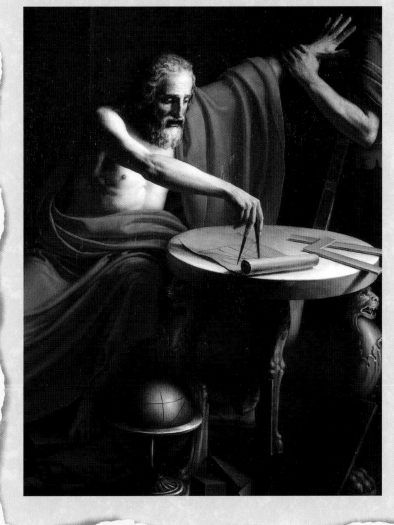

Suddenly it dawned on him that since gold is more dense than silver, he could test the "gold" crown by putting it into a container full of water and measuring how much water was displaced. If it displaced more water than an equal weight of solid gold, then it was a fake.

Archimedes is said to have been so excited by this discovery that he forgot to get dressed and ran naked through the streets to his home, shouting *"Eureka!"* ["I have found it!"]

After the capture of Syracuse by Roman forces in 212 B.C.E., Archimedes was murdered by one of the soldiers.

dealer. Having failed in business, in his mid-thirties he went to study at the Mint in Munich, where he learned the craft of engraving dies. He made perfect copies of Greek, Roman and medieval coins, which he struck in gold and silver. Becker sold these to dealers, among whom was T. E. Mionnet, the author of a vast work on ancient coins, who in turn sold them to private collectors.

To enhance the deception, many of the coins were treated to make them appear older than they were. There is a story that Becker aged them in what he called his *Kütscherbüchse* [carriage can]. This was a metal box filled with iron filings, attached to the axle of his carriage.

Like many forgers, Becker made only a small profit. A set of 269 coins, sold to Mionnet for 1,350 florins, cost him 550 florins to make. It is estimated that a genuine set (and no one knows whether Mionnet sold the fakes as genuine) would have been valued at 67,000 florins.

By 1826, Becker's eyesight was failing, and he could no longer continue engraving. When he died two years later, his widow used the 331 dies he left behind to produce cheap copies of coins in lead. The dies went later to the Imperial Museum in Berlin.

Although it is now relatively rare, people are still counterfeiting coins to this day. False copies of new euro coins, worth only U.S. $1 and U.S. $2, have been found in circulation.

WORTH ITS WEIGHT IN METAL?

For some time during the nineteenth century, platinum, which is slightly heavier than gold, was used for coinage in certain countries, including Russia. When output of the metal exceeded demand, the price of platinum fell below even that of silver, and counterfeiters were able to produce platinum coins, thinly covered with gold. Because the coins felt like the right weight in the hand, many people were deceived.

More enterprising counterfeiters realized that the price of gold bullion was often less than the face value of coins minted by the state authorities. Some forgers have therefore been able to copy the coinage with genuine gold. When real gold is used, this activity is defined as "illegal manufacture" rather than counterfeiting. It is still

FORGER'S FILE
DON'T GET CLIPPED!

All sorts of ingenious methods to produce fake money have been developed over the last 2,000 years. But fake currency threatens the economy of the state, so for many centuries counterfeiting was defined as a crime of treason, punishable by death. Petty criminals avoided this penalty by cutting small pieces from genuine coins, melting the fragments together and casting new pieces, earning them the name "clippers." When caught, having their ears or noses similarly clipped made such criminals immediately identifiable.

considered a crime, however, because it makes illegal use of official marks.

During the twentieth century, gold and silver coins gradually went out of use in most developed countries. The only coins now produced for circulation are those of relatively small denominations, made from base metals such as copper and nickel. The cost of the metal may well be equal to, or greater than, the face value of the coin, and this, combined with the workmanship involved, has made the counterfeiting of coinage generally uneconomic.

Although it is now relatively rare, people are still counterfeiting coins to this day. False copies of new euro coins, worth only U.S. $1 and U.S. $2, have been found in circulation.

A BIG CHANGE IN SMALL CHANGE

At one time in the 1970s, coins of small denominations vanished from circulation in Italy. To compensate, typewritten notes, subway tickets, telephone tokens and even candy were used as change. Apparently, some enterprising Japanese had discovered that the metal content of the coins was worth more than their face value and steadily bought up all that was available.

PROBLEMS FOR COUNTERFEITERS

Producers of counterfeit money faced, and still face, two difficulties: One is the technical problem of manufacturing imitations without getting caught. The other is putting the imitations into circulation in order to make a profit.

A small-scale counterfeiter can use the false money to purchase necessities, using a high-denomination piece and receiving genuine money in change. But there is a constant danger of being caught using this method.

An intermediary organization with the means of passing counterfeit money into general circulation undetected is needed for large-scale production. This is most often an international criminal gang, but recent evidence suggests terrorist organizations are also involved. Such gangs are also out to make a profit, so they

During the Crusades (between 1096 and 1303), Christian forces fighting Islamic soldiers in the Holy Land struck copies of the local currency. Although relatively crude forgeries, these were nevertheless in gold and silver, and could be used in trade.

FORGER'S FILE
TAKE A CLOSER LOOK

F ew people look closely at the banknotes they handle, which is all to the advantage of the forger, as it decreases the chances of the forgery being detected. When color photocopiers were first introduced, for example, a number of counterfeiters successfully passed photocopied currency in small-time operations. These were recognized on closer inspection, of course, but by then the forger had vanished into thin air.

Magnified details from a new Bank of England £5 note (left) and a counterfeit copy (right). The difference between the sharply engraved lines of the genuine note and those of the copy is clearly visible.

pay the counterfeiters only a percentage of the face value of the forgeries.

An alternative, medium-scale scheme involves the establishment of a small criminal gang. Here's how they operate: First, using genuine currency, one or more members of the gang will purchase jewels, furs or other valuable merchandise that can easily be sold elsewhere. Shortly afterward, they will revisit the merchant and purchase a larger amount, this time with counterfeit currency. By the time the merchant discovers that the cash is counterfeit, the criminals will be long gone.

PAPER MONEY

A Scottish financier and speculator named John Law (1671–1729) introduced the use of paper banknotes into France in 1716.

These were, in effect, promissory notes, by which Law's Banque Générale accepted the deposit of coins and promised to repay on demand. Unfortunately, the scheme collapsed only four years later in what is known as the "Mississippi bubble."

At that time, Louisiana was French, and Law allied the bank with a company that planned to exploit the vast resources of the Mississippi Valley. When the bank failed, Law was forced to flee France.

Despite this false start, the use of paper money was later widely adopted. The proliferation of small banks during the nineteenth century naturally encouraged the forging of banknotes, and nowadays this has remained the principal activity of counterfeiters. However, currency is not the only paper that gets forged. Checks, stock certificates, government bonds, even postage stamps attract the attention of creative crooks.

Larger quantities of counterfeit banknotes find their way into organized crime, particularly networks that deal in drugs and arms. When a bundle or even a suitcase of notes is handed over surreptitiously in a dark alley, no one is likely to inspect it closely on the spot. Often, each bundle has a genuine note on the top and bottom. Subsequently, the fake notes in between may well be dispersed into general circulation, only to be detected upon examination by a bank.

When U.S. Secret Service agents raided a printing company in Milwaukee, Wisconsin, they seized uncut sheets of $10 and $20 bills with a face value of over half a million dollars.

THE U.S. SECRET SERVICE

Before 1862 American paper currency consisted of notes issued by local banks operating under charter. There was no federal currency, and Congress left the detection and prosecution of counterfeiters to state and local authorities and bank associations. The U.S. Treasury then passed several acts of Congress, culminating in the National Bank Act of 1863, which authorized the issue of federal banknotes ("greenbacks.")

However, the successful suppression of counterfeiters in order to maintain confidence in the federal currency was a problem in need of a solution. Hugh McCulloch, Secretary of the Treasury, initiated a plan by establishing the U.S. Secret Service in Washington, D.C., in July 1865. William P. Wood, who already claimed experience in detecting counterfeits, was put in charge.

Currency is not the only paper that gets forged. Checks, stock certificates, government bonds, even postage stamps attract the attention of creative crooks.

Despite strenuous efforts on the part of the Secret Service, counterfeiting continued. Seventy years later, for example, it was calculated that the victims of banknote fraud were losing over $770,000 every year. When Frank J. Wilson was appointed head of the service in 1937, he decided to instruct the public on how to detect bogus notes. Thousands of circulars were distributed to banks and retailers, bearing descriptions of fake notes currently in circulation. Secret Service agents visited banks and stores and gave demonstrations of counterfeits. A movie, *Know Your Money*, exposed

counterfeiting, while millions of leaflets described how to identify counterfeits.

This program was very successful at first, reducing the annual loss from counterfeiting to only $48,000, a decrease of 93 percent. Later, however, the volume of counterfeit notes increased dramatically, and although the Secret Service seized huge quantities before the notes went into circulation, the average loss was estimated to be around 12 percent of the total. In 1971, for example, the quantity seized totaled $23 million, and subsequently, $3.4 million was detected in circulation.

THE ROLE OF THE U.S. SECRET SERVICE

It is widely thought that the activities of the Secret Service involve only the protection of the president, the president's family and fellow officers, visiting foreign dignitaries and also the detection of certain cases of espionage. However, the investigation of counterfeiting remains an essential part of its work. Recently Secret Service activities have been extended to include credit card and computer fraud, identity theft and terrorist threats to financial security. In March 2003, part of the Secret Service was

Genuine U.S. $1 bills emerging from the printing press.

transferred from the U.S. Treasury to the newly created Department of Homeland Security.

WILLIAM BROCKWAY, UNREPENTANT COUNTERFEITER

Born William Spencer in 1822, notorious American counterfeiter William Brockway was an adopted child, who assumed the surname of his adoptive parents. He was largely self-educated but managed to sit in on classes in law and electrochemistry at Yale. Prior to the Civil War, commercial printers produced local banknotes while an official from the issuing bank stood guard over the paper and plates. One day in a bank in New Haven, Connecticut, Brockway succeeded in diverting the attention of the bank official as he slipped a thin sheet of lead through the press. This produced a positive impression of the $5 note being printed, and from this, applying techniques learned at Yale, he was able to print about 1,000 notes for his own use.

Temporarily a rich man, Brockway set himself up in Philadelphia, where, passing as a stockbroker in a sober suit, he married.

In 1860 he made the acquaintance of a British-born engraver, William Smith, who worked by day as a banknote engraver in New York, and his skill, coupled with a flawless memory, enabled him to produce perfect reproductions. At the same time, Brockway found a suitable business partner in James B. Doyle, a man with extensive interests in ranching and land purchase. Doyle had numerous bank accounts through which counterfeits could be passed.

For 15 years Brockway, Doyle and Smith continued their successful career. In 1880, Smith engraved a $1,000 bond due for redemption the following year, the special paper for the bond having been stolen from the mill at which it was made. At that time, Brockway's wife was consulting a lawyer about a divorce, and he half-jokingly suggested to an acquaintance, Agent Drummond of the Secret Service, that Brockway's affairs might be worth looking into.

Brockway was placed under surveillance and his connection with Doyle noted. Doyle was then tailed to Smith's home and seen leaving with a small packet. When later

The twentieth-century Italian artist "Mariolino da Caravaggio" (real name Feraboli) included reproductions of postage stamps in his paintings and earned the title of "counterfeiter."

detained in Chicago, Doyle was found to be in possession of 204 forged bonds. Brockway was also arrested but made a deal with Drummond, handing over 23 sets of plates, a cache of special paper and $50,000 worth of printed counterfeits in exchange for immunity from prosecution. At Doyle's trial Brockway testified that the protesting Doyle had had no idea the bonds were forged. Despite this, Doyle was sentenced to 12 years' imprisonment.

THE LAW CATCHES UP WITH BROCKWAY

In 1883, Drummond caught Brockway in possession of forged railroad bonds.

FORGER'S FILE
PRINCIPAL TYPES OF PRINTING USED IN BANKNOTE PRODUCTION

INTAGLIO

This was the original process used to print banknotes. A metal plate can be engraved by hand or machine. Or a photographic image can be transferred to it, then etched into the metal. The plate is inked overall and wiped clean, leaving ink in the hollows of the engraved image. When this is printed, the ink is raised on the paper so it is detectable; in many cases it can even be felt by rubbing the fingers over the surface of the paper.

OFFSET LITHOGRAPHY

A metal plate is coated with chemicals and then exposed to a negative of the image to be printed. This "fixes" the image on the plate while the unfixed coating is washed off. On the printing press the plate is first wetted, then inked. The ink adheres only to the fixed image and is transferred (offset) to a rubber roller and from there to the paper. Under the microscope, the printed result is flat.

LETTERPRESS

Metal type is assembled, or a single metal plate is made photographically in a way not unlike that for lithography, then etched so that the image stands proud of the surface. This reverse relief image can then be inked and printed. If stiff ink is used heavily, microscope examination might reveal a slight prominence to the print. Banknotes are given serial numbers in this way, using a "numbering box" that works rather like the mileage gauge of a car, clicking forward with each impression.

DRY OFFSET

Effectively similar to letterpress, it employs plates that have been etched to leave a relief image, which is then offset as in lithography.

SCREEN PRINTING

Also called serigraphy, this makes use of a stretched screen of silk, nylon or metal, on which a stenciled image has been produced by a photographic process. An inked roller passed over the screen transfers the image to the paper beneath.

Brockway was sentenced to five years in Sing Sing, of which he served three. On his release he took up counterfeiting once more but was eventually informed upon and served a term of ten years more. In 1905, Brockway, age 83, was observed buying tracing paper and brought in for questioning. However, he was released the next day, the judge ruling that he was too old to be suspected. Brockway survived 15 more years, dying in 1920 at the ripe old age of 98.

ENGRAVING A BANKNOTE PLATE

Genuine banknotes and other securities are printed wholly or in part from engraved plates. This type of printing is known as "intaglio" (see Principal Types of Printing Used in Banknote Production on opposite page). During the nineteenth century and into the twentieth, skilled engravers and etchers made these plates by hand, and counterfeiters had to use the same techniques. This is why we have the popular cartoon figure of the counterfeiter, wearing his eye shield, crouched in a secret cellar with his forged notes, each printed independently on a hand press and hanging from a clothesline to dry.

By the middle of the twentieth century, a rather complicated process was being used officially to duplicate engraved plates. The

An intaglio printing plate for a Bank of England £5 note. To ensure that the engraving is accurately reproduced, any minor imperfections are polished off by hand.

original steel engraving was hardened and impressed a number of times into a soft steel cylinder, producing a raised image. This was then also hardened and impressed in turn into a sheet of steel or copper, being duplicated many times in precise printing position. The sheet was electrically plated with chromium to resist wear, then wrapped around the cylinder of the printing press.

MONEY TO BURN?

At the end of World War II in Europe in 1945, four victorious Allies (the United States, Britain, France, and the Soviet Union) occupied Germany and Austria. Each conqueror governed a sector. There was a severe shortage of food and essential services, and also of Western cigarettes. In this situation cigarettes very soon became a valuable item of currency. They could be exchanged for goods of all kinds or used as bribes to obtain preferential treatment from a local official. However, because cigarettes were valuable to the economy, nobody would smoke what they had, because that would be like setting fire to $10 bills. Shady small-time crooks operating in the black market could be seen clutching small attaché cases packed with hundreds of loose cigarettes. And as this "money" passed from hand to hand, the tobacco would dry and gradually fall out, leaving empty tubes

An agent of the U.S. Secret Service using a comparison microscope to investigate a suspected counterfeit bill. The microscope brings the images of a genuine bill and the suspect bill side by side, so that tiny details can be compared.

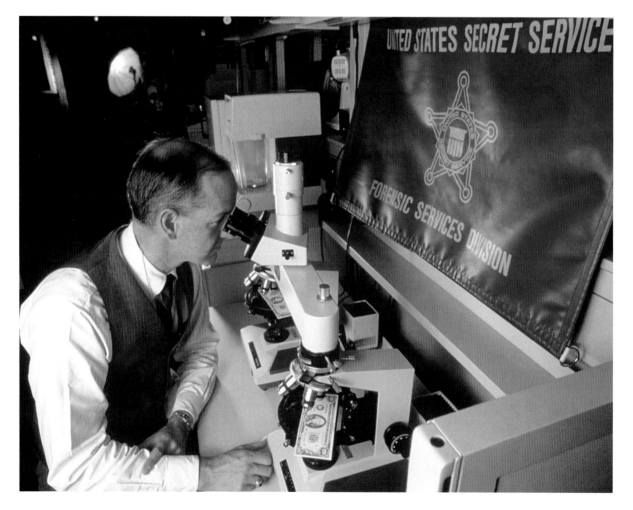

of paper that nevertheless kept their nominal exchange value. It is not known whether anyone entered this market with counterfeit tubes of cigarette paper that had never seen a tobacco factory, but such an opportunity did exist.

STAYING AHEAD OF THE FORGERS

In their constant struggle to outwit the counterfeiters, U.S. Treasury officials and their counterparts around the world have devised ingenious means to make it impossible to copy their notes. Designers have adopted photographic methods of adding details to the engraved plates, a technique impossible for forgers to follow.

For a time, forgers had no choice but to continue engraving by hand or to attempt to pass off crudely colored photographs as genuine notes. The situation changed dramatically in the 1950s, however, with the development of photolithography (see Principal Types of Printing Used in Banknote Production on page 20) and the rotary offset lithographic press.

Color separation photography and the so-called "small" offset press (not really so small and correspondingly expensive) became the tools of the modern counterfeiter during the 1950s. The necessary equipment is found in many legitimate businesses not primarily dedicated to printing, where few questions are likely to be asked of a prospective purchaser.

Since the 1980s, counterfeiters have increasingly turned their attention to the use of high-definition color scanners linked to computers. The final output from the

Now that computerized equipment is readily available, desktop counterfeiting has become the greatest danger. Genuine banknotes can be scanned electronically—reproducing all but the most microscopic details —and then reproduced in passable color by laser printer.

scanner can be a set of four-color separation negatives, ready to be made into plates and printed on a conventional offset press. This was the process used by English forger Stephen Jory, who flooded the market with forged £10 and £20 notes during the 1990s. He was not himself a printer but had access to a German he nicknamed "Herman the Scan-man," who supplied the negatives. This man "signed" his forgeries by changing the color of a small pot in the engraving found on the reverse side of the £20 note.

The new issue of notes that Jory's printer forged no longer had a continuous metal strip embedded in the paper; rather, the metal was revealed as a broken line on the surface of each side. Jory was able to

> "If you took every bank robbery that occurred in the United States in 1992...there were $63 million in losses. But in the same year, those same financial institutions lost $4.2 billion in fraud. The person who steals money with a pen steals far more money than the person who steals with a gun."
>
> —FRANK ABAGNALE

duplicate this by fusing a discontinuous pattern of metal foil onto the notes. He was eventually caught in 1998, when an associate, who had been given the job of destroying proof sheets, was found instead to have kept them in storage.

DESKTOP FORGERY

The latest development in counterfeiting comes from the widespread adoption of desktop publishing and the ready availability of laser printers. The product can be identified relatively easily by experts, but it still passes muster in the open market. The ingenuity of counterfeiters is remarkable: The output from the scanner can be modified on a computer so that security features such as watermarks and metal foils are "whited out" and subsequently restored. On checks, in particular, items such as amounts and signatures can be changed with ease.

Back in 1989, an international criminal organization swindled $750,000 from First Interstate Bancorp in Los Angeles. They stole a genuine dividend check issued by the corporation, altered the amount and the payee's name on a computer, and printed a counterfeit with a laser printer. The resulting forgery was good enough to deceive First Interstate's clearinghouse.

A number of design changes have been introduced into the printing of both checks and banknotes in order to combat these developments. One is to incorporate details so small that they are below the resolution of most copiers and scanners. In 1993, for example, Imperial Bank of Los Angeles began marketing "SafeChecks." These included patterns of tiny dots that could not be scanned, leaving the word "VOID" visible on copies. (This is comparable to the visual tests that are commonly used in diagnosing color blindness, in which only those with full color discrimination can distinguish

figures within a field of multicolored dots.) The bank later claimed that check-fraud losses were cut by 90 percent after the introduction of SafeChecks.

Other precautions include the use of fluorescent ink, and a chemical coating on the paper. The coating reacts to the use of any ink eradicator. However, the technology of color scanners is continually being upgraded. Since 1991, the oval line that bordered the portrait of Benjamin Franklin on a $100 bill had included "microprinting," with the words "The United States of America" repeated several times in tiny letters. An advertisement for a color

Some of the almost undetectable details in a Bank of England £5 note, incorporated to make counterfeiting very difficult. A pattern of microprinting is incorporated within the background of the note (top), while this printed value (bottom) shows up only in ultraviolet light.

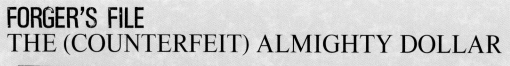

FORGER'S FILE
THE (COUNTERFEIT) ALMIGHTY DOLLAR

A counterfeit $20 United States Treasury bill.

The most widely counterfeited currency in the world is the U.S. dollar. In 1993 it was reported that $20 million in counterfeit notes had been seized within the United States, but another $121 million had been seized in other countries. In addition, large quantities of counterfeit dollars circulate in Asia, the Middle East and Eastern Europe without ever returning to regions where they can be identified. For example, Lebanese authorities reported that since 1992, more than $2 billion in high-quality counterfeits, mostly of dollars, had been produced by Shiite fundamentalists, allegedly with the encouragement of Iran and Syria. An estimated one-fifth of all banknotes in Russia—dollars and rubles alike—are fakes. India is also a major source of counterfeit documents.

scanner, marketed by a company called Envisions for only $1,799, revealed that this detail could be copied. Envisions was soon visited by agents of the Secret Service and obligingly withdrew the advertisement, but the capability remains.

As a result, several scanner manufacturers have already incorporated anticounterfeiting features into their machines. A specially programmed microchip recognizes a range of the major currencies, and the copier prints only a blank sheet of paper. Another development prints the copier's serial

number in microscopic dots, which are invisible to the eye but can be decoded by special equipment. In January 2004, Adobe Systems admitted that its popular Photoshop software incorporated a detection device meant to make it more difficult to copy currency.

The U.S. Secret Service estimates that most counterfeit currency is still produced by offset printing and that the machinery used is relatively easy to trace. However, "desktop" counterfeiting uses equipment similar to that in millions of homes and businesses. This fraud is spreading rapidly and is growing every year as a threat. In June 2004, the Bureau of Engraving & Printing estimated that counterfeit money produced digitally could represent as much as 40 percent of the total.

FOILING THE FORGER

As part of its ongoing effort to defeat counterfeiters, beginning in 1996 the United States Bureau of Engraving and Printing issued a new generation of Treasury bills, representing the first major redesign since 1929. Small changes in design had been made quite frequently over the years without affecting the overall appearance of the note. In particular, the use of microprinting and a security thread was introduced. Now a new series has been issued every two years or whenever a new Secretary of the Treasury is appointed.

There are a number of novel features incorporated in the new notes. The use of watermarked paper (adopted for the original greenbacks but abandoned in 1879 to make way for a special paper containing tiny colored threads) has been reintroduced. The most noticeable visual change is a larger, slightly off-center portrait, incorporating more detail. The background includes very fine line printing, difficult for counterfeit printers to duplicate.

The numeral in the lower-right-hand corner of each banknote is printed in "color-shifting" ink, that changes color according to the angle at which it is viewed. The position of the security thread varies with each denomination and glows in a different hue under ultraviolet light. The denomination is also printed along each thread: For example, "USA TWENTY" and an American flag are repeated along the length of the thread in a $20 note, with the figure "20" within the star field of the flag.

Microprinting is used in the border of some of the portraits. On the $50 note it is found in President Grant's collar, and on the $100 note it appears on the lapel of Benjamin Franklin's coat. Beginning in September 2004, a new design of the $50 note was introduced, following the new $20 note of October 2003. Features added include subtle background colors of red and blue, images of a waving flag and a small silver-blue metallic star.

FORGED POSTAGE STAMPS

The very first postage stamp, the British "Penny Black" issued by Sir Rowland Hill in 1840, was forged within a year.

Examination under the comparison microscope can quickly reveal the differences between a genuine banknote and a forgery, as in these details of the face of Benjamin Franklin on a 1959 $100 bill. The genuine engraving is on the left.

The first postage stamp in the world was the "Penny Black" issued by Sir Rowland Hill of the British post office in 1840. Although it was of such low face value, it soon became the target of counterfeiters, and the first forgeries were made within a year of its issue.

Nowadays, however, forging postage stamps currently in circulation is seldom profitable because their denominations are relatively small. Collectors, on the other hand, are willing to pay high sums for rarities; many are also happy to buy identified forgeries. The oldest surviving forged Penny Black, for example, was sold in 1991 for £1,350,000.

The early stamps produced by many different countries soon became rare, and by the middle of the nineteenth century, a number of forgers were already at work. Among the pioneers was Samuel Allan Taylor (1838–1913), who headed the so-called "Boston Gang." Born in Scotland, he moved to the United States as a child, began dealing in stamps and produced his first forgery in 1863. Years before countries such as Paraguay or Guatemala were producing their own stamps, the Boston Gang was merrily printing fakes for sale. At that time also, some U.S. post offices and carriers issued their own local stamps. Taylor forged hundreds of these as well, sometimes incorporating his own portrait. He was jailed for a period in 1893 but apparently continued producing fakes until 1905.

In the early years of stamp dealing, many dealers bought up the plates of obsolete issues, then sold stamps printed from them as originals. They included George Hussey and J. Walter Scott in the United States, Stanley Gibbons in England and J. B. Moens in Belgium. Legally these were forgeries, although if challenged, these dealers described them as "facsimiles." In Hamburg, Germany, the Spiro firm produced hundreds of forgeries

FORGER'S FILE
MEDAL-WINNING FORGERIES

François Fournier (1846–1927) was born in Switzerland but became a French citizen and served as a soldier in the Franco-Prussian War (1870–1871). He returned to Switzerland, settling in Geneva, where he produced innumerable stamp facsimiles. At that time, this was legal. Indeed, gold medals were awarded for these copies at international philatelic exhibitions. One of those who won a medal was Louis-Henri Mercier, also of Geneva. In 1904, Fournier purchased all of Mercier's stock, and Fournier continued to offer the facsimiles. When Fournier died, his widow sold everything, including his printing and perforating equipment, to the Swiss Union Philatelique de Geneva. The society overprinted the stamps FAUX (fake) and prepared albums of Fournier's work. After this the remainder of his stock was burned.

from the 1860s through 1880, and the Senf brothers did the same from the 1870s through 1890.

The problem of facsimiles became so great that the Royal Philatelic Society in England set up a committee of experts who would examine any questionable material for a fee. Other countries followed suit, but the production of facsimiles continued.

FAKING JUST FOR FUN

The so-called "king of stamp counterfeiters" was Jean de Sperati (1884–1957). He began faking stamps in his native city of Pisa, Italy, at an early age. Like many modern forgers of works of art, Sperati relied upon the authentication of his products by experts. Deceived, the experts would provide a certificate of genuineness, and Sperati would

Italian-born Jean de Sperati has been called the "king of stamp counterfeiters." He always insisted that his replicas were only "imitations," and he once won a defamation suit for being described as a forger.

then put the stamps up for auction. During the 1920s, he made his forgeries look even more authentic by overprinting them with fake post office cancellations.

During World War II, rare stamps became even more desirable. It was easy for people to conceal them to avoid their confiscation by the Germans. Sperati was caught smuggling stamps out of France and forced to confess that they were forgeries in order to avoid imprisonment. He pointed out that all the stamps had markings on the back, but as these were in pencil, his intentions seem clear.

Throughout his life, Sperati insisted publicly that he produced only "imitations," and he was once awarded damages for having been called a forger. When Sperati reached the age of 70, his eyesight was failing, and the British Philatelic Association, hoping to put an end to his illegalities, bought him out for a reputed £20,000. At his death three years later, however, it was discovered that he had continued his faking. "Just for fun," he so confessed on his deathbed.

FORGERIES THEY COULDN'T STOP

Buying up a forger's stock seems to be the only way to withdraw it from the market. In 1967 the American Philatelic Society (APS) struck a deal with Belgian-born Raoul de Thuin (1889–1975), who had been forging thousands of stamps and cancellations in the Yucatán peninsula of Mexico.

Colonel James DeVoss, executive secretary of the American Philatelic Society, said: "We had known about his activities for nearly 20 years, but had been unable to stop them. If de Thuin had been in the United States, he would have been thrown into jail, but he was not violating Mexican law, since he worked only with old stamps, mostly using his skill to create postmarks and overprintings that added to their rarity. The U.S. postal authorities issued fraud orders against him, which prevented him from sending mail to the United States, but his forgeries continued to circulate through other channels."

The APS bought 1,636 plates and what they believed to be all de Thuin's other equipment, including the inks he used, allegedly for a very small sum. Legally they were not allowed to own the material, so they used it to illustrate a book, *The Yucatán Story*, after which, so they were told, everything had to be handed over to the Secret Service. De Thuin then left for Guayaquil, Ecuador. After his death there, it was found that he had kept some of his materials and had continued with his stamp forgeries.

In 2004 it was revealed that a dealer on the eBay website, Juan Canoura Sr., had

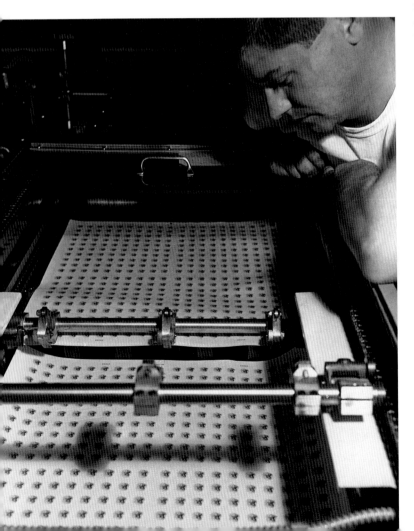

Checking the quality of British postage stamps as they are delivered, sheet by sheet, from the printing press.

acquired some of de Thuin's materials. Canoura, who had been in business for at least 16 years, announced that he was selling out and retiring. "I am just finish [*sic*] as a forger. I just want to enjoy the years of my life that I have left," he reportedly said.

THE PORTUGUESE BANKNOTE SWINDLE

One famous counterfeiter who did not print false notes, but instead persuaded a leading security printer to carry out the work for him was a young Portuguese, Artur Alves Reis. Born in 1896, Reis arrived in the Portuguese West African colony of Angola with his young wife in 1916. He carried a university engineering diploma, which he had forged, and rapidly found employment as an engineer.

The Angolan economy was then in dire straits, and the Portuguese government had done nothing to help. At the age of 24, Reis was able to take over the ailing railroad company he worked for and subsequently began fraudulent dealings in its shares. However, his activities were detected, and upon returning home to Lisbon in 1924, he was arrested and spent two months in prison.

While there, he hatched a fantastic scheme to make money. As soon as he was released, he forged a document drawn up between the Angolan authorities and himself, authorizing him to issue Portuguese banknotes in Angola to the value of 100 million escudos, against an imaginary loan of £1 million. He then recruited a small team of accomplices, none of whom was permitted to know more than the barest details of the project.

One of these, Karel Marang, approached a security printing firm in Holland; they gave him a letter of introduction to the printers of Portuguese banknotes, Waterlow & Sons in London. Armed with this letter, Marang arranged a meeting with Sir

One famous counterfeiter did not print false notes but instead persuaded a leading security printer to carry out the work for him.

William Waterlow, the company's chairman. Marang told Sir William that the issue of the notes had to be kept secret. The political consequences would be serious if it became known, and Marang said he would be dealing directly with the governor of the Bank of Portugal. Moreover, the notes were to be duplicates of notes already printed, which would be overprinted with the word "Angola" as soon as they arrived in the colony. When Sir William agreed (he did not even inform his fellow directors), Reis forged two more letters, ostensibly from the Bank of Portugal, approving the deal.

Early in 1925, two hundred thousand 500-escudo notes were printed and mixed up so that their serial numbers were out of sequence, then taken to Lisbon. Meanwhile, Reis had formed a banking company, Banco Angola & Metropole, with offices in Lisbon and Oporto, which he financed with the duplicate notes. The bank did so well, by offering loans at lower interest and better foreign exchange rates than its competitors, that in July, 380,000 more notes were ordered from Waterlow & Sons.

In an effort to cover his tracks, Reis began to buy Bank of Portugal shares. He reasoned that if he and his accomplices became major shareholders, it would be impossible for any banking official to instigate an inquiry into the existence of duplicate notes. However, while he was abroad on a trip to Angola, a bank teller in Oporto noted that foreign exchange dealings had not been properly recorded in the ledger and reported it.

Sir William Waterlow, pictured with his wife. In 1924 he authorized the printing of 580,000 genuine 500-escudo Bank of Portugal notes on the basis of two letters forged by Reis—without consulting his fellow directors.

One of the 200,000, apparently genuine, Bank of Portugal 500-escudo notes that Reis persuaded the London security printers, Waterlow & Sons, to produce.

An exhaustive search through all the Banco Angola's holding of notes eventually uncovered two with the same serial number. There was, of course, no way of telling which was the genuine issue and which the duplicate. When the news leaked out, there was panic: Everyone holding 500-escudo notes became desperate to change them. When Reis came ashore on his return from Angola, he was arrested.

The Bank of Portugal was forced to buy in all 500-escudo notes, and for a time it looked as if the Portuguese economy would collapse. After a complicated trial in 1929, Reis was sentenced to 20 years in prison. But the matter did not end there.

The following year the Bank of Portugal sued Waterlow & Sons in London. Waterlow argued that the case concerned mere pieces of paper; the Bank of Portugal had taken back the suspect notes and issued others at only the cost of their printing. The prosecution, on the other hand, sought exemplary damages. In the end, the case went to the House of Lords on appeal, and the Bank of Portugal was awarded damages equivalent to 60 million escudos.

FORGER'S FILE
BETTER THAN THE REAL THING?

Until well into the twentieth century, the value of a state's currency was based on the gold standard, dependent on how much gold a country had in its reserves. Britain came off the gold standard in 1931, after which the sovereign (a gold coin with a face value of £1) was no longer legal tender. But the Royal Mint continued to produce the sovereign as an item that could be used in trade with developing countries. It proved of great importance during World War II, when, for example, it was used to finance groups of Resistance fighters against the Germans. It remained a valuable item of international finance after the war.

Jose Beraha, a member of a wealthy family of Sephardic Jews, was born in 1907 in the Macedonian city of Skopje. When the Germans occupied Yugoslavia in April 1941, most of his family were transported and put to death in concentration camps. But Beraha and two young nephews escaped to Albania, where, using sovereigns, they paid their boat passage to Italy.

In Italy, Beraha learned the language and was able to set himself up in business. At the end of the war, he entered the export trade but found himself frustrated by complicated rules of currency control. The British sovereign was the key that opened all doors. Beraha soon discovered, however, that while it then commanded the equivalent of some $20 in the market, its value in metal was only around $9.

Beraha set up a small mint on the Via Andrea Doria in Milan and began manufacturing sovereigns. His were, in fact, better than those produced by the Royal Mint, containing about one percent more gold. By 1951, Beraha was a millionaire; he sold his business to his production manager and retired with his family to Switzerland.

The British authorities had soon become aware of Beraha's activities, and in 1952 they applied to the Swiss government for his extradition on charges of counterfeiting. However, he hit upon an argument to defend himself. Since the sovereign was no longer legal tender in Britain, it could not be used to purchase goods or services there and was of interest only to collectors or dealers in gold bullion. Beraha sent his lawyer on a trip to prove this: Every shop, and even the British Treasury, refused to accept the coins. "Try selling them to a coin dealer," they said. At Beraha's extradition hearing, the Swiss judges dismissed the application, accepting that he had not been guilty of counterfeiting.

A counterfeit gold sovereign, with the head of King George V, dated 1918. Interestingly, this was the one year in which sovereigns were not produced at the London Mint. The forger may have made a careless mistake. Or, because it is only illegal to forge legal tender, he may have deliberately created a coin that never existed so that he could not be charged with a criminal act.

CHARLES BLACK, MAN WITH AN EYE FOR DETAIL

Charles Black was born in 1928 and trained as an instrument maker. He put his skill to good use for three years, inventing a new system of thermostatic heating for aquariums. But his knowledge of engineering led him into the used car trade, and he was eventually convicted of dealing in stolen cars. While in prison, he had many conversations with fellow inmates who had been convicted of forgery and, not long after his release in 1969, decided to make use of his skills as an amateur photographer and take up counterfeiting.

By his own good fortune, there was an international printing fair (IPEX) being held in London. Black spent time there with salesmen who were only too pleased to explain and demonstrate their products. Very soon he had his "shopping list," and a casino owner (identified only as "Fred") provided the capital. Black told suppliers of his equipment that he intended to print catalogues, and he told his wife that he was going to produce pornographic magazines. He built a large shed in his garden to accommodate the printing press and plate-making equipment, and turned his study into a photographic darkroom. Within days he had taught himself the intricacies of color printing.

Black's time in prison had given him a developed contempt for other forgers. As he has said, they were content with a product that was superficially passable, whereas he meticulously worked to make his forgeries as close to the original as possible. Black spent many hours in his darkroom, making photographic negatives from which he would print in magenta, blue, yellow and black, in the same way photographs are printed in high-quality magazines. He was not satisfied with making a single negative for each shade, however, but instead made enlargements

and painstakingly patched different pieces together to get exactly the right tones in different areas.

Black and an associate, Stanley Le Baigue, began by producing £250,000 worth of travelers' checks in £50 denominations. Fred then distributed these through the criminal underworld at one-third their face value.

Checks and banknotes are numbered in succession, using a small "numbering box" and magnetic ink. Black was able to persuade an acquaintance at a security printer, who previously had offered him genuine checks that he himself had stolen, to steal three numbering boxes and a

Above: British counterfeiter Charles Black, with a handful of £20, £10 and £5 notes.

Opposite: Jean de Sperati at work on one of his "imitations."

quantity of the necessary ink. Black made overprinted stamps in the name of several issuing banks, perforated the checks and stitched them ten at a time into printed card covers. It was only when the checks returned to the issuing banks that they were discovered to be forgeries and the entire genuine issue was withdrawn.

ELECTRICAL CORD AND GLYCERINE

Black then decided to forge $50 and $20 bills, but these presented a new problem. The paper on which U.S. Treasury bills were printed included a mix of fine red and blue filaments as a precaution against counterfeiting. Black's solution was typical of his approach. He shredded the fabric covering of some old-fashioned electrical cord, scattered the pieces over a sheet of paper printed in light green and photographed it. When the photograph was reduced to size, it finally looked right. It took a long time to find the right shade of green and even longer to get the engraving correct. Black even discovered (by a visit to the local library) the correct relationship between the prefix letter in the numbering of the notes and the issuing bank. Finally, to give the paper the silky feel of a new issue, he dipped each bill in glycerine and dried it over a heater.

But then an accomplice was arrested for passing stolen but genuine checks, and Black was implicated. In 1971 the police searched his house for evidence, but since they had no suspicion that he was a counterfeiter, they failed to search his garden shed. While Black was remanded in custody for seven weeks, Le Baigue happily continued turning out forged dollar bills. Released on bail to await trial, Black immediately set about counterfeiting a new series of £5 notes that had just been issued by the Bank of England.

The new notes had been widely publicized as being "forge-proof," but Black took up the challenge. The paper was watermarked in a precise position, with the head of the Duke of Wellington; in addition, a fine metal strip was incorporated in the weave. Only by pulling the two layers of paper apart could the metal strip be revealed, something that busy bank tellers and storekeepers were very unlikely to do. They contented themselves with holding the note up to the light, to see both the watermark and the shadow of the strip.

Black's solution was simple but typical of his painstaking methods. He printed a plain black line in the position of the strip, then overprinted the paper with opaque white ink, leaving the ghostly image of the Duke transparent. After this it was easy to print the colored features of the notes and the serial numbers in his usual way.

Black stood trial in February 1972, accused of "using forged instruments to obtain goods," and was convicted and

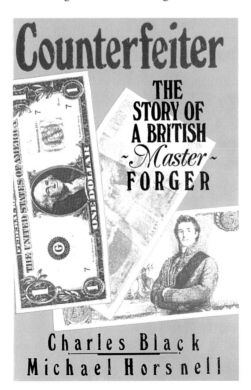

Charles Black, with the assistance of journalist Michael Horsnell, described his career in this best-selling book. It was published in 1989, after he had vowed to "go straight."

sentenced to five years in prison. Ironically, while he was there, he worked in the print shop. A year or so later, he learned that his home had again been raided by the police, all his equipment had been seized, and two men (including Le Baigue) were "assisting the police with their enquiries." Le Baigue and the other man were each sentenced to five years, but Black took advantage of his status as a prisoner to refuse to be questioned. Nevertheless, because of the suspicion surrounding him, he was not released on parole until late in 1973.

Back home, Black was happy to discover that a spare set of $50 negatives, which he had concealed in a cavity in the bottom of the kitchen door, was still there. For a while

he tried to pursue an honest living as an instrument maker, but another printing exhibition in London in 1975 proved too great an attraction. There he met an old acquaintance, Brian Katin. The printing firm for which Katin had worked had closed down, and Katin had an offset press concealed behind a false wall at his home at Pagham, in Sussex.

"I felt ready to resume my career and needed the partnership," Black later said, "but upon inspecting his forgeries at Pagham decided that he needed me rather more badly. I've seen more realistic currency on a Monopoly board."

Black introduced a further refinement into his techniques. As described on page 20,

A copy of a Byzantine coin struck by Carl Wilhelm Becker, together with the body and face of the die with which it was struck.

genuine notes are printed by intaglio, leaving a relief image, whereas Black's offset-printed image was flat. He tried using thermographic powder, such as is used for letterheads, to make them look as if they had been embossed. But, he said, "they looked like that short-lived phenomenon of late 1950s cinema, the 3D film: The image leaped from the paper like a psychedelic experience." Finally, Black engraved a pattern of minute dots into a brass plate, following the printed image, and embossed the notes so that they felt (and superficially looked) as if they had been engraved.

At the subsequent trial in 1979, a U.S. Treasury official was forced to admit that Black's forgeries were the finest he had ever seen.

However, there was one point that the wily Black had not taken into account. Banknotes and other legal documents are printed on a special paper. It does not contain the "whiteners" that are added to ordinary paper. These cause the paper to look brighter in daylight, but under ultraviolet light they fluoresce a brilliant blue. In 1976 banks everywhere had begun to install ultraviolet scanners to examine notes passed over the counter. These are now common, not only in banks but also in stores.

Black learned of this when one of his clients was arrested in Switzerland. He was fortunate enough, however, to discover a large stock of old legal paper that had lain for a long time at the back of a warehouse and began to use this. In February 1977, Black and Katin received an order for $2 million worth of bills to be delivered to

Beirut. Although they were to get only 14 percent of the face value, they still stood to make $140,000 each.

A CHANCE ARREST PROVES BLACK'S DOWNFALL

Black and Katin thought they were going to be rich at last, but a driver carrying a quantity of Black's bills (presumably to buy drugs) was arrested in Turkey and asked why he had so much money with him. An official from the U.S. Treasury was dispatched to Ankara from Paris but admitted that he could not tell whether the notes were genuine or not. However, Black's telephone number was found scribbled in the driver's passport.

Once more the police raided Black's home. They found no counterfeiting equipment but did find $85,000 worth of forged notes hidden under a box of potatoes. More importantly, they also found a note written in pencil that gave the frame number of Katin's press. Questioning the manufacturer soon led to Katin's garage, where bills totaling $3.6 million were discovered.

At the subsequent trial in 1979, a U.S. Treasury official was forced to admit that the forgeries were the finest he had ever seen. They were so good, he said, that detection equipment that had taken years (and millions of dollars) to develop was rendered obsolete overnight. Katin was sentenced to three years, while Black received a total of 21 years.

A KNIFE-THROWER GOES STRAIGHT

Released on parole in 1982, Black at last decided (or so he has said) to go straight. His wife divorced him, he married a Thai woman, and together they set up an agency to supply Thai brides for British men. "You might be the best knife-thrower in the circus," said Black, "but you sleep better at night if you're one of the clowns."

Bank of England notes are produced, under the highest security, at the bank's printing works in Loughton, Essex. Every printed sheet must be inspected visually to ensure that each conforms to the highest standards.

CHAPTER 2
FAKE ART

Works of art by leading artists become ever more valuable over the years. Many skilled craftsmen, embittered by their own lack of success, have turned to more profitable forgery.

The faking and forging of works of art have gone on for many hundreds of years, but it is only during the past century that real efforts have been made to detect forgeries. There are a number of reasons for this. For example, many artists' studios, particularly during the fifteenth and sixteenth centuries, encouraged the production of close copies, either as training for apprentices or to supply a demand in the market. As a result, there was no clear-cut distinction between a "genuine" work of art and a copy, particularly if the master of the studio had signed both. When the passion for collecting works of art became fashionable during the eighteenth century, many copies—and fakes—changed hands, usually without documentary proof of their origins. For 200 years the forgeries were considered genuine.

Opposite: Tom Keating, a British art forger, with one of his "Sexton Blakes"—Cockney rhyming slang for "fakes."
Left: One of the many supposedly fifteenth-century fake heads produced by Italian forger Giovanni Bastianini during the mid-nineteenth century.

Opposite: Roman sculptors made many copies of ancient Greek statues. These were in honest admiration of their quality and cannot be considered forgeries, but they deceived many experts into thinking that they were Greek originals.

In addition, copying the style of a known artist was regarded as an act of homage. For example, the great British painter J.M.W. Turner (1775–1851) was happy to produce paintings based on the work of Dutch painter Willem van de Velde (1611–1693) and French painter Claude Lorrain (1600–1682).

Lack of communication among experts, who could also be guilty of a certain self-interest, also contributed to the problem of detecting forgeries. Experts tended to concentrate (and still do) on the work of a single artist, or a closely related group, and seldom consulted with experts on other artists. They were also likely to collect lesser-known works by this artist and so had a vested interest in the authentication of his or her work.

The prices paid at auction for well-known works of art have risen astronomically in the last hundred years, making forgery a far more profitable business. When it comes to making money, forgers are no different from anyone else. Profit provides them with a great incentive to improve the quality of their work.

Finally, it is only during the past century that a wide range of scientific analytical

"The hardest deception to detect is usually one that has been made recently.... The forgery is closer to our time and to our viewpoint, and therefore is more appealing."

—JOSEPH VEACH NOBLE, FORMER VICE-DIRECTOR, METROPOLITAN MUSEUM OF ART, NEW YORK

techniques has been developed. Investigators are now able to identify and date the material used in a work, examine its structure and compare that with other authenticated works. Perhaps most important of all, they can communicate rapidly with other experts in distant parts of the world.

DETECTING FORGERIES

Before the availability of scientific methods of examination, only two criteria could be applied to the authentication of works of art: style and provenance. Provenance is the documentation that should be produced to show how the work

FORGER'S FILE
PROFIT AND MISCHIEF

The principal purpose of art forgery is undoubtedly fraudulent profit. However, it is interesting that in many cases the forger claims also to be motivated by something very different: a desire (mischievous or bitter) to outwit the experts. To produce a plausible forgery, a great deal of artistic ability, knowledge and skill is necessary. Frequently forgers have found that they are unable to gain recognition (and a reasonable price) for their own work. However, if the work is attributed to some well-known artist, preferably dead, it can command high sums. The temptation to produce a forgery is often too great to resist.

has passed on from owner to owner through the years in order to confirm its genuineness. In the case of a forgery, these documents must also be forged.

The known style and subject matter of a famous master can be copied meticulously by a skilled forger. On the other hand, a painting may be signed "Goya" or "Rembrandt," but if to the eye of the expert, it does not "look right," it will be dismissed as a fake.

Nevertheless, as Joseph Veach Noble, a former vice-director at the Metropolitan Museum of Art in New York wrote in the *Encyclopedia Britannica*: "The hardest deception to detect is usually one that has been made recently.... The forgery is closer to our time and to our viewpoint, and therefore is more appealing. As a forgery ages, the contemporary viewpoint shifts, tastes change, and there is a new basis of understanding. Consequently, a forgery rarely survives more than a generation."

HOW OLD IS OLD?

In the museum world the situation can be complicated whenever a piece long thought to date from ancient times is discovered, or suspected, to be a copy from a more recent period—but still very old. A good example is the sculpture of the head of Dionysus, the Greek god of wine, which was unearthed in a vineyard near Naples in 1771 and is now in the British Museum. It was thought at first to be ancient Greek in origin, but it is now known to be a copy (made by a Roman sculptor of the second century C.E.) of an older head, possibly the work of the fifth-century B.C.E. Athenian master Phidias. As pointed out in the Introduction, there is no reason to suppose that the Roman sculptor intended this as a forgery, and it is, of course, of great value in itself. Many other museum pieces throughout the world have a similarly uncertain history.

ART BECOMES A PROFITABLE BUSINESS

For many centuries there was no market in Europe, or indeed anywhere in the world, for works of art. They were produced on commissions from religious or state authorities. Artists were sometimes (but not always) paid well and/or highly respected, but their work remained in specific locations, and their names were seldom recorded. However, this situation changed forever during the fifteenth century when wealthy merchants emerged as a new class of patrons. The nouveau riche of their day, merchants were eager to prove their importance and standing in the community and began to rival the church as buyers of fine works of art.

THE RENAISSANCE

The fifteenth century is known as a time of renaissance (rebirth) of art. Individual artists became famous and competed with one another for valuable commissions. It was then that art forgery first became profitable.

A growing band of wealthy collectors would buy anything attributed to a famous artist, whether genuine, a copy from the artist's studio or a plausible forgery. Artists came from other countries to Italy to study the new art of the Renaissance; sometimes

FORGER'S FILE
THE CARDINAL AND THE FAKE CUPID

In *Lives of the Most Eminent Architects, Painters and Sculptors of Italy*, Giorgio Vasari (1511–1574) wrote: "Michelangelo carved a sleeping Cupid, life-size. A friend said, 'I am certain that if you bury this statue for a time and then send it to Rome as an antique, you will get more for it than if you sell it here in Florence.' This Michelangelo is said to have done, though some say the friend took it to Rome and buried it there. In any case the Cardinal of San Giorgio [Raffaello Riario] bought it for 200 crowns. Others say that the friend delivered only 30 crowns to Michelangelo, told him that was all he could get, and kept the difference. In the meantime the cardinal discovered that the Cupid was no antique; it had, in fact, been made in Florence, and he insisted on getting his money back. He was laughed at and even blamed for not being able to appreciate the merit of the work, which was really perfection. 'What matter, they laughed, whether it were modern or not?'...The whole affair increased Michelangelo's reputation."

they would return home to produce work "in the style of" a recognized Italian artist. Rich collectors in other countries also sent agents to purchase expensive work. This proliferation of works of art, many of which were copies or deliberate forgeries, was to cause huge problems in later centuries.

MICHELANGELO: AN ACCOMPLISHED FORGER

The great Italian painter, sculptor, architect and poet Michelangelo Buonarroti (1475–1564) was not above producing forgeries in his early years. As a 14-year-old, he was apprenticed to the painter Domenico

Ghirlandaio (1449–1494) and spent much of his time studying the work of his elders.

In his book on the life of Michelangelo, Giorgio Vasari wrote: "He also copied drawings of the old masters so perfectly that his copies could not be distinguished from the originals, since he smoked and tinted the paper to give it the appearance of age. He was often able to keep the originals and return his copies in their stead."

The most famous of Michelangelo's forgeries was an "antique" sculpture of a life-sized *Sleeping Cupid* that he produced in 1496. The sculpture is now lost, but a sketch among his drawings is believed to be the

original design. During the sixteenth century, the *Sleeping Cupid* was in the d'Este collection in Mantua. Visitors were shown it alongside a genuine antique, no doubt to allow them to marvel at Michelangelo's skill.

A REAL REMBRANDT?

The great difficulty in distinguishing between original work by an old master, copies made under his direction, or imitations and intentional forgeries, is exemplified in the case of the Dutch painter Rembrandt van Rijn (1606–1669). Rembrandt's work is greatly admired and very valuable, and large numbers of paintings are associated with his name. For example, the records of the U.S. Customs Service in New York list no fewer than 9,428 works "by Rembrandt" being imported into the United States between 1909 and 1951. He certainly was prolific, but for this to be correct, throughout his working life Rembrandt would have had to produce two of these every three days, and this accounts for none of the many other authenticated works held in state collections throughout the world or for those attributed to Rembrandt in private hands.

A large part of the confusion is partly Rembrandt's own doing. He maintained workshops in which his pupils produced Rembrandt-like work, which he himself often signed and sold as his own. After his death, in honest admiration, other artists produced imitations in the style of Rembrandt. An obscure eighteenth-century English painter, Thomas Worlidge, is among those credited with producing etchings that at one time were thought to be by Rembrandt.

Modern art forgers spend much time studying the lesser-known works of famous artists of the past. These minor works by Rembrandt, shown at a recent exhibition at the Scottish National Gallery, no doubt attracted a degree of criminal attention.

FORGER'S FILE
BY BOTTICELLI'S BRUSH?

Another Renaissance artist who set up workshops to meet the demand for paintings was Sandro Botticelli (1444–1510). It is known that apprentices produced several of his works under his supervision. Afterward Botticelli would add the finishing touches, perhaps making significant changes, and offer the painting as his own. Strictly speaking, this is neither fake nor forgery. But when we admire a wonderful work attributed to Botticelli, we cannot know how much of the brushwork is actually his.

A typical painting by Botticelli— a Madonna and Child with Saint John the Baptist, in the Accademia gallery, Florence, Italy. Although it has been authenticated as a Botticelli, it is impossible to be certain whether any part of the work is that of his apprentices.

Opposite: Rembrandt's *An Elderly Man in a Cap*. Although catalogued as a forgery, it is believed to be genuine by gallery experts. Art historians, however, refuse to accept this finding.

At the same time, the profusion of "non-Rembrandts" has led to doubts about paintings that may well be genuine. The National Gallery in London possesses a painting, *An Elderly Man in a Cap*, which was catalogued as "an imitation of Rembrandt, possibly an eighteenth-century one" and the signature, *Rembrandt f/1648*, was considered a forgery. However, investigation by the gallery's scientific department has revealed that it dates almost certainly from the seventeenth century and reveals characteristics of Rembrandt's own technique.

The head of the fifteenth-century firebrand monk Girolamo Savonarola, sculpted by Bastianini. The Italian faker produced many similar pieces of work before he died at the age of 38.

As the publication accompanying the British Museum's 1990 exhibition *Fake? The Art of Deception* puts it: "The most natural conclusion of this would be that the painting is not an imitation but a genuine Rembrandt. But no connoisseur of Rembrandt's work would be convinced by these scientific arguments. Any dispute about the painting's authenticity has long been exhausted."

Art auction houses use a subtle code to distinguish work that they are not prepared to confirm as being by a named artist. The categorization starts off with work that is "said to be by" the artist, to "studio of" the artist, "school of" the artist and, finally, work they are fairly sure is by another hand.

THE BIG MONEY

The nineteenth century might fairly be called the golden age of art forgery, and it is no coincidence that this was the era when the great national art galleries were first established. The Louvre, in Paris, began as a historic palace built mostly while Louis XIV reigned over France (1643–1715). In the nineteenth century it became the first art museum opened to the public and was soon followed by the National Gallery in London, the Prado in Madrid, the Staatliche Museum in Berlin and the Alte Pinakotheck in Munich. By the end of the century, Cairo, Tokyo, Melbourne, Montreal and other cities had their own galleries. In the United States the Metropolitan Museum of Art in New York, the Boston Museum of Fine Arts, together with those in Philadelphia, Chicago, Detroit and a dozen other American cities, were all established.

The result was that all these galleries competed to purchase major works of art, particularly those from ancient times, and the temptation for forgers rose to its height. Craftsmen and artists became embittered by a realization that the work of their predecessors had become more valuable than their own. Meanwhile, individual collectors became excited by the prospect that what they had bought could be sold at a considerable profit.

At first the greatest demand was for Egyptian, Greek and Roman antiquities. When museums began to publish illustrations of works in their possession, fakers found it even easier to make copies or forge imitations. Interest grew in medieval artifacts; all sorts of fakes were produced, including coins, carved ivories and even illuminated manuscripts.

FORGERY, ITALIAN STYLE

Italians were particularly skilled in the production of fake antiquities. One of the most prolific was Giovanni Bastianini. When he himself proudly confessed to one of his forgeries, doubts suddenly arose about other works.

Born in 1830, the young Bastianini was hired by Florentine antiquarian dealer Giovanni Freppa, who provided him with clay and marble to sculpt. Bastianini's bust of the fifteenth-century Dominican reformer Girolamo Savonarola was such a convincing fake that it became regarded as a great discovery and was immediately sold by Freppa for a large sum.

Collectors became convinced that the work of an unknown fifteenth-century studio had been discovered. Soon enough, busts of the philosopher Marsilio Ficino and Lucrezia Donati, mistress of Lorenzo de'Medici, appeared. The latter bust was judged by a leading art historian as a masterpiece by a fifteenth-century Florentine sculptor, but a year after Bastianini's death in 1868, its purchaser discovered it to be a fake. Nevertheless, it was considered of such exceptional quality that the Victoria and Albert Museum in London bought it, as a forgery, for £84 — a price comparable with that currently paid for genuine Renaissance work.

TAKING ON THE LOUVRE

The most notorious of Bastianini's fakes was a bust of Girolamo Benivieni, who had been a friend of Savonarola's. The only known "likeness" was an eighteenth-century engraving, so Freppa and Bastianini found a tobacco worker named Bonaiuti, whose features closely resembled the engraving, to sit as a model. The resulting bust convinced the Louvre, which paid the record sum of 14,000 francs for it in 1866.

Controversy arose almost at once. The following year, Freppa announced that he

Restoration of a painting is a delicate business, requiring the skills of more than one expert retoucher. This painting, *Danae,* by Rembrandt, was vandalized in the Hermitage museum in St. Petersburg, Russia, in 1965, and required extensive repair.

had commissioned the bust from Bastianini. The director of the Louvre, Comte de Nieuewekerke, defended his museum's purchase. Soon a battle raged in the press between French sculptor Eugène Lequesne, for the Louvre, and Bastianini himself.

When a newspaper reported that de Nieuewekerke had offered Bastianini 15,000 francs to produce a companion piece to the bust, the forger announced that he would make it for a fee of 3,000 francs, together with busts of all 12 Roman emperors for a fee of 1,000 francs apiece. But there was no response from the Louvre, and by June 1868, Bastianini had died.

Ten years after Bastianini's death in 1878, another Italian art forger, destined to become the most successful of the early twentieth century, was born in Cremona. He was Alceo Dossena. An apprentice to a stonemason, he had learned the secrets of the sculpture of the past by working on the restoration of old buildings. In 1918 he moved to Rome, where he was hired to produce fakes by two antiquarian dealers— Alfredo Fasoli and Roman Palesi—and at the same time acquired a mistress.

DOSSENA'S "RECONSTRUCTIONS"

Dossena's forgeries were so accomplished that they even fooled reputable art

"I never copied works. I simply reconstructed them. Perfectly familiar with the various styles of the past...I could not assimilate them in any other way. And that was how I produced."

—ALCEO DOSSENA

institutions that had paid serious money for them. Among his forgeries, an "ancient Greek" Athena and a Madonna and Child attributed to Giovanni Pisano (c.1250–1320) were sold to the Cleveland Museum of Art. An "Etruscan" Diana, in 21 fragments, was sold to the City Art Museum in St. Louis. An Annunciation attributed to Simone Martini (1284–1344) was sold to the Frick Gallery in New York City for $225,000. A tomb attributed to Mino da Fiesole was sold to the Boston Museum of Fine Arts, accompanied by a forged receipt, allegedly from Mino.

In 1928, when Dossena learned that Palesi had received nearly six million lire for the fake tomb sold to Boston, while he had been paid a mere 25,000 lire, he brought a complaint before a magistrate. His mistress had just died, and he wanted to give her a suitably lavish funeral. He claimed 1,250,000 lire in back payments while acknowledging the forgeries for which he was responsible. Dossena protested: "I never copied works. I simply reconstructed them. Perfectly familiar with the various styles of the past, not as represented by any particular treatment but as manifest in the spirit, I could not assimilate them in any other way. And that was how I produced."

After his confession the court dropped the case. Dossena then exhibited work under his own name in Naples and Berlin, but as a magazine review of the Berlin show reported: "The faker is finished, but the artist does not appear." In 1937, Dossena died in a charity hospital.

HOW FORGERS WORK: PAINTINGS

All forgers must be highly skilled craftsmen because the most important element in a forged work of art is that it should look genuine. Forgers must have a knowledge and understanding of the artist and the work they are copying, and be able to duplicate it exactly.

A fake "Madonna and Child" by Italian forger Alceo Dossena. It was bought by the Victoria and Albert Museum in London and only later identified as a forgery.

But this, in itself, is not enough. The forger's materials must also deceive the experts. For example, some old masters painted on wooden boards, others on canvas. In order to forge a painting on board, the forger must first find old wood of approximately the right age or know how to treat a modern piece to age it. Panels from antique furniture are ideal, but buying antiques and then breaking them up is expensive. New panels can be steamed, "cooked" in boiling water or left to stand for a year or more out in the open. Then they must be stained to darken them. It is occasionally possible to buy bad paintings on boards quite cheaply, but this is rare. In such a case some forgers rub the painting down to the original "ground," while others just paint on top.

One characteristic of very old wood is that it may be worm-eaten. In the past, fakers of antique furniture have achieved the same effect by firing lead shot at the wood, but then the lead had to be removed. Some forgers simply drill holes into the wood. But drills and lead shot only make holes in a straight line, unlike genuine woodworm. Eric Hebborn (see page 71), in his book *The Art Forger's Handbook*, recommends beating the surface of the wood with a very coarse file to give it the appearance of age.

COPING WITH CANVAS

Modern canvases (the term used to describe the canvas on its wooden stretcher) differ from those used a century or more ago. Today the wood of the stretchers and wedges is cut by machine and will appear as new. The fabric itself will have been woven by machine and will be very uniform in appearance, unlike that of the past, which was woven by hand and is slightly uneven. Fortunately for the forger, there are many old, badly damaged or poor-quality paintings on canvas. These can be bought relatively cheaply and painted over. Alternatively, the back of a new canvas must be roughened and stained to look as if it had been affected by dampness.

PAINTS, PIGMENTS AND VARNISH

The next problem to be dealt with is the paint. Until the late nineteenth century, artists used only natural coloring matter, in

the form of minerals and plant dyes. Nowadays zinc and titanium white have almost entirely replaced white lead. Alizarin and other organic pigments have taken the place of ground-up minerals. But careful forgers know this too well and use only original materials. Van Meegeren, for example, made his ultramarine from lapis lazuli, his indigo from the juice of the indigo plant, his vermilion from cinnabar and his earth colors from traditional clays.

To add to the apparent authenticity, these pigments must be ground with linseed oil on a glass slab. When the paint is used, this mixture is thinned with turpentine and more oil. Linseed oil or other oils used in the past dry quite slowly, and new paint can remain soft for many years. It also darkens with age, while at the same time becoming more translucent. The forger can allow for this by making the painting, particularly the highlights, slightly darker than usual. Heating the finished work or any

A bottle of smalt, a deep blue pigment, formerly used principally for coloring glass and pottery glazes. It is a mixture of minerals, including silica, potash and cobalt oxide.

Because etchings and prints are themselves copies, it can be almost impossible to detect the fake if the forger is really skilled.

intermediate stages in a warm (but not hot) oven may help to harden the paint.

Many paintings are varnished. Originally this was done partly to slow down the darkening, both of the oil and of the white lead used. Over the centuries the varnish and the surface layer of paint beneath it will crackle. This is called *craquelure* and is not the same as other cracks that can penetrate all the paint layers. Expert forgers use two varnishes specially made for picture restorers by the French company, Lefranc et Bourgeois. These are called *Vernis à veiller* [varnish to add age] and *Vernis craqueleur* [crackle varnish]. Elmyr de Hory used both in the latter part of his career, though Van Meegeren employed a different technique.

Finally, the forger must make the painting and the back of the canvas dirty. This can be done by blowing ordinary household dust into the crackling or using smoke from a candle or a tobacco pipe. Once the work is set into an old picture frame to make it seem even more genuine, it is ready for sale.

HOW FORGERS WORK: DRAWINGS, ETCHINGS AND PRINTS

Far fewer problems have to be solved when forging works on paper than in forging paintings. This requires a considerable degree of artistic ability but somewhat less than that needed to fake painted work. Because etchings and prints are themselves copies, it can be almost impossible to detect the fake if the forger is really skilled.

Many works on paper have disappeared into private collections, sometimes into attics or into the archives of lawyers for safekeeping. It is not uncommon for a genuine or seemingly genuine work to be rediscovered after many years. Unrecognized pictures can also turn up in antique shops or flea markets. Of course, these don't have provenance and therefore need the authentication of experts. Art historians and museum curators publish lists of the known works of major artists, but nobody knows what else they might have produced or how many copies of each.

IMITATING OLD PAPER

The principal problem for a forger is to obtain the sort of paper on which the drawing has been done or the copy printed. Since 1945, almost all paper manufactured commercially has had "whiteners" added to the mix to increase its brightness. Under ultraviolet light this will fluoresce blue. Experienced forgers buy old books of approximately the right age and make use of the flyleaves or any blank pages. When these are carbon-dated (see page 64), they will appear genuine.

Modern artists, of course, are likely to employ modern paper, so this problem does not arise. Paper intended for legal documents may also be without whitener. However, it will still have to be aged if the forger is faking an old piece of work. Luckily for the forger, tea or coffee can be very effective in staining paper, or the paper can be heated in an oven.

Prints are reproduced by lithography (see page 20), and even the most meticulous forger is likely to use modern inks. However, while suspect paintings can be chemically analyzed by taking a tiny chip of paint, perhaps from the very edge of the painting under its frame, the film of lithographic ink is so thin that it defies normal analysis.

HOW FORGERS WORK: SCULPTURE AND CERAMICS

As with all other art fakes, the skill of the forger lies in reproducing, exactly, the style of the artist. A sculptor, however, is unlikely to create two identical pieces of work, and so the forger must design and create a new sculpture. And here the question arises: "Is it any less desirable as a work of art?"

As the story of Michelangelo's *Sleeping Cupid* forgery (see page 44) shows, the

Manufacturers of reproduction antique furniture have been known to fire lead shot into the wood to imitate the worm-eaten appearance of genuine pieces.

easiest way to give an appearance of age to a sculpture or a bronze cast is to bury it for some time, then "discover" it. Marble will develop a surface patina that has a characteristic fluorescence under ultraviolet light, and bronze develops a blackish-green patina. On marble that is supposed to be ancient, an expert can often detect when modern electric tools have been used in fashioning the stone.

Copies made during the life of the artist should bear the name of the founder. But what happens after the artist dies and what of the founder's heirs?

As with prints, a bronze cast is a copy, and as in the case of Guy Hain (see page 75), this raises an interesting point. Genuine casts are, in principle, made under the supervision of the artist. Copies made during the life of the artist should bear the name of the founder. But what happens after the artist dies and what of the founder's heirs? They will often continue to manufacture copies for amateur collectors, at which point, legally, the name of the founder should be changed. Hain's forgery lay in replacing the modern founder's name with that of his grandfather.

Ceramics present a serious problem, even for the most expert forgery detective, because they also are produced in quantity. A clever forger can make an exact copy of a piece of fifteenth-century Ming pottery, and it has been estimated that a large number of Chinese "antiques" in public and private collections are in fact modern fakes. However, the techniques employed by the old Chinese potters were relatively crude, and the modern electric kiln may produce a glaze that can be slightly different. Nevertheless, present-day analysis by thermoluminescence (see page 64) is really the only way to detect forged ceramics.

THE MICHELANGELO *MODELLO*

In 1986 two dealers with dubious reputations in the art world were involved in the "discovery" of a tiny piece of sculpture. If genuine, it would have been valued at as much as $90 million. One dealer, Dutchman Michel van Rijn, was a self-confessed smuggler of icons and other works. Van Rijn had managed to sell a self-portrait by Rembrandt (van Rijn) to a Japanese collector who believed him to be a descendant of the painter. The other suspect dealer was Frenchman Michel de Bry, who had famously sold a head of Achilles, which he claimed was the work of the fourth-century B.C.E. Greek sculptor Skopas, to the Getty Museum for $2.5 million.

The piece in question was part of a plaster *modello* of the famous statue of David by Michelangelo. It was known that Michelangelo had made a preliminary model. According to Giorgio Vasari, friend and biographer of the artist, it had been made of wax. There was also a rumor that a second model, made of plaster, had been stored in the Palazzo Vecchio in Florence, Italy, part of which was destroyed by fire in 1690. There were signs that flames had scorched the fragment.

Determined to obtain authentication for his find, de Bry contacted Frederick Hartt, Emeritus Professor of the History of Art at the University of Virginia and one of the world's experts on Michelangelo. De Bry invited Hartt, as his guest, to Paris and showed him the *modello*. Hartt was delighted and flattered. He even convinced himself of how the statuette had fallen forward to become burned in the way it was. When de Bry announced that he would have to sell it, Hartt thought of the wonderful book he could write and found a suggested commission of 5 percent for his expertise irresistible.

The history of the *modello* from that time forward is complex. Sotheby's, the art dealer,

became involved. Van Rijn, who was negotiating the sale of another, possibly genuine, Michelangelo statuette, was drawn into the matter as an intermediary. Meanwhile, de Bry had named a fictitious "Honegger Foundation" in Geneva, Switzerland, as the owners of the statuette and claimed it had been found in a shoebox among the possessions of the dead composer Arthur Honegger. It now remained locked up in a bank vault, with all the players in the drama jealously refusing access.

Finally, when it became known that Professor Hartt had agreed to receive a

The original painting of fourteen sunflowers made by Van Gogh in August 1888, now owned by the National Gallery in London. A copy made by the artist in January 1889 is presently in Amsterdam. A similar, recently disputed, painting was exhibited by the National Gallery for ten years, and throughout that time its authenticity was never questioned. In 2002 a panel of experts declared all three versions to be genuine.

commission on the sale of the *modello*, his authentication was discredited and little more has been heard of it. Van Rijn now has an Internet site, on which he carries on a personal vendetta against the marketplace in fakes and forgeries and against the corrupt dealers who handle them.

VAN GOGHS IN DOUBT

In 1997 an investigation by *The Art Newspaper*, London, alleged that at least 45 paintings and drawings attributed to post-Impressionist Vincent van Gogh (1853–1890), then held in many of the world's leading museums, were fakes. Altogether, said the journal, some 100 were "very doubtful."

Van Gogh may have been forged "more frequently than any other modern master," so the late John Rewald, a leading scholar in the field, declared.

The claim provoked a storm of protest, but it also stimulated many museums to reexamine their holdings. What emerged was that experts had for many years regarded a number of well-known and well-loved "Van Goghs" as "doubtful," although few agreed on which were fakes. As the results of the investigation were gradually published, the name of Frenchman Claude-Emile Schuffenecker was regularly mentioned.

HOW MANY SUNFLOWERS?

Schuffenecker (1851–1934) was a painter, a contemporary of Van Gogh's and a friend of Paul Gauguin's (1848–1903). In 1901 he was involved in an exhibition of Van Gogh's paintings in Paris, to which he contributed several he owned and several others owned by his brother Amédée. He also spent some time restoring one of the *Sunflowers* paintings owned by the Van Gogh family.

Van Gogh had made four paintings of sunflowers in August 1888 to decorate a

room in Arles, France, where Gauguin was coming to stay with him. The paintings were of 3, 5, 12 and 14 sunflowers. Gauguin was delighted with the set and asked for two, so Van Gogh made copies of the 12- and 14-sunflower paintings in January 1889. The original 14-sunflower painting is now in the National Gallery in London, and its copy is in Amsterdam. The letters of Van Gogh refer only to these six paintings, but a supposed seventh appeared at the 1901 Paris exhibition as "the property of Monsieur E. Schuffenecker."

German dealer Otto Wacker was found guilty of fraud. He had put 33 "previously unknown" Van Gogh paintings on sale, 30 of which turned out to be copies.

At that time, E. Schuffenecker had a large collection of contemporary paintings. When his wife sued him for divorce, he was compelled to sell them to his brother Amédée, an art dealer. The name Schuffenecker had already been mentioned in connection with the selling of fakes by the 1920s. The name emerged once again in 1932, when German dealer Otto Wacker was found guilty of fraud. He had put 33 "previously unknown" Van Gogh paintings on sale, 30 of which turned out to be copies. He had obtained three from the Schuffenecker brothers.

In 1987 the Chester Beatty family sold the seventh sunflower painting to the Japanese firm Yasuda Fire & Marine Insurance for £24,750,000. The suggestion that this painting was a Schuffenecker fake naturally horrified the company, which announced that the Yasuda Kasai Museum of Art had never doubted that it was a genuine work. The Van Gogh Museum in Holland also

A self-portrait by Claude-Emile Schuffenecker, suspected of having forged at least three paintings attributed to Van Gogh.

found itself in an embarrassing position, since it had recently accepted a large donation from Yasuda to build an extension.

In 2002 all three 14-sunflower paintings were exhibited in Amsterdam, and a panel of experts concluded that all were genuine. London's National Gallery stated: "The version of the *Sunflowers* belonging to the Yasuda Fire & Marine Insurance company hung on our wall for ten years, and its authenticity was never questioned."

Claude-Emile Schuffenecker's own paintings can be found in a number of collections, but he never achieved the fame of Van Gogh. He died in 1934 in Paris, an embittered retired art-school teacher.

DOUBLE IDENTITY

An extraordinary case of forgery emerged in 2000. A painting by Paul Gauguin entitled *Vase des Lilas* (not one of his greatest, but still valued at several hundred thousand dollars) was offered for sale simultaneously by Christie's and Sotheby's, both leading international auction houses. When they discovered this, the two houses flew both paintings to the Wildenstein Institute in Paris to be examined by their Gauguin expert, Sylvie Crussard. She quickly announced that the painting being offered by Christie's was, in the language of the trade, "not right." The genuine work was sold by its owner, New York Iranian-born dealer Ely Sakhai, for $310,000, while Christie's had to inform the Gallery Muse in Tokyo that sadly, theirs was a fake.

The FBI was called in, and after several years of international investigations, in March 2004, Sakhai was arrested on eight counts of fraud. According to the FBI, Sakhai had bought the original some years earlier, acquired a duplicate and sold it to a Tokyo collector. It was a one-in-a-million coincidence that both paintings had come up for sale at the same time.

Also according to the FBI, Sakhai had carried on this type of deception for years, accumulating profits of $3.5 million. The Bureau explained that Sakhai would sell a copy of a painting, authenticated by the original's certificate to establish provenance,

to a buyer in Asia. Later he would sell the original in Europe. Sakhai reasoned, so the FBI said, that the sales were too far separate for the news to spread and that the paintings were always relatively unfamiliar and of middle-market value, so their sale would attract little attention.

It is yet to be determined where Sakhai had the forgeries made. China and Taiwan, where it is known that entire workshops are busy producing "old" paintings, are two possibilities. It is unlikely, however, that such a scheme could ever work again. Nowadays dealers all over the world are in constant touch on the Internet, and it would quickly become apparent that the same painting was on sale at two different auction houses at the same time. Sakhai pleaded guilty to forgery charges in December 2004.

USING MODERN SCIENCE TO DETECT FORGERIES

To examine a work of art, the scientific departments of major galleries use a

FORGER'S FILE
THE SCANDALOUS SCAMS OF SAKHAI

In 1990, Sakhai bought La Nappe Mauve by Marc Chagall (1887–1985) for $312,000 at Christie's and in 1993 sold what seemed to be this painting, accompanied by its authentication certificate, to a Tokyo collector for $514,000. In 1999, he sold the genuine La Nappe Mauve, through Christie's, for $340,000. Meanwhile, the other painting had passed through several hands and ended up being offered for sale at the Galerie Koller in Zurich, Switzerland, where the gallery owner compared it closely with the photograph on the accompanying certificate. "The colors were strange, a little bit," he decided, and withdrew it from sale.

In 1995, Sakhai sold a "Marie Laurencin" painting, Jeune Fille à la Mandoline, to a Tokyo buyer for $28,100. Two years later it was put up for sale at Christie's, at which point Christie's discovered that Sakhai still owned the same work.

In 1998, a buyer in Taipei bought a supposed Chagall, Le Roi David dans le Paysage Vert, from Sakhai for $80,000. He sent it to France for verification. It was immediately declared a fake, and the French authorities destroyed it.

The apparatus used to
carry out radio-carbon
dating at the Research
Laboratories for
Archaeology in Oxford,
England.

number of techniques, most of which were developed in the twentieth century. These include the use of ultraviolet, infrared and X-ray radiation; sophisticated chemical analysis, including spectrography; thermoluminescence; and radiocarbon dating. There are plenty of scientific

techniques available for catching forgers; unfortunately, few dealers have the time or the money to put their works on sale after such detailed examination.

Ultraviolet illumination can quickly reveal additions or changes to a painting because the various layers of paint and varnish will fluoresce in different hues. Old marble develops a patina that fluoresces yellowish green, while a modern marble, or an old piece that has been newly cut, will fluoresce a bright violet.

In a typical case a triptych, painted and gilded in fifteenth-century Sienese style, was shown to contain modern machine-made nails.

Infrared light, photographed through an appropriate filter, will penetrate the layers of paint, disclosing painting underneath the surface layer. This can reveal an earlier painting on the same canvas (not necessarily in itself an indication of forgery, as many artists have painted over their own work) or a signature that has been covered up and replaced by one more valuable. Radiation from X-rays can be employed in the same way.

X-rays can be employed in a similar way. These rays are also useful for looking inside an object. If, for example, a supposedly medieval wooden carving is shown to have nails or other metal supports deep inside that are obviously of modern manufacture, it is clearly a forgery.

In a typical case a triptych, painted and gilded in fifteenth-century Sienese style, was shown to contain modern machine-made nails. Even more revealingly, the X-ray examination showed that the wood panels were already worm-eaten before the

painting and gilding had been applied.

X-rays can also be used to induce fluorescence in an object, as secondary X-rays. Comparing these secondary emissions with those from known materials, an analyst can identify the elements present. The technique has been used, for example, in analyzing the proportions of manganese and cobalt in the blue glaze of Chinese porcelain.

Chemical analysis can detect the presence of paint pigments that were not used by artists in the past. Until the nineteenth century, the only white pigment available was white lead. At that time, people burned coal to heat their homes, and the fumes of burning coal caused the paintings to darken. Modern white

pigments are manufactured primarily from titanium dioxide, which does not darken and is easily detected by analysis. Other colors, too, are now generally available as modern synthetic products.

SPECTROGRAPHIC ANALYSIS

Unfortunately, any chemical analysis requires the removal of a sample of the paint from the work. However, the development of spectrographic analysis means that the sample need be only a minute speck. The tiny fragment, perhaps removed from someplace unseen, such as underneath the frame, is burned in a flame. This produces a spectrum that reveals the characteristics of every element in the fragment. Photographing this spectrum

Opposite: This portrait
of Pope Julius II was
long believed to be only
a copy of a painting by
Raphael. Eventually,
detailed analysis
revealed that walnut oil
had been used to thin
the paint. As Raphael
was known to have
employed this oil, the
painting has now been
accepted as a genuine
original.

shows how much of each element is present.

The oil used by a painter to dilute pigments can also be analyzed. In one case it showed that what was believed to be a copy of a papal portrait was actually the original. A portrait of Pope Julius II was long thought to be only a copy of a painting by Sanzio Raphael (1483–1520). However, analysis established that the medium had been walnut oil, as was used by Raphael. In addition, X-ray photography revealed that the paint underneath had been reworked a number of times, which is not something that happens when an artist is simply making a copy.

DATING POTTERY USING THERMOLUMINESCENCE

Thermoluminescence is a technique that is mostly used for the dating of pottery and other ceramics. It is based on the principle that when pottery is fired, it loses any inherent radioactivity. However, over the years it will gradually reabsorb radioactive material from its surroundings, particularly if it remains buried in the

earth. When a sample of the ceramic is heated to above 640°F (340°C), it glows. The brighter the glow, the older the sample. By comparing the intensity of the glow with that made by materials of a known age, experts can estimate the age of the pottery being tested.

Counterfeiters have come up with all sorts of tricks to defeat thermoluminescence analysis. In one case a restorer glued together a number of ancient cups and bowls, then covered them with a thin ceramic coating to make the shape of a Persian bull. Other restorers use genuine broken fragments, of little value in themselves, and assemble them into pieces that look highly valuable.

RADIO-CARBON DATING

Another important technique, carbon dating, is based on exactly the opposite principle called thermoluminescence. All organic materials contain a small proportion of the radioactive isotope carbon-14. Once the material has been made into an object, the amount of carbon-14 present steadily

FORGER'S FILE
SCIENCE CATCHES UP WITH DOSSENA

Thermoluminescence was used to prove that several "ancient" sculptures were actually the work of Alceo Dossena (see page 50). One was the terra-cotta figure of Diana, said to have been unearthed in 21 separate pieces from an Etruscan site. Doubts had been raised quite early when Dossena, in confessing to being a forger, produced a photograph of the assembled pieces in his studio. But supporters of the statue's authenticity dismissed this as "a photographic trick." Eventually, in 1968, a dental drill was used to take a tiny sample from one of the pieces. There are no prizes for guessing that thermoluminescence analysis confirmed that the figure was only some 40 years old.

FORGER'S FILE
FAKE ART BUT A GENUINE SCAM

One ingenious use of a forged artwork may not come to light for many years, if ever. The perpetrator of the scam obtains a high-quality forgery, together with fake provenance papers, and an authentication that may be genuinely mistaken or itself another forgery. With these in hand, he insures the work for a huge sum and lodges it in a bank vault. The insurance document is now supposedly proof of the work's value, and investors are invited to buy shares in it. Few ever see the forged item, of which they believe they own a piece, as it is held under lock and key. In reality it may already have been taken from the vault and sold elsewhere on the market.

decays with the passing of time. By analyzing the amount of carbon-14 still present in an object, scientists can make a relatively accurate estimate of its age. Carbon dating cannot be used on materials that are less than 50 years old, but it does give reliable results on specimens even up to 40,000 years of age. However, the analysis requires the destruction of a fragment of the object about the size of a postage stamp. This amounts to significant damage to the piece, so carbon dating is seldom used in the examination of works of art.

Other scientific methods have been developed recently to detect forgeries or authenticate artwork. These can be very expensive, however, and in some cases, there may be only one person in the world who is expert in the technique.

PAINTER, FORGER, CONVICT

French forger Francis Lagrange (1894–1964) trained as a painter; he was known as "Flag" to his friends. In the years following World War I, Lagrange survived for some time by selling pornographic art, but in 1926 he won a prize in a competition for the design of a new French postage stamp. This attracted the attention of the underworld, a

member of which offered him 20 percent of the proceeds if he would undertake the forging of rare items sought by philatelists. He accepted and later grew confident enough to start forging $100 bills.

Then one day his underworld contact brought him a dealer who had an American customer determined to acquire a painting by Fra Lippo Lippi (1406–1469). The difficulty was that almost all of Lippi's work was in major museums. However, there was a three-panel altar painting (a triptych) in a cathedral in Rheims, in northern France.

For two months Lagrange worked in a rented attic studio near the cathedral, carefully copying the work in exquisite detail. What he did not know was that his criminal associates had planned to steal the original and replace it with his copy. All went well until 1929, when the American stock market crashed and the buyer of the original was forced to sell it. The triptych was included in the list published to advertise a London sale, to the amazement of the director of the Rheims museum. He made his way to London, convinced that he could denounce the painting as a forgery, but he was assured it was indeed authentic. On his return to Rheims, the director had the

work in his museum examined, and it was soon exposed as a copy.

DEVIL'S ISLAND

Meanwhile, the underworld gang had lured Lagrange back to Paris, and it contrived to have him arrested for counterfeiting money. In 1931 he was sentenced to ten years in the penal colony in Cayenne, French Guiana. He managed to escape in 1938 but was soon recaptured and committed to Devil's Island, where he was allowed to take up painting again. Finally released in 1946, he settled in Cayenne, where, apart from another three years in prison for fraud (but not for forgery), he continued painting.

An American who visited Cayenne showed an interest in Lagrange's work, and this persuaded Lagrange to move to the United States. There he held exhibitions of his work and published his autobiography, *Flag on Devil's Island* (1961). He eventually returned to Cayenne and died there in 1964.

What became of the Lippi triptych remains a mystery. The original was returned to France, but the Rheims museum was damaged during World War II and never reopened. There is a story that this "original" was also found to be a copy and that it still exists, stored in the basement of a Paris museum.

The flamboyant Spanish artist Salvador Dalí (1904–1989) had a wicked sense of mischief. Shortly before his death, and knowing exactly what he was doing, Dalí signed hundreds of sheets of plain paper. Their later history is likely to trouble art historians for many years.

THE MAN WHO FOOLED GOERING

Han van Meegeren was born to a large
and devout Catholic family in Deventer,
Holland, in 1889. He showed considerable
talent as a painter and before the age of 30
held two successful one-man shows.
However, like so many others trying to
make a living as an artist, he grew
disillusioned with the arrogance of art
experts and, in particular, with one Dr.
Abraham Bredius.

In 1932, van Meegeren relocated to the
south of France. He made a reasonable
living producing portraits, but he also spent
the following four years quietly planning
how to fake seventeenth-century paintings.
He worked out a way of making paint dry
hard quickly, using a mixture of oil of lilac
with components of Bakelite (an early form
of plastic) and reproducing the *craquelure*

[crackling] of old works. He bought minor
seventeenth-century paintings and removed
the top layers down to the original ground
color, then applied a coat of paint and
baked the canvas in an oven. This caused
the crackling that formed to reappear
through whatever was painted over it.

To avoid detection, van Meegeren used
only the pigments that had been available to
artists in the seventeenth century. Such
pigments were often expensive and difficult
to obtain, but he used them to make his
paints appear original. He started with
imitations of Terborch, Hals and Vermeer,
using elements from their known paintings.
Once he had mastered the technique, baking
the finished painting to produce further
crackling and then rubbing ink into the
cracks to simulate the dirt of centuries, he
embarked upon his masterpiece.

Art experts believed that Vermeer (1628–1691) had painted several religious subjects between 1654 and the time he began his familiar domestic interiors and that these were undiscovered or perhaps lost. The only identified work was *Christ with Martha and Mary*, which had been authenticated in 1901 by Dr. Bredius. In 1937, van Meegeren astounded the art world by "discovering" a new Vermeer, *The Disciples at Emmaus*. The 83-year-old expert Bredius welcomed it with joy, and it was sold to the Boymans Foundation for 550,000 florins, of which van Meegeren

Van Meegeren answers his accusers in the dock of the Dutch court. He was convicted of forgery and died in prison shortly afterward.

received two-thirds. But the financial reward might have formed only part of van Meegeren's satisfaction. Bredius was utterly fooled. In 1937 he wrote: "It is a wonderful moment in the life of a lover of art when he finds himself suddenly confronted with a hitherto unknown painting by a great master, untouched, on the original canvas, and without any restoration, just as it left the painter's studio." Van Meegeren was now a rich man, but he could not resist the temptation to continue faking.

Between 1939 and 1942 another six "Vermeers" appeared. Holland was under German occupation beginning in 1940, and van Meegeren sold one painting, *The Adulteress*, to Nazi field marshal Hermann Goering. Fate finally caught up with van Meegeren after Holland was liberated in 1945, when he found himself accused of being a collaborator and of selling national treasures. He was forced to confess that the painting was a fake, and he was found guilty of forgery in 1947. He died a few weeks later.

ERIC HEBBORN, MASTER FORGER

One of the most successful twentieth-century art forgers was an Englishman named Eric Hebborn (1934–1996). Born into a poor and violent family in London, he had a miserable childhood. After setting fire to his school in a form of frustrated protest, he was sent to a reform institution. There Hebborn's teachers recognized his talents as a painter and encouraged him. He was eventually accepted into the Royal Academy Schools, where he was awarded a silver medal and a Rome Scholarship to study in Italy.

While still a student, Hebborn worked for a picture restorer named George Aczel. He learned not only to clean and retouch but how to produce crackling in new areas of paint to imitate the effect produced by age. He also discovered how to "improve" paintings by adding small details. Adding a balloon to an unimpressive landscape made it a rare and valuable record of pioneer aviation. Putting a cat in the foreground of a painting, according to Hebborn, immediately made it much more desirable.

Hebborn was without doubt a master craftsman. His book, *The Art Forger's Handbook* (1997), provides extensive information on how to find old paper for forging drawings and how to make the ink and tools for forgeries appear truly authentic. He describes the pigments employed by various old masters in their palettes and how to mimic them. He details the kind of wood panel or canvas they would have used.

An active member of the gay community, Hebborn made the acquaintance of Sir Anthony Blunt, then director of the Courtauld Institute in London. Blunt was later exposed as a spy and stripped of his title. He is known to have authenticated at least two of the forgeries produced by Hebborn. Whether it was done innocently or otherwise remains in doubt. However, other experts were unquestionably fooled.

Hebborn moved to Rome, where, like so many other forgers, he found that his own paintings were not well received by critics. In the years that followed, he produced more than 1,000 drawings, which he attributed to a wide range of old masters.

Below: Many ancient Egyptian works of art sold to tourists are in fact forgeries. This statuette of Queen Tetisheri is held in the British Museum's collection of fakes.

Opposite: Van Meegeren's forged Vermeer painting, *The Adulteress,* is inspected by experts during his trial.

He also forged bronze sculptures, and paintings accepted as those by Corot, Boldini, Augustus John and David Hockney. He sold his forgeries through a small gallery he established, and they found their way into the collections of the British Museum, the Pierpont Morgan Library, the National Gallery in Washington and countless private collections. Hebborn grew wealthy and lived the high life in Rome's gay community.

A temporary setback in Hebborn's career occurred in 1978, when the respectable London dealer Colnaghi realized that a number of drawings it had sold to the Pierpont Morgan Library and to the British National Gallery had been faked by Hebborn. Detected, Hebborn nevertheless announced that he would flood the market with 500 more drawings. To confuse the experts even further, he

Eric Hebborn, forger of an unknown number of works of art. Even when he had been unmasked, he threatened to flood the market with many more.

"There is no such thing as a fake…. Only fake experts and their fake labels."

—ERIC HEBBORN

boldly claimed in his autobiography, *Drawn to Trouble* (1991), that he was the creator of a number of works that are still believed to be genuine.

"There is no such thing as a fake," wrote Hebborn. "Only fake experts and their fake labels." He was found in a Rome street on January 8, 1996, his skull smashed in by a blunt instrument, and he died three days later. Hebborn's death echoed that of Pier Pasolini, the Italian moviemaker murdered outside Rome by a male prostitute in 1975.

FORGER'S FILE
TOM KEATING AND HIS "SEXTON BLAKES"

Seventeen years older than Eric Hebborn, Londoner Tom Keating (1917–1984), an immensely likable rogue, pursued a successful career as a forger. What is remarkable about Keating, though, is that he took none of Hebborn's care in the use of authentic materials. As he later wrote in his book, *The Fake's Progress* (1978), concerning some of the drawings he produced: "I used watercolor, sepia ink, wax and varnish…except, of course, that mine were of the modern synthetic variety." In the London vernacular rhyming slang, he described his works as "Sexton Blakes" (fakes).

At the age of 27, Keating got a medical discharge from the Royal Navy, but it was not until six years later, in 1950, that he obtained a grant to study art for a diploma. He failed in this, however, and could not get the art-teaching job that he had hoped for. He spent the next few years working as a picture restorer, in which pursuit he learned many of the same shady techniques used by Hebborn.

Then, claiming he was acting in protest against the exploitation of artists by dealers, Keating turned to forgery. During the next 20 years or so, he said, he faked the work of more than 100 different artists, including Rembrandt, Goya, Turner, Van Gogh, Degas, Monet and Sisley.

Tom Keating with one of his paintings, attributed to John Constable.

FORGING "THE GUV'NOR"

In 1965, Keating suffered an injury to his back and was unable to get around for a while. He describes how he began to produce a number of watercolor drawings by the English draftsman Samuel Palmer (1805–1881), who had lived in Shoreham, Kent, and whom he always referred to as "the guv'nor."

"I got my drawing board and a pile of pristine paper together and began to draw very rapidly in the style of the guv'nor, banging in a couple of sheep here, a shepherd there, the moon, trees and Shoreham Church. Sometimes I put in the hallowed figure of Christ, sometimes a barn and sometimes a three-arched bridge...."

Opposite: Tom Keating at work on one of his "Sexton Blakes." Unlike van Meegeren, he used modern synthetic materials, but they were not detected.

FORGER'S FILE
SOME MODERN FORGERS

CHANG DIA CHIEN (Chinese, 1899–1983)
In the course of his long life, Chang was a bandit, a Buddhist monk and the creator of some 30,000 paintings, most of which were fakes. It is estimated that every major collection of Chinese art, including the Freer Gallery in Washington, D.C., the Boston Museum of Fine Arts and the British Museum, has a Chang forgery among its collection.

WILLIAM BLUNDELL (Australian, born 1947)
Charged with producing some 4,000 forgeries, mostly of native Australian painters, Blundell also forged works by Monet, Picasso and Jackson Pollock.

GUY HAIN (French, active 1990s)
Hain obtained bronze casts of sculptures by Auguste Rodin (1840–1917) that had been legally manufactured by the Rudier foundry, but he replaced the modern founder's signature with that of his grandfather to suggest that these had been cast with Rodin's approval. He served a term of imprisonment in 1997 but continued his forgeries, including bronzes by other artists, until he was apprehended again in 2000. An estimated 6,000 forgeries by Hain are currently in circulation.

JOHN MYATT (English, born 1946)

A former art teacher and pop songwriter from the English Midlands, Myatt, desperately short of money, placed an advertisement in a London magazine, offering "Genuine Fakes for £250" in 1986. One of his clients was John Drewe (see page 84), who commissioned a painting copied from a drawing by French artist Albert Gleizes (1881–1953), forged the provenance documents and sold the work for £25,000, of which Myatt received half. Using modern emulsion paint (nothing like the materials used in the works he faked), Myatt nevertheless deceived experts with more than 200 works attributed to acknowledged modern masters. Drewe's ex-girlfriend informed on the two men in 1995, and both forgers were given prison sentences for fraud. Investigators calculated that Drewe had made some £2,500,000, of which Myatt received a mere £100,000.

"I gave some of them to the kids who'd been so kind to me while I was laid up with my back. I think they flogged a few in local junk shops, but I like to think they kept one or two and still have them on their walls now that they're grown up. I rarely bothered to frame them; I just handed out slips of paper with Palmer drawings on them. I gave them to all kinds of people, like the gas man who came to read the meter; casual acquaintances and complete strangers; and I even sent them to my family and friends as Christmas cards—I expect they chucked them in the dustbin on Twelfth Night."

Keating had relocated to Norfolk in 1965 with a former pupil, Jane Kelly, and they set up a small business in cleaning and restoring paintings. Some of his Samuel Palmer fakes were, however, sold to London dealers by Jane. In 1976, Geraldine Norman, the Art Sales correspondent of the *Times* in London, began to investigate stories of suspect Samuel Palmers that had appeared on the market. Norman's investigations led her first to Jane Kelly and then to Keating. He was persuaded to confess at a press conference and admitted to forging many other works. Consternation reigned in the London art market.

Keating became a popular hero, and criminal charges brought in 1977 were later dropped on account of his state of health. He won a television award for a series of talks on great artists and their working methods, and was about to begin another when he died in 1984. A posthumous sale of his work brought £274,000, about seven times the estimate that had been expected. This success must be attributed to the popularity of Keating himself because few of his paintings, with the exception of some of the Samuel Palmers, could be taken on close examination, to be the work of the artists to whom they were attributed.

GETTING AWAY WITH IT

What is notable is that few modern forgers of works of art, when they have been unmasked and have confessed, have been charged with fraud. This is because they have usually protected themselves by selling their work through dealers, scrupulous or unscrupulous, who, having charged much higher sums to buyers, are in a more precarious legal position. When a reputable dealer learns that a work he has sold is a fake, it is customary to buy back the work and accept the loss. Less scrupulous dealers will often try to bluster their way through, challenging the buyer

Opposite: One of three supposed "Etruscan warriors," presumably dating from the sixth to fifth centuries B.C.E., purchased by the New York Metropolitan Museum between 1915 and 1921. In 1960 close analysis revealed that the statues were forgeries.

Below: The man who made the fakes, Alberto Fioravanti, was still alive. He proved he was the forger by producing a missing thumb from one of the statues.

FORGER'S FILE
THE EMBARRASSING CASE OF THE "ETRUSCAN" SARCOPHAGUS

In 1871 the British Museum acquired a huge collection of classical objects from an Italian dealer named Alessandro Castellani. But the British Museum ended up deeply embarrassed when many of them were subsequently declared fakes.

The best of the collection was a life-sized terra-cotta sarcophagus (burial casket), apparently from the sixth century B.C.E. Castellani had bought it from one Pietro Pennelli, who said he had excavated it at Cervetri, in Etruria. The sarcophagus was in pieces, which were painstakingly reassembled at the museum over a period of two years. Then, in 1875, Pietro's brother Enrico claimed that it was he who had made the huge object. Controversy over its authenticity raged on for many years.

There were a number of doubtful aspects of the sarcophagus that should have made curators immediately suspicious. The nudity of the male figure was very unusual. The pose of the figures was unlike that in any other known work, and not only that, the female appeared to be wearing nineteenth-century underwear! It was also shown that an inscription inside the lid had been copied from a gold brooch in the Louvre. Nevertheless, for 60 years the British Museum preferred to regard the work as genuine, and it was not removed from display until 1935. Unfortunately, by then photographs of it had been used to illustrate countless books on Etruscan art.

to prove that the work is a forgery, something the buyer might be unwilling to do. Ironically, many works reenter the market and can still command quite high prices, even though they are known or suspected forgeries.

THE ENGLISH VICE

Interestingly, several of those who have been described as "master forgers" of the second half of the twentieth century were Englishmen. This is due in no small way to the fact that London remains the central city for buying and selling art, and the leading London dealers maintain auction houses in the major cities of the world.

What London dealers offer for sale often requires careful restoration by highly skilled people. And part of learning the craft of restoration is learning the methods and styles of the old masters. Both Eric Hebborn and Tom Keating worked for restorers in London, and both claimed that their forgeries were a protest against the high profits made by dealers.

One fact will have become very clear from these stories: The art forger seldom, if ever, earns the "big money." The forger works away, often for a mere pittance, while the dealer, whether genuinely deceived or knowingly dishonest, makes the major profit. Nothing could better exemplify this than the career of Elmyr de Hory, widely described as the leading forger of the twentieth century.

ELMYR DE HORY, THE PRINCE OF CHARM

Hungarians, among all people, are particularly renowned for their charm and their ability to survive by means of it—none more so than art forger Elmyr de Hory. He was born in 1906 and claimed that his family owned large estates in central Hungary. Revealing some promise as an artist, de Hory was sent to Budapest to study at the art school, and at age 18, he continued his studies at the Akademie Heimann in Munich.

Two years later De Hory went to Paris, where he studied under the painter Fernand Léger (1881–1955). A poor struggling artist, de Hory nevertheless (he claimed) employed his charm to make the acquaintance of every artist and writer in Montparnasse, the quarter of Paris where artists and writers lived and congregated. In 1938, de Hory returned to Budapest for some reason, but in 1941 he found himself in a German concentration camp, where he was badly beaten by the Gestapo and ended up in a hospital outside Berlin.

One day, noticing that the hospital gates were open, he calmly walked out and, after many adventures, made his way once more to Paris in 1945, in time for the end of World War II. He began to paint again, selling whatever he could to wealthy acquaintances. Then, in April 1946, the widow of British racing driver Sir Malcolm Campbell visited him in his cheap little room. Spying a line drawing de Hory had done of a girl's head, she asked, "Isn't that a Picasso?" He just sighed tragically and agreed reluctantly to sell it. Lady Campbell was hardly out the door before he had dashed off seven similar drawings.

A LUCRATIVE PARTNERSHIP

Now fortune smiled on de Hory, because in the period just after the war, there was a passion among collectors for work by Pablo Picasso (1881–1973). Picasso could produce a characteristic drawing as swiftly as de Hory, and he was prolific in his output. Elmyr confessed his ability to replicate Picasso to a close friend, Jules Chamberlin. Chamberlin, whose father had been a well-known collector, suggested that they go into partnership, selling

Elmyr's work as the remainder of his father's collection.

Two "Picasso" figure studies were sold to the director of the Musée des Beaux Arts in Brussels, Belgium, and others were disposed of all over Europe. But then came the inevitable dispute with Chamberlin over how to divide the spoils, and Elmyr flew off alone.

Elmyr de Hory (1906–1976) was perhaps the twentieth century's most famous and prolific art forger.

De Hory was forced to leave Los Angeles in a hurry when dealer Frank Perls threw him out of his gallery, being convinced that the drawings de Hory had brought him were fakes.

After his exposure, de Hory hoped that his fame would enable him to sell his own paintings, but he had little success during his lifetime.

De Hory turned up later in Rio de Janeiro, where he rapidly established himself as a successful portrait painter. But he soon tired of Brazil and, after obtaining a three-month visa for the United States, went to New York.

From there he made his way to Hollywood, where he became known as

Baron de Hory and began to sell a succession of fake Picassos. Tiring of this, he tried his hand at Matisse and Renoir drawings: "I sold three Matisse pen-and-ink nudes on the spot [at a fashionable gallery in Beverly Hills].... After that, the owner always bought everything I offered him. He passed them along to the film colony at 500 percent profit."

However, de Hory was forced to leave Los Angeles in a hurry when dealer Frank Perls threw him out of his gallery, being convinced that the drawings de Hory had brought him were fakes. De Hory returned to New York, but by now he was starting to show his age, was beginning to dye his hair and, perhaps most important, was without papers.

His charm was also starting to pall. One of de Hory's New York acquaintances later recalled: "He was rather frantic about his sex life, and that became a bit of a bore. The name-dropping, too—he couldn't tell a story without a dozen digressions about this baron or that young prince he'd slept with in Paris or Cannes or Kitzbühel."

In late 1952, de Hory returned to Los Angeles, intending to give up forgery and sell his own paintings. But before long he needed cash and knew only one way to get it. With a companion, he went back to New York once again, where he sold a visiting French dealer three

"Matisse" drawings for $500 apiece. The two men then left for Miami. From there de Hory, using the name L. E. Raynal, wrote to galleries and museums all over the United States, announcing that he had a work for sale, a drawing, a gouache, a watercolor or a small oil by Matisse, Picasso, Braque, Derain, Bonnard, Degas, Vlaminck, Modigliani or Renoir. Within two years he had sold some 70 drawings and paintings in New York, Philadelphia, St. Louis, Chicago, Seattle, Baltimore, Washington, D.C., Boston, Cleveland, Detroit, Dallas and San Francisco for a sum he claimed to be more than $160,000.

THE NET TIGHTENS

Learning that both the FBI and dealer Frank Perls were asking questions about him, de Hory acquired a passport in the name of L. E. Raynal and escaped to Mexico City. But he had trouble with the police there and returned once more to New York. In his typical manner he immediately threw a party, and he claimed later that Marilyn Monroe had been one of the guests. But another guest was to cause him nothing but trouble for the rest of his life. His name was Ferdinand Legros—a thin, shabbily dressed young man, half French and half Greek.

Et voila! Elmyr de Hory could turn out a passable forgery of a Henri Magritte drawing in ten seconds, but he said that he had a problem in making the work look authentic. Magritte's drawing line would be interrupted when he turned from his easel to look at the model; but working solely from his imagination, de Hory tended to make his line continuous.

Legros proposed a partnership. He would sell de Hory's forgeries, taking 40 percent and giving Elmyr 60 percent. But de Hory soon discovered that while he was forced to stay in a second-rate hotel steadily producing his fakes, Legros and a French-Canadian beach bum named Réal Lessard were living in the best hotel in town. After six months and regular bitter fights, de Hory decided to leave for Europe. He settled in Rome and took up painting again. Using the name Joseph Boutin, he had a modest success with a one-man show in Milan.

It has been estimated that if the thousands of works of art de Hory distributed around the world had been genuine, they would have had a market value of more than $60 million.

But in 1960 he made a nostalgic visit to Paris, where the familiar shabby figure of Legros tracked him down. Legros asked if de Hory had any forgeries to sell. De Hory replied that all he had were stored in a trunk in the Hotel Winslow in New York. Legros left at once, telephoned the hotel posing as Elmyr de Hory and announced that a young man named Ferdinand Legros would collect the trunk within a week.

Meanwhile, completely unaware of this, de Hory returned to Rome. There he found it impossible to make a living selling his own paintings, and within a month he had put together a portfolio of Renoir and Degas pastels, Chagall and Derain watercolors and Matisse drawings. He set off in his car to sell in Switzerland, Germany and Holland. Finally, he decided he would settle down in the little island of

Ibiza, in the Balearics, off the eastern coast of Spain. The authorities there knew him as Joseph Elmyr Dory-Boutin.

He could not resist the lure of Paris for long, however, and there again he ran into Legros and Lessard. But now they were well dressed and obviously prosperous. Unbeknown to de Hory, Legros had sold the contents of his trunk and set himself up as a successful dealer. Legros once more proposed a business partnership: de Hory should return at once to Ibiza, where Legros would send him a regular allowance, together with his share of whatever price he could obtain for his forgeries. In 1963, Legros made what seemed an even more generous gesture when he built Elmyr a fine house above the sea in Ibiza, with a roomy studio.

Legros could well afford this, as he and Lessard were now rich. The second half of the twentieth century had seen an unprecedented boom in the sale of art. The United States in particular seemed full of rich men who, aware that prices were rising, could easily be persuaded that art was a sound investment as a hedge against taxation. By far the best customer for Legros was Texas millionaire Alger Hurtle Meadows, head of General American Oil. He had spent around $1 million in Madrid on a number of questionable Goyas and El Grecos, and between 1964 and 1966, Legros sold him 46 works, all by de Hory, at least half of which were oil paintings.

However, while in Dallas, Legros and Lessard had a bitter dispute, and Meadows began to be suspicious of the two. He invited a number of experts, including two who already had their doubts about de Hory, to view his collection. The experts unanimously declared them to be fakes.

Legros escaped to Paris and at once demanded more paintings from de Hory, which immediately went on sale in an auction in the small French town of

Pontoise. An auction-house employee, thinking that a painting described as executed in 1906 by Maurice Vlaminck (1876–1958) looked a little dirty, began to clean it. He was more than a little surprised when some of the blue sky came away on the cloth: The paint was still soft. The news precipitated a panic throughout the art world. Were all the works sold by Legros and by de Hory himself fakes?

IBIZAN EXILE

Gathering up what he could of his stock, Legros fled to Egypt but was arrested in Switzerland in April 1968. Elmyr had also been on the run, but learning of Legros's arrest, he returned to Ibiza. Elmyr reasoned that since his most notorious fakes had been made outside Spain and none had been sold there, he had committed no crime under Spanish law.

However, on his return to Ibiza, de Hory was arrested on a number of relatively flimsy charges and spent two months in the local jail. He was allowed his deck chair, books, sleeping pills, clothes and other comforts, and it is even reported that he kept his stock of drink in the refrigerator of the town hall next door. He was released in October 1968 and told he must leave Spanish territory for a year, which he spent in Portugal.

Meanwhile, another resident on Ibiza, Clifford Irving (whom we shall meet again in chapter 3) published a book entitled *Fake!*, which was based on many conversations with de Hory. Orson Welles subsequently made his film, *F for Fake*, in which both Irving and de Hory were featured. De Hory's name and reputation had become known everywhere.

For the next eight years, de Hory spent a precarious life on Ibiza as a popular party-giving member of the expatriate

Elmyr de Hory forgeries now sell for prices as high as $20,000—and there are also fakes of his fakes on the market!

FORGER'S FILE
SENTIMENTAL PROVENANCE

Forged works of art sell much more easily if they are authenticated as genuine. One day, for example, Réal Lessard visited the aged Kees van Dongen (1877–1968), asking him to authenticate an Elmyr de Hory version of a woman's portrait Van Dongen had painted 60 years earlier. The artist, then in his eighties, took one look at it and with tears in his eyes told Réal how beautiful the woman had been and how many times he had made love to her during his painting of the portrait.

A sketch of John Drewe (above right), in court during his trial for fraud. He and John Myatt, the artist who produced the forgeries, were both found guilty. A former school friend, Daniel Stoakes (above left), who had unwittingly acted as a seller for Drewe, was cleared of complicity.

community. Then, in 1976, he learned that Legros, who had escaped from Switzerland to Brazil, had been extradited to France and sentenced to two years for defrauding Alger Meadows. De Hory also faced extradition, and in December he took a fatal overdose of sleeping pills at his home.

JOHN DREWE

Drewe was a document forger. However, the fact that he forged provenances of the paintings of the forger John Myatt makes this chapter the most appropriate place for the story of his career.

Born John Cockett in 1948, in Sussex, in southeast England, he changed his name to Drewe in 1965. Even as a child, he had

lived in a fantasy world of his own creation. Drewe later claimed to have studied physics for six years at Kiel University in Germany, where there is no record of his attendance or graduation, and to have taught for a year at Sussex University. All that is known of Drewe until 1980 is that he briefly held a clerical post in the British Atomic Energy Authority. During the early 1980s, he taught physics at a private school in London. Then, in 1986, he read John Myatt's advertisement, called him on the phone and introduced himself as "Professor Drewe," a nuclear physicist. He then commissioned several of Myatt's "genuine fakes."

FORGER'S FILE
BERENSON AND DUVEEN, THE ARTFUL PARTNERS

Bernhard Berenson (1865–1959) was born in Lithuania but raised in Boston. He became an acknowledged expert on Italian Renaissance paintings, many of which he had bought for himself. With an enviable reputation as a "fake buster," he became an adviser to the English dealer Joseph Duveen (1869–1939). Duveen was later raised to the peerage for his aid in building additional galleries to the Tate Gallery, London, and the British Museum.

Duveen's motto was "Europe has the art, America has the money." Using Berenson's authentication, he was able to sell hundreds of works of art to Andrew Mellon, J. P. Morgan, the Rockefellers, the Metropolitan Museum of Art in New York and many other prestigious American collections.

It was not until 1986 that the writer Colin Simpson published his book, *Artful Partners*. Allowed access to archives that had been closed previously, Simpson was able to show that a secret agreement existed between Berenson and Duveen. It worked very simply. Following the sale of a painting he had endorsed, Berenson would be paid a considerable commission. These made him a wealthy man.

Wealthy English art dealer Joseph Duveen, who was made Lord Duveen for his donations to London museums.

Berenson knew every forger and faker in Italy, where he lived for most of his life. Simpson maintains that he authenticated a number of sculptures as being by Lorenzo Ghiberti (1378–1455) or Antonio Rossellino (1427–1479), both highly regarded Renaissance artists, when in fact he knew full well that they had been created by Giovanni Bastianini.

Simpson cites many other instances of works that were "improved" to increase their value. For example, a painting of a middle-aged woman in mourning, attributed to Sebastiano Mainardi (died 1513) was "restored" to reveal a young girl in a fashionable dress. And an alleged Giorgioni portrait had come to Berenson from the hands of his friend, the restorer Luigi Grassi. Now questions are being asked in the art world about every one of the works that Berenson authenticated and Duveen later sold.

Bernhard Berenson was a famous expert on Italian Renaissance art throughout his life. He owned a beautiful villa, near Florence, Italy. On his death in 1959, the villa, with its striking art collection and magnificent library, was bequeathed to Harvard University, and it is administered as a Center for Italian Renaissance Culture.

Drewe soon revealed to Myatt that Christie's had accepted one of his paintings, and the near-penniless artist was caught up in a web of deception. At Drewe's insistence he rapidly began to produce work in a wide range of styles: Giacometti, Nicolas de Stael, Braque, Ben Nicholson, Matisse and many more. "I was flattered," Myatt later said, "into thinking I was a man of importance."

At first, in order to provide provenance for the fakes he was selling, Drewe forged letters from nonexistent owners or persuaded acquaintances to pose as sellers. Then he hit upon a scheme that was to cause havoc in London's art archives. He pretended to be an expert researching art that had been lost to the Nazis during World War II, and he insinuated himself into the libraries of the

Institute of Contemporary Art, the Tate Gallery and the Victoria and Albert Museum. Once there, he altered and fabricated hundreds of documents in order to provide persuasive proof of the provenance of Myatt's paintings.

Alan Bowness, former head of the Tate Gallery, London, and son-in-law of the English painter Ben Nicholson, was deceived into authenticating two of Myatt's "Nicholsons." It wasn't that they were particularly good examples of the artist's work, he said, but that Drewe had provided unquestionable documentation of their provenance.

Myatt's "Giacometti" was sold for $175,000. Drewe had inserted a photograph of the painting into the catalogue of a 1955 exhibition in the archives of the National Art Library. As Melanie Clore, head of the modern art department at Sotheby's put it: "You go to the Tate Gallery archives, and you look through the stock book of the most reputable gallery in London in the fifties, and you find the picture reproduced in black and white. You can't be more diligent than that."

The directors of the Tate Gallery and the Victoria and Albert Museum were forced to admit that they might never discover to what extent their archives had been altered by Drewe. At New York's Museum of Modern Art, a program of meticulous reexamination of paintings and archives was begun. A spokesman for the museum reported: "It will take years, probably, before it is fully accomplished."

A genuine painting by Alberto Giacometti (1901–1966), a 1921 self-portrait in the Kunsthaus, Zurich, Switzerland.

FORGER'S FILE
THE FAKE-BUSTER FOOLED

The Italian art forger Ilicio Federico Ioni once took a genuine fourteenth-century Sienese painting for Bernhard Berenson's approval. "Tell Signor Ioni," said Berenson, "he is getting better as a faker." Ioni retorted, "It's always the same. When I bring him a fake, it becomes genuine, and when I bring him a genuine work, it becomes fake!"

CHAPTER 3
FALSE PAPERS

The faking and forging of documents are among the oldest of criminal activities. Although usually done for fraudulent purposes, they can also be mischievous rather than criminal.

Among the earliest "documents" found are accounts by ancient Egyptian nobles, painted on the walls of their tombs to record their accomplishments. Many of these wall paintings, to put it charitably, exaggerate somewhat. Others tell outright lies. In more modern times papers establishing a person's ancestry can be forged, particularly if there is a question of inheritance, and so, of course, can wills. Letters of credit, IOUs and receipts, lading bills, certificates of provenance for works of art, autographs, professional credentials—the list is endless. In most instances, however, forgeries amount to mundane cases of fraud that occur almost every day. Far more entertaining is the history of literary forgery.

Opposite: The original Constitution of the United States (1787) was written with a quill pen. Examination under a low-power microscope can easily detect any later copy written with a metal nib.

Left: William Ireland (1775–1835), who enjoyed brief fame in the 1790s with his Shakespeare forgeries.

A history of the early Christian church, written by Eusebius of Caesarea, included the text of letters allegedly written by Christ—more than a century after his death.

EUSEBIUS
BISHOP OF
CÆSAREA in PALÆSTINE.

EUSEBIUS CÆSARIENSIS.

One of the earliest known examples of faked correspondence appears in the history of the early Christian church written by Eusebius of Caesarea (264–340 C.E.). It is based on letters that were alleged to have been exchanged between King Abgar of Edessa and Christ. But there's one minor hitch in the story: Abgar did not rule until more than a century after Christ's death.

Early church policy was actually based on a forged document, known as the "Donation of Constantine." Possibly written in Rome during the eighth century, it purported to be an authorization by the Emperor Constantine (274–337) to Pope Silvester I (314–335), giving the Roman church supremacy over all others. It was used for hundreds of years to justify papal power and went unchallenged until the sixteenth century.

THE MAN FROM FORMOSA

Some of the most interesting examples of literary forgery appeared in England during the eighteenth century. In 1704 a book entitled *An Historical and Geographical Description of Formosa* was published in London. The author's name, certainly not his true one, was given as "George Psalmanaazaar." Formosa ("an island subject to the Emperor of Japan," as described on the title page) is a real island (present-day Taiwan), but it was a place that almost nobody in the Western world, apart from a few Dutch traders, knew anything about when the book was published.

The book sold well. It was illustrated with a dozen or so good engravings and described the manners and customs, crops and houses and gold mines on the island. It included details of the "Formosan" language, illustrated in an alphabet of symbols reading from right to left. It also contained an account of the author's conversion to Christianity and criticized the activities of Jesuit missionaries in the Far East.

Early church policy was actually based on a forged document, known as the "Donation of Constantine."

But who was (as his contemporaries spelled it) "Psalmanazar?" It seems he was born in France in 1679 and spoke French, Latin and English, as well as "Formosan." He claimed to have spent many years on Formosa but by the age of 22 had been wandering in Europe for some time,

George Psalmanaazaar, who claimed a detailed knowledge of the island of Formosa (present-day Taiwan) and invented a "Formosan" language.

Ossian, the legendary Irish warrior-poet and son of Finn MacCool, who supposedly lived around 250 B.C.E. His name became well known in 1760–1763 when James Macpherson published what was later found to be his own verse as an alleged translation of the bard's tales.

motive for Dr. Samuel Johnson's tour of the Highlands and Islands with James Boswell in 1773 was to seek them out. Johnson concluded: "The editor, or author, never could show the original; nor can it be shown by any other. Whence could it be had? It is too long to be remembered, and the language formerly had nothing written. He has doubtless inserted names that circulate in popular stories, and may have translated some wandering ballads."

Johnson was mistaken in his assertion that "the language formerly had nothing written," but he nevertheless dismissed Macpherson's work as "insolence" and "stubborn audacity."

In spite of doubts expressed by some readers of his work, Macpherson continued to insist that the original sources existed. Many years were to pass before it was generally agreed that he had faked the poems of Ossian. He took up a political career and in 1764 was appointed surveyor-general of Florida. He entered the British parliament in 1780 and died at his home near Inverness in 1796. He was buried, at his own expense, in Westminster Abbey.

RECOGNITION COMES TOO LATE
Another poet, even younger, emerged in 1762. He was 10-year-old Thomas Chatterton (1752–1770), born after his

schoolmaster father had died, in Bristol, in western England. His poems had merit, but he soon turned to faking fifteenth-century manuscripts that were allegedly the work of a priest named Thomas Rowley. Chatterton had access to many old documents kept in the Church of St. Mary Radcliffe, Bristol, where his uncle was sexton, and he copied their style and spelling.

At the age of 15, Chatterton was apprenticed to an attorney in Bristol. He passed what spare time he had by writing articles for local magazines, continuing his own poetic output and faking more manuscripts by "Rowley." These excited three Bristol antiquarians, so Chatterton obliged by drawing up a fictitious family tree for one of them.

In April 1770, Chatterton decided to seek his fortune in London's literary world,

"This ys mie formaunce, which I nowe have wrytte, The best performance of mie lyttel wytte."

—FROM THE POEM *TO JOHN LYDGATE*
BY "THOMAS ROWLEY"

but he found that writers there had already been denouncing his manuscripts as forgeries. In despair, he took arsenic and died in his garret in Holborn on August 24. It was only after Chatterton's death that later poets hailed his abilities. Among others, William Wordsworth called him "the marvellous Boy," and John Keats dedicated his poem *Endymion* to Thomas Chatterton.

Thomas Chatterton, only 17 years old in 1770, lies dead of suicide in the garret of his lodging in Holborn, London. This painting was made in 1856 by Henry Wallis in the actual room in which Chatterton died.

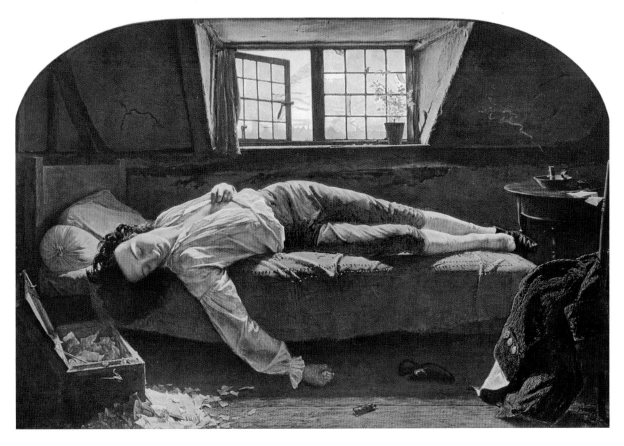

The intrepid Baron Munchausen is carried aloft by a string of ducks in a typical illustration to his *Adventures,* which were in fact fabrications by penniless geologist Rudolf Erich Raspe. Many of Raspe's tales were told in a semi-scientific tone that made them appear plausible.

THE AMAZING BARON

Yet another literary hoax was published in eighteenth-century England. This was entitled *The Adventures of Baron Munchausen* and appeared in 1786.

Because there was a real, living Hieronymus Karl Friedrich, Freiherr von Münchausen (1720–1797), this work can be considered a forgery, even though the baron himself suffered no financial loss from it. He had served as a soldier with the Russians, along with many other Germans, in the war against the Turks in 1738–1740. Münchausen was a passionate hunter, and after he retired to his estates in 1760, he became famous locally as a teller of humorous tales about his life as a soldier and sportsman.

The author of the fake *Adventures*, Rudolf Erich Raspe (1737–1794) may well have known the baron personally and certainly was familiar with his anecdotes. Raspe was born near the Münchausen home. He spent much of his life in debt, although after leaving university, he wrote a book on geology that quickly became a classic. In 1767, Raspe was appointed keeper of the valuable gem collection of the Landgraf Frederick of Hesse-Cassel, and he proceeded to steal from the collection to cover his debts. When his thefts were discovered, Raspe fled Germany. He arrived in England in 1775.

The fame of Raspe's geology book secured him election to the Royal Society, and he made a number of important improvements to mining technology. He was among the first to champion James Macpherson's Ossian poems. The talented Raspe also translated plays and wrote a history of oil painting.

When a German warrant was issued for the arrest of Raspe, the news soon reached London and he was expelled from the Royal Society. To support himself, he began to anonymously publish fictional stories concerning Münchausen. The collected edition of 1786 was entitled, in full, *Gulliver Reviv'd: The Singular Travels, Campaigns, Voyages and Sporting Adventures of Baron Munnikhousen, commonly pronounced Munchausen; as he related them over a bottle when surrounded by his friends.*

Only a few of the incredible stories that Raspe and his publishers assembled came from Münchausen himself. Others were popular legends from past centuries, gathered together in a German magazine that Raspe had read. Still others were derived from genuine journey memoirs, and the story of the baron's voyage to the moon was based on a true account of the Montgolfier brothers' hot-air balloon ascent in 1783. However, the style of writing was Raspe's own. He wrote in a dry, semi-scientific tone that made the extraordinary incidents he described seem credible. Before the end of the century, eight editions of the work, with additions, had been published.

An imaginary portrait of the imaginary Baron, as it appeared on the title page of one of the many editions of Raspe's work. The real-life Münchausen had nothing to do with the *Adventures* and suffered from their publication.

The book was soon translated into German, and the unfortunate real-life baron suffered as a result. Crowds of sightseers arrived at his home, hoping to hear more incredible tales. His beloved wife died, and he turned from a jolly raconteur into a morose loner. Although he married again late in life, his only faithful companion was his longtime huntsman and he died in

1797. By then Raspe was already dead, and his authorship of *Munchausen* was not revealed until 1847.

SHAKESPEARE DISCOVERED

Maybe it was the fame achieved by James Macpherson, or even the posthumous praise for Chatterton, that inspired William Henry Ireland (1775–1835). His father, Samuel, was a London dealer in rare books and prints and a great lover of the works of William Shakespeare. In early 1794, Ireland went with his father to Stratford-upon-Avon, the birthplace of Shakespeare, and met a certain John Jordan, a local poet with a fund of doubtful anecdotes concerning the playwright.

Back in London, Ireland went to work for a solicitor who had a store of ancient parchments. Using a piece of parchment from an old rent agreement and a wax seal, he copied the handwriting from an early-seventeenth-century deed and forged a mortgage agreement between William Shakespeare and an actor named John Heminge—who really existed. He copied Shakespeare's signature from one of his father's books. The College of Heralds was fooled by the forgery and duly agreed to authenticate the document.

Over the next few months Ireland faked a wealth of documents, all written on blank pages cut from 200-year-old books. They included two "newly discovered" historical dramas, revisions to other plays, a letter from Queen Elizabeth to Shakespeare, correspondence between the playwright and the Earl of Southampton and a letter and love poem to Anne Hathaway, Shakespeare's wife. Ireland said he had found the documents while sorting papers at the home of a "Mr. H.," who wished to remain anonymous.

William's father, Samuel Ireland, delightedly mounted an exhibition of these finds in early 1795, and London society

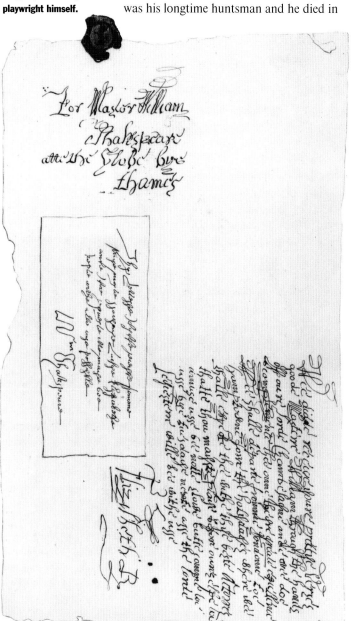

A letter from Queen Elizabeth I to William Shakespeare, forged by William Ireland in 1794. He added a note allegedly written by the playwright himself.

FORGER'S FILE
THE MYSTERIOUS MR. H.

Perhaps William Henry Ireland revealed an unexpected witty streak when he attributed his discoveries to the papers of "Mr. H." For centuries scholars have argued over who "Mr. W. H." was, the man to whom Shakespeare had dedicated his *Sonnets*.

One of several imaginative portraits of Shakespeare.

crowded to see them. James Boswell, the Scottish biographer of Dr. Johnson, fell on his knees and kissed the "relics." But scholars were already expressing doubts, and by December the game was up. An authentic signature by John Heminge was discovered, appearing not at all like that on the mortgage deed.

The press began to attack the Irelands for what it called "a gross and indecent imposition." William Henry produced a transcript of one of the "new" plays, the tragedy of *Vortigern*, which opened at the Drury Lane Theatre on April 2, 1796. It closed after a single performance; the packed audience jeered at its complex plot and feeble writing and collapsed in helpless glee during the last act as the leading actor, John Kemble, intoned the line "When this solemn mockery is ended."

John Payne Collier deceived Shakespearean scholars for many years with his forgeries, often adding Shakespeare's name to otherwise genuine historical documents.

The British Museum examined the "Perkins" volume in detail and revealed that pencil tracings could be found under the ink of many written alterations.

A detailed exposure of Ireland's forgeries, written by Shakespeare scholar Edward Malone, was published at the same time. The culprit admitted all, shortly afterward, in *An Authentic Account of the Shakespearian Manuscripts*. When the fuss eventually died down, Ireland found honest employment with a London publisher. He died in London on April 17, 1835.

THE COUNTERFEITS OF COLLIER

Although Ireland's exploits can be considered inconsequential, some 15 years later much more serious Shakespearean forgeries began to appear. These were the work of John Payne Collier (1789–1883), a respected Shakespeare scholar and critic. As a teenager, he had bought a seventeenth-century edition of Shakespeare's plays and later became an expert on medieval English literature. In 1831 he published *A History of English Dramatic Poetry to the Time of Shakespeare*. Although this book contained a wealth of valuable documentary material, Collier still could not resist inserting details he had invented himself. One was the

addition of Shakespeare's name to a supposed request by a company of actors that they be allowed to renovate a playhouse in London. The date was seven years earlier than that of any document mentioning Shakespeare that had been known until then.

Four years later Collier published *New Facts Regarding the Life of Shakespeare*, with many more invented details. In this work he made even more exciting "discoveries": evidence that *Othello* had been performed before Queen Elizabeth in 1602 and a contemporary ballad that could have been Shakespeare's inspiration for *The Tempest*. Collier then began to tamper with existing historical documents, adding the dramatist's name to certain letters and deeds. He founded the Shakespeare Society, which published these and other finds.

Collier brought out an annotated edition of the plays, which he claimed was based on manuscript additions to an early edition, and *A Life of Shakespeare* (1844) that contained many more inventions. All this work was widely praised, but other scholars began to express doubts. Joseph Hunter, a keeper at the Public Records Office, was particularly critical, and a fellow member of the Shakespeare Society went so far as to opine that Collier was a forger.

In 1852, Collier announced his greatest "find," an old volume of plays that contained thousands of manuscript alterations. Punctuation and stage directions had been changed, lines crossed out or altered, and as many as nine lines added in places. Had an actor, whom Collier identified as Thomas Perkins, made these changes on Shakespeare's own instructions? To add to his deceptions, Collier later claimed to have found the long-lost notes of poet Samuel Taylor Coleridge (1772–1834) for his lectures on Shakespeare.

This proved too much for Collier's critics. In 1859, Sir Frederick Madden of the British Museum examined the "Perkins" volume in detail and revealed that pencil tracings could be found under the ink of many written alterations. Nevertheless, it was only as he lay dying, in September 1883, that Collier at last confessed to his forgeries with "a bitter and sincere repentance."

UTTERLY AUDACIOUS FORGERIES

It is remarkable what some forgers imagine they can get away with. Constantine Simonides (1820–1867) was born on the Greek island of Symi and as a young man went to study in an ancient monastery on Mount Athos. The monastery held many extremely old manuscripts, and Simonides learned to copy and make excellent imitations of them. Around 1845 he left for Athens, carrying with him a large number of manuscripts. Some were copies of originals, others pure fakes.

In Athens, Simonides announced that he had discovered a hoard of previously unpublished—in fact, totally unknown—manuscripts by ancient Greek and Byzantine writers. He even claimed to have a copy of the work by the poet Homer, author of the *Iliad* and *Odyssey*. Scholars cannot agree when Homer lived or even if he had lived at all. But if it were to have proven genuine, the manuscript would have to have been at least 2,400 years old. Simonides succeeded in selling it to the king of Greece.

FORGER'S FILE
WAS COLLIER INNOCENT?

In his book on Collier, *Fortune and Men's Eyes,* Professor Dewey Ganzel has suggested that the pencil tracings found in the "Perkins" volume were made by Sir Frederick Madden and that Collier was innocent. He compares some of the notations to the text with the same word written by Madden in his diaries.

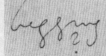 And crooke the pregnant Hindges of the knee, Where thrift may follow faining. Dost thou heare?

The word "begging" written in the margin of the Perkins folio.

The word "begging" as it appears in Madden's 1856 diary.

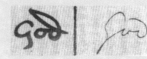

The word "God' as it appears in two places in the Perkins folio.

"God" written in Madden's diary.

In 1849–1850, Simonides published two entirely fictitious books. One was attributed to a "Eulyrus Pylareus"; the other was an account of an imaginary philosophical "Apolloniad School of Symi." Two Greek scholars quickly published an article declaring the works to be forgeries, and Simonides was forced to leave Greece.

A REPUTATION IN RUINS

Simonides made his way to Germany and then to England, selling his manuscripts to various unsuspecting scholars. While in England he published a book of *Facsimiles of Certain Portions of the Gospel of St. Matthew, and of the Epistles of SS. James and Jude*, which he claimed to have found "written on papyrus in the first century" in a private collection in Liverpool. Because of the reputation that had preceded him, the work was at once denounced, although it has never conclusively been proven to be a forgery.

Once again Simonides was compelled to move on, this time to Alexandria, Egypt, where he sold manuscripts to tourists until his death in 1867.

FORGING FOR FRANCE

A near-contemporary of Simonides proved to be even more audacious. A Frenchman named Denis Vrain-Lucas (1818–1888) was the son of a peasant from Châteaudun. Lucas made his way to Paris after working for some time in a lawyer's office. A dealer in rare manuscripts took him on, and Lucas soon learned to become a first-class copyist. When the dealer died, Lucas acquired part of his stock and discovered that he could sell forged copies as easily as the real thing.

About this time a new librarian, Michel Chasles (1793–1880), had just been appointed to the French Academy. A distinguished scientist, he was eager to build up the library's collection. As fate would have it, a colleague put him in touch with Lucas in 1861. Lucas, spotting an opportunity, spun him the tale that he had come across papers belonging to an aged descendant of an eighteenth-century count, who had been obliged to sell them.

In 1867, Chasles announced that he had letters written by the French mathematician Blaise Pascal (1623–1662) to fellow scientist Robert Boyle (1627–1691), a leading member of the Royal Society in London. They purportedly proved that Pascal had discovered the laws of gravitation, some 30 years before their publication by Sir Isaac Newton in 1687. Some Academy members were delighted at the thought that a Frenchman had beaten the English genius

FORGER'S FILE
"I FAKED THIS!"

Once he had been unmasked as a forger, Simonides made what is perhaps his most barefaced claim. In 1844 a fourth-century manuscript, now known as the *Codex Sinaiticus*, was discovered by the German biblical scholar Konstantin von Tischendorf in the monastery of Saint Catherine on Mount Sinai. The *Codex* contained parts of the Bible in Greek; Tischendorf published a facsimile but kept where he had found the original a secret. Not long afterward Simonides claimed the manuscript to be one of his forgeries.

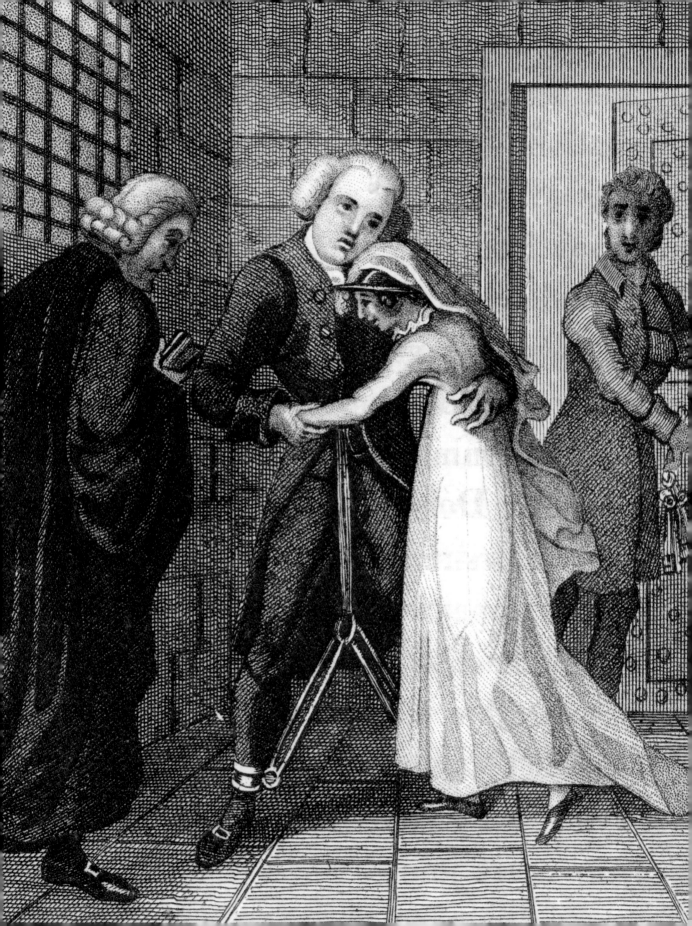

One of the 27,320 historical documents forged in Paris, France, by Denis Vrain-Lucas. It is in the form of a letter to the aged Italian astronomer Galileo Galilei from French mathematician Blaise Pascal. Apparently dated 1633, it would, if authentic, have been written when Pascal was only ten years old.

to the discovery by a generation. However, other more experienced scientists pointed out that there was nothing in Pascal's known writings to suggest that he understood the math involved. In England, of course, the claim was vigorously denied. Eventually, when numerous anomalies had been discovered in the text of the letters, Chasles confessed that he had always suspected them to be forgeries.

ANCIENT PEN PALS

Lucas went on trial in Paris in February 1870, accused of selling 27,320 forged historical documents. It emerged that, carried away by his successes, Lucas had produced a vast number of writings that were patently false. These included letters from Alexander the Great (356–323 B.C.E.) to the philosopher Aristotle; others from

Cleopatra to Julius Caesar; still others from Lazarus, Charlemagne and Galileo. There were even letters from Mary Magdalene: "You will find the letter I spoke of to you which was sent me by Jesus Christ a few days before His passion." Fascinating, except that all these were written in French, and on paper, which was not used in Europe until the fourteenth century. Lucas was sentenced to two years in prison. Chasles admitted that he had paid the forger some 170,000 francs for the documents but maintained that Lucas had told him that the oldest originals had been gathered at the Abbey of Tours during the eighth century and later translated into French by the writer François Rabelais (1494–1553). Chasles was not charged with deliberate deception, and he died, still respected, ten years later.

FORGING FIRST EDITIONS

Until well into the nineteenth century, people bought books, including rare old books, more for their content than for their rarity. By around 1870, however, the way in which the public regarded books had changed, and an interest in collecting first editions began to develop. Quite often the publisher would test the market with the first printing of a book, so the number of

FORGER'S FILE
DE LUNA BYRON

Major George Gordon de Luna Byron (died 1882) claimed to be the illegitimate son of the poet Lord Byron (1788–1824) and a Spanish countess. He served with the British army in India but by 1841 was farming in Wilkes-Barre, Pennsylvania. He journeyed to London and acquired a number of his "father's" letters, meanwhile making copies of others.

De Luna announced that he was preparing a three-volume biography of Byron, but in 1849 he sold many of the letters, together with others allegedly written by Shelley and Keats, and sailed for New York. There, still proclaiming himself Byron's son, he tried unsuccessfully to obtain publication of the letters.

In 1852 a book of de Luna's "Shelley" letters was published in London, and de Luna was soon exposed. A reader noticed that one passage was an almost exact copy of an article that his father had written some years earlier. As a result of accusations of forgery, the entire stock of the book was withdrawn. De Luna left England once more but never gave up claiming his parentage. To this day a controversy continues over which of the Byron letters de Luna sold were genuine and which were fakes.

One of a number of letters supposed to have been forged by de Luna Byron. Written in 1822 from Pisa in Italy to a certain Captain Hay, the letter is in Byron's characteristic style: "I am more likely to kiss the Pope's toe than to subscribe...the sum of two thousand pounds for a man with an income of twenty thousand...."

copies printed would be relatively small. This meant that copies of first editions would quickly become rare. Nowadays, even contemporary popular fiction can command very high prices at auction. One such example is Ian Fleming's first James Bond novel, *Casino Royale*, published in 1953.

The earliest collectors of first editions, however, still had an interest in their importance as works of literary worth.

"A terrific read and a stunning first novel" *Wendy Cooling*

Quite often these collectors belonged to societies devoted to the work of a single writer, and such societies would often produce facsimile reprints of early editions that their members could not otherwise afford. One such group was dedicated to the writings of the poet Percy Bysshe Shelley (1792–1822), and around 1886 they put Thomas James Wise (1859–1937) in charge of their reprints.

The printing firm Wise recruited for the job was Richard Clay & Sons, of Bungay, Suffolk, in the east of England. In the beginning Wise's methods were simple. In addition to a facsimile edition of the poet's works that had been ordered by the Shelley Society, Wise had extra copies run off on paper of a higher quality, which he sold for his own profit. Then he instructed the unsuspecting printers to put an earlier year of publication on the title page. What he was actually doing was faking a "first edition" that had never existed. In the year 1887 alone, Wise reprinted 33 Shelley books and pamphlets, including one unknown compilation of poems, which had been apparently published by an American literary society that did not, in fact, exist.

Nobody suspected Wise's activities, and he quickly gained a reputation as an antiquarian book collector, who had exciting "discoveries" to his credit. Wise soon had an accomplice by the name of H. Buxton Forman (1842–1917). An experienced literary editor, Forman gave Wise much useful advice, and Forman himself produced a number of forged books of Tennyson's poetry. The two men produced a range of forged first editions by George Eliot, Elizabeth and Robert Browning, and Swinburne and Ruskin, among others.

As early as April 1888, Swinburne wrote to Wise, denying all knowledge of a pamphlet, *Cleopatra*, dated 1866, that Wise

The two inveterate forgers of nineteenth-century first editions: H. Buxton Forman (left) and Thomas J. Wise.

had shown him. As it was a forgery, this denial was hardly surprising, but Wise kept the news to himself and Swinburne had no reason to suspect him.

Forman and Wise worked together for 12 years. In 1890 they forged William Morris's *The Two Sides of the River*, dating it 1876; in 1896 they produced a copy of Tennyson's *The Last Tournament*, dated 1871. Their last known collaboration was the printing of Rudyard Kipling's *The White Man's Burden*, which they had lifted from its publication in the London *Times*.

Wise was now building up a huge collection of antiquarian books, called the Ashley Library, at his home. He bought and sold, finding collectors, particularly in the United States, through his dealer Herbert Gorfin. His reputation appeared unassailable. It was not until 1934, when Wise had only three years to live, that two English booksellers, John Carter and Graham Pollard, became suspicious. Browsing through sale catalogues, they noticed that "very rare" works had been turning up remarkably often during the course of the 1920s.

THE CARTER-POLLARD INVESTIGATION

The two booksellers decided to focus their attention on one particular pamphlet. This was a collection of 43 sonnets written by Elizabeth Barrett Browning, wife of Robert Browning. The provenance of the pamphlet was a charming fiction. According to it, one morning Elizabeth had slipped some papers into her husband's pocket. He discovered that they were love poems dedicated to him and arranged for them to be privately printed. They were not published until 1850, together with Elizabeth's collected works, but the pamphlet was dated 1847.

Carter and Pollard soon showed that the paper on which the pamphlet was printed contained esparto, first used in 1861, and chemical wood pulp, not introduced until 1874. To clinch matters, they found that the type used was "Clay's No. 3 Long Primer," which the printers had bought in 1876. Examining other books, Carter and Pollard discovered that in places the text contained differences from the accepted first editions and in fact had been taken from later

THE LAST TOURNAMENT

The "private edition" of Tennyson's *The Last Tournament* was forged by Forman and Wise in 1896 and dated 1871.

editions. Forman, it seems, had made careless mistakes.

Carter and Pollard published their findings as *An Enquiry into the Nature of Certain Nineteenth Century Pamphlets* (1934). They were careful not to accuse Wise directly, but their evidence pointed to him. However, there was no suggestion at this point that the contents of the Ashley Library included any of Wise's own forgeries. After his death, Wise's widow sold the library to the British Museum, which made a disturbing discovery. As a respected collector, Wise had been allowed ready access to the museum's antique-book shelves, and it was found that he had stolen pages from rare volumes to complete imperfect copies in his own collection.

THE VINLAND MAP

The jury is still out on the question of who the first Europeans to visit North America were. Two Icelandic sagas record that Viking sailors reached the coast they called Vinland around the year 1000. Scholars argued for many years about its exact location, and in 1965, Yale University Press published a book that described an ancient map on parchment, recently donated to the Beinecke Library at Yale. It was proposed that the map had been drawn in the 1430s by a monk in Basel, Switzerland, and was in fact a copy of an even earlier map. A Latin inscription in the upper-left-hand corner gave a brief description of the Vikings' voyage.

The map, bound up with an unrelated document, showed the continent of Europe,

FORGER'S FILE
PRESIDENTIAL SIGNATURES

It is estimated that the signature of Abraham Lincoln has been forged more often than any other, although those of other notables from American history, including George Washington, Benjamin Franklin and Andrew Jackson, come close. This is a genuine signature.

North Africa, Asia and the Far East, together with Iceland and Greenland, in relatively accurate detail. To the west was an island named Vinland, its eastern coast pierced by a huge inlet, with a river running from a great lake.

Almost at once, scholars proclaimed the map a recent fake. Admittedly, its provenance was obscure. Little more was known than that a dealer in New Haven, Connecticut, had bought it from an Italian bookseller. If it was genuine, however, it documented a knowledge of the North American East Coast at least a half-century earlier than John Cabot's 1497 voyage and a full century earlier than those of Giovanni da Verrazzano in 1524 and Jacques Cartier in 1534–1542.

In an effort to resolve the map's authenticity, the Smithsonian Institute held a conference on the subject in 1966, but each of the experts present held to his own opinion. Yale therefore decided to have the map examined by Walter McCrone, who has been described as "the world's leading microanalyst." He revealed that the black ink lines were superimposed over lines in a yellowish ink, which McCrone suggested was to give the effect of age. Analysis of a minute sample of this ink revealed traces of anatase,

FORGER'S FILE
FORGERS OF AMERICAN DOCUMENTS

ROBERT SPRING (1813–1876) was born in England. As a young man, he opened a bookshop in Philadelphia and soon began selling hundreds of copies of faked letters by George Washington. He was convicted of forgery in 1869.

JOSEPH COSEY (1887–early 1950s) was born Martin Conneely in Syracuse, New York. After several criminal convictions, leading to incarceration in San Quentin Prison in California, he took up forgery of Franklin's signature in 1929. Cosey also forged the autographs of John Adams, James Monroe, Patrick Henry, George Washington, Abraham Lincoln, Edgar Allan Poe, Mark Twain, Walt Whitman and many others. His most daring forgery was a draft of the Declaration of Independence in Thomas Jefferson's handwriting. Cosey was arrested in 1937 and served a year in prison, but he continued forging documents until his death.

HENRY WOODHOUSE (1884–1970) was born Mario Casalegno in Turin, Italy. He left Italy for the United States in 1905 and around 1910 founded a successful magazine, *Flying*. A wealthy man by the 1920s, Woodhouse began to collect rare documents, then turned to forging them. Although experts can easily distinguish his copies from Lincoln's true signature, he fooled many innocent collectors. Woodhouse was never convicted of criminal activities.

CHARLES WEISBERG (died 1945) has a reputation as one of the most skilled Lincoln forgers. But he served several prison sentences and died in a prison in Lewisburg, Pennsylvania.

JOHN LAFLIN (born in Nebraska, died 1970) was one of the most prolific document forgers of the twentieth century. Notoriously, he produced a "Personal Narrative with Santa Ana," allegedly written by Jose Enrique de la Peña, a document long believed to be a rare account of the Battle of the Alamo. Very recently it has been suggested that another document from the Alamo (1836), the "Isaac Millsaps" letter (held by the University of Houston) is also a Laflin fake. His Lincoln forgeries were many. Some, perplexingly, were written in German, a language Lincoln was not familiar with. It is not known whether Laflin ever served a prison sentence.

Passy, April 22, 1779

My Dear Sir,

Will you call upon me this afternoon, I have just received my letters from Boston, among them one from Mr Quincy, mentioning you in the kindest manner;— I am sorry a very severe attack of the gravel prevented my accompanying you, and the Marquis de la Fayette yesterday to Versailles, but do not imagine the old mans company was greatly missed;— I regreted my sickness for I have always met with the kindest reception from their Majesties, and feel great pleasure in paying my respects to them, but disease and pain, are better away, tho' some would endure more, for a less friendly reception than I should have received;— Come if you can. —

Yours affectionately,

B Franklin

Mr Bradford

a form of titanium dioxide, a modern white pigment first produced by the Titanium Corporation of America about 1920.

Yale accepted this finding, and its experts decided that the map was a fake. The controversy did not end there, however. In 1986 physicists at the University of California at Davis employed an analytical technique called particle-induced X-ray emission (PIXE) and concluded that there was no reason why the ink should not have contained naturally occurring anatase. This is also the view of one expert at the Smithsonian Center of Materials Research.

Reports of further investigations appeared in 2002. A paper in the journal

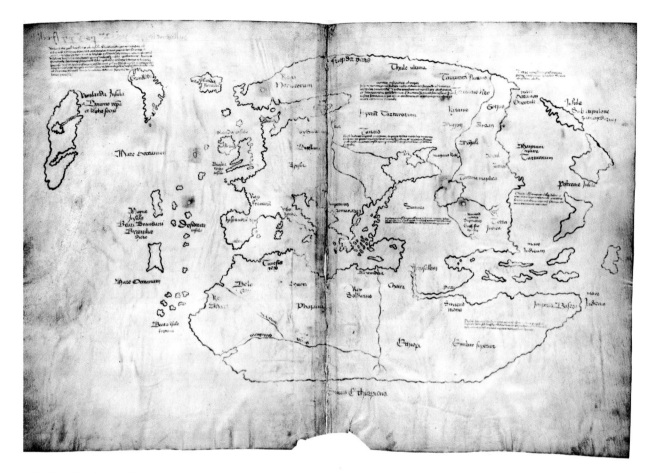

If the Vinland Map is genuine, it documents a knowledge of the North American East Coast at least a half-century earlier than John Cabot's 1497 voyage.

Radiocarbon announced that carbon dating established a date around 1434, thereby determining the age of the parchment. Simultaneously, a paper by British researchers, in the journal *Analytical Chemistry*, repeated the assertion that the inks used were modern.

There, for the moment, the matter rests. It is agreed that a clever forger would certainly have used an old piece of parchment, so the argument concerns the composition of the inks. Multimillionaire Paul Mellon paid an estimated $1 million for the volume containing the map in 1957, and it has recently been valued by insurers at $25 million. Will its authenticity, or its status as a forgery, ever be proven beyond doubt?

THE "DIARY OF JACK THE RIPPER"

For three months in the fall of 1888, the East End of London was in a state of near panic. A serial killer roamed the streets at night. Between August and November that year five women, all known prostitutes, were murdered and brutally mutilated. A letter received by the police, allegedly from the killer and written in red ink, identified him as "Jack the Ripper." No further murders occurred, nobody was ever

The Vinland Map. What could be a part of the North American East Coast, with the St. Lawrence River flowing from Lake Ontario to Long Island Sound, is at far left. Above it, an inscription in Latin provides a brief account of the Viking voyage.

conclusively proven to be "Jack," and the case remains unsolved. For more than a century "ripperologists" have put forward a number of possible culprits, among them Queen Victoria's grandson, the Duke of Clarence, and also the English painter Walter Sickert (1860–1942).

In 1991, Michael Barrett, a small-time scrap dealer in Liverpool, England, announced that he owned a 63-page diary, written on the pages of a Victorian scrapbook, that finally solved the mystery and also explained why the murders had abruptly ceased. A friend, who he said had since died, had passed the book to him.

Significantly, the discovery hinged on another notorious Victorian case of murder. On May 11, 1889, James Maybrick, a Liverpool cotton merchant who traded with the United States, died after having suffered for several weeks. His American-born wife, Florence, 23 years younger than her husband, was found guilty of poisoning him with arsenic and sentenced to life imprisonment. She persistently claimed her innocence and was released after 15 years. Florence Maybrick died in the United States in 1941.

It was known that Maybrick had regularly taken arsenic as an aphrodisiac, and in 1887, Florence discovered that her husband had a mistress. She found consolation in the arms of Maybrick's friend Alfred Brierley, an affair her husband discovered in March 1889. The prosecution's case against Florence rested on her subsequent purchase of a dozen flypapers containing arsenic and the

A page from the recently "discovered" diary of James Maybrick, in which he identifies himself as the perpetrator of the notorious "Jack the Ripper" murders in London in 1888. The killer has never been authoritatively identified. Most experts condemn this as a forgery.

James Maybrick, a wealthy cotton merchant who, it is suggested, carried out the "Jack the Ripper" murders in nineteenth-century London. The diary in which he supposedly admitted the crimes, published in 1993, was later found to be a fake.

discovery in her room of a packet with the label ARSENIC: POISON FOR CATS.

The startling claim made by the diary was that James Maybrick had been the "Ripper" and that he had expressed his pain at the discovery of his wife's infidelity by viciously murdering prostitutes on his occasional trips to London. His death in May 1889 explained why no further

"Ripper" murders had taken place, and it was even suggested that he had asked Florence to poison him.

The Diary of Jack the Ripper, with an accompanying text by Shirley Harrison, was published in 1993. In its introduction the publisher described the steps that had been taken to establish the diary's authenticity. These included an assessment by Dr. David Forshaw of the Maudsley Psychiatric Hospital in London and an analysis of the ink by Dr. Nicholas Easthaugh. Dr. Forshaw considered that the diary's content was consistent with the mind-set of a psychotic serial killer, while Dr. Easthaugh reported only that there was nothing specific to suggest that the materials were modern.

The startling claim made by the diary was that James Maybrick had been the "Ripper" and that he had expressed his pain at the discovery of his wife's infidelity by viciously murdering prostitutes on his occasional trips to London.

Among the many "ripperologists" consulted, each had his own theory about the identity of the Ripper, and they could not reach a consensus. It was suggested that only the police and the killer had known certain details in the diary, but as these had been made public in 1987, they were secret no longer. Principal doubts arose concerning glaring grammatical and spelling errors and the fact that the handwriting in the diary did not appear to be of the right period. Nor did it resemble the only available specimens of Maybrick's writing, found on his marriage certificate and his will. The publisher dismissed this last criticism with the claim that the will had been forged.

Before its publication in the United States, the diary was submitted to two handwriting experts, one of whom was Maureen Casey Owens, formerly the Chicago Police Department's forensic document expert for 25 years. She concluded that it was a fake.

In 1994, Michael Barrett confessed to forging the diary. He said he had bought the old scrapbook at a garage sale and the ink at an art supplies store. Later he retracted his confession, leading to yet further confusion.

Inquiries led to the probability that the ink was Diamine black manuscript ink, which contains a small amount of chloroacetamide as a preservative. Subsequent analytical reports are conflicting, but one laboratory reported six positive findings for this chemical. To complete the confusion, an American expert, who claimed to be able to estimate the age of the ink from its degree of spread in the paper, provided a date of 1921, plus or minus 12 years. If his estimate were correct, the diary was clearly a forgery, although not one committed by Barrett. Otherwise, the handwriting and chemical analyses do apparently implicate him.

EXAMINING SUSPECT DOCUMENTS

Faked or forged documents can be of many different kinds, and qualified document examiners must have wide experience in the ways they can be produced. If these are to be questioned in a court of law, an examiner must fulfill all the requirements placed upon any forensic expert called to give evidence. It is rarely enough just to establish a single point of similarity, or one difference, between the suspect document and a genuine one. Many points of comparison must be demonstrated to make a convincing case.

As with forged works of art, two criteria to be considered are provenance and style. To establish provenance, generally the forger will claim to have discovered the document among other old papers. So a verification of the history of the document showing to whom it belonged, where it came from originally and so on, is at best doubtful. Next must come an analysis of how the supposed writer expressed himself

or herself. But most important is scientific examination of the material as it makes use of many of the techniques described in the previous chapter.

A given document may be written by hand, generally in ink but sometimes in pencil, and can be on parchment, vellum or paper. If it is allegedly old or of a specific date, the ink must be analyzed. This may require no more than examining it under a microscope. But in most cases it means a small sample of the ink must be scraped off and analyzed using spectrographic analysis, carbon dating or neutron activation.

EARLY INKS

The earliest inks were made from carbon, in the form of lampblack or soot, mixed with gum and water. Since carbon does not fade over time and cannot be bleached by chemicals, it will remain black for centuries. However, carbon remains only on the surface of the material and can be removed by accidental or deliberate scraping.

In the second century C.E, a new type of ink had been developed that was still in use late into the nineteenth century. It was prepared by mixing an extract of nutgalls with a solution of the mineral copperas (ferrous sulfate). It was slightly corrosive and gradually "bit" into the parchment, so it was difficult to scrape away once it had become fixed. On the other hand, it eventually turned a rusty brown as the iron in the ink oxidized. To overcome this browning effect, dyes such as indigo were later added.

Detail from an illuminated psalter on vellum from the former monastery of Suben, Austria, dating from around 1200 C.E.

THE INK IN YOUR PEN

Synthetic aniline dyes were developed after 1856 and were soon used in inks. Today most inks are composed of synthetic matter. Those used in ballpoint pens are thick and oily, similar to printers' ink, while felt-tipped pens use ink based on petroleum products.

STYLUS, QUILL OR NIB?

Aside from analyzing the ink, an examiner will look for evidence showing what type of pen had been used. The ancients used a stylus, a brush or a reed pen. Until the late eighteenth century, writers predominantly used quills. Originally these had a broad edge similar to a chisel, but later they were sharpened to a point. Steel nibs appeared in 1780 but were not widely used for another 50 years or more. Then, in succession, came gold nibs, fountain pens and a variety of other types. Examination under a microscope can frequently reveal the type of pen used, which in many cases is found to be of a later date than the date on the faked document.

Genuine early documents are unique and extremely valuable. Unfortunately, in order

Identification of the type of pen used to write a document can prove valuable in the detection of a forgery. Modern fountain pens and others provided with a metal nib are "scratchier" than the quills used in earlier centuries, and this can be detected under a microscope.

There are ways to tell if the ink used on the paper is truly old. Ink on a good grade of new paper leaves a sharp impression.

to test them for authenticity, examiners sometimes have no choice but to damage the document slightly by carefully removing a small piece of material. Carbon dating is used to test parchment and vellum, and the properties of the paper can also be analyzed further.

Sometimes simply placing the document under ultraviolet light may offer enough proof that the paper has been manufactured too recently to be a genuine antique, as described in chapter 2 and in the case of the "Hitler diaries." When a variety of specimens is available, as in the case of the Carter-Pollard examination of the Wise pamphlet described on page 107, the partial destruction of one can be justified to verify that the whole set is fake.

There are ways to tell if the ink used on the paper is truly old. Ink on a good grade of new paper leaves a sharp impression. However, treating the paper first to make it look old causes it to become absorbent. Any ink applied to the surface will spread slightly and look "fuzzy" under a microscope. Examiners also check to see if the ink has been blotted and how this has been done. For example, before the introduction of blotting paper, fine sand was used to soak up excess ink, and tiny particles should generally still be present. Signs of the use of blotting paper include a gradual fading of the ink from one end of the document to the other, as the freshest ink will be absorbed more than that which has begun to dry. The fresher ink is also likely to be slightly smudged.

use of a new and simple piece of equipment known as ESDA (electronic static detection apparatus). ESDA makes use of the fact that pressure on paper will permanently increase its capacity to hold an electrostatic charge. This can reveal any faint indentation on paper that had been produced by writing on a sheet placed above it.

The document is laid on a flat bed of porous metal, and a thin sheet of transparent Mylar is placed over it. Vacuum suction through the metal bed draws the two sheets tightly together, and an electrical discharge is then passed over the "sandwich." The indented parts of the document become electrostatically charged. A mixture of photocopier toner powder and tiny glass beads is then sifted over the Mylar, revealing the charged image beneath.

THE HOWARD HUGHES "AUTOBIOGRAPHY"

To this day Clifford Irving (born 1930) insists that the Hughes fraud began as a joke. One December morning in 1970, Irving was on a boat taking him back to Ibiza, in the Spanish Balearic Islands, where he was living with his family and where he had very recently written his book *Fake!*, about the career of Elmyr de Hory (see chapter 2). Irving had arranged a brief meeting with a friend and fellow writer, Dick Suskind, during a stopover at Mallorca.

Irving had just read an article in *Newsweek* about Howard Robard Hughes, "the invisible billionaire." Hughes, the self-described "richest man in the world," lived like a hermit on the top floor of the Desert Inn in Las Vegas (which he owned), surrounded at all times by a protective "palace guard" of Mormons. Hughes had

Novelist Clifford Irving, who conceived a fictitious autobiography of the reclusive billionaire Howard Hughes. The "hoax" soon got out of hand, and Irving was eventually convicted of fraud.

"Invisible?" said Suskind. "I wouldn't be surprised if he were dead." Irving was struck with a sudden inspiration: "Suppose I went to a publisher, let's say my own publisher McGraw-Hill, and cooked up a scheme to pretend I'd met Hughes and he'd commissioned me to write his authorized biography?"

Irving's first idea was "a hoax, a gorgeous literary caper, in which publisher and author would collaborate," but he decided that was impossible. However, he did decide to write to his editor, Beverly Loo, at McGraw-Hill: "I sent a copy of *Fake!* to Howard Hughes and to my surprise received a note of thanks and praise from him." He then sat down with an American yellow legal pad of the kind Hughes was known to use, and using a photograph of a letter from the *Newsweek* article as a model, Irving forged himself three letters.

The first, dated December 10, 1970, was the letter of thanks. The second, dated January 8, 1971, was just a brief note: "I have had your most recent letter. I have taken note of its contents and will give the matter my very serious consideration." The third, dated January 20, was longer. It read, in part: "It would not suit me to die without having certain misconceptions cleared up and without having stated the truth about my life.... I would be grateful if you would let me know when and how you would wish to undertake the writing of my biography...."

NO GOING BACK

A few days later Irving flew to New York and showed the letters to Beverly Loo and to Albert Leventhal, a vice president of McGraw-Hill. They immediately offered Irving $100,000 on signature of contract, $100,000 on delivery of a preliminary manuscript and $300,000 for the completed manuscript. Irving was now committing

In his later years Howard Hughes became a virtual recluse, leaving the administration of his vast fortune to the Hughes Tool Company.

not been seen in public for 15 years, and he communicated with his extensive network of business interests only by telephone and dictated memoranda. He also owned a hideaway on an island off Nassau in the Bahamas, and it was here that Hughes was believed to be staying when Irving and Suskind met.

himself no longer to a simple hoax but to a major forgery.

For several years Irving had enjoyed an on-and-off affair with Nina van Pallandt, one-half of the former folk-singing duo Nina and Frederick. Irving and Van Pallandt had arranged to meet in New York and spend the weekend on Nassau, where Irving had told McGraw-Hill he was to meet with Hughes. Unfortunately, the couple were unable to get a flight to Nassau and went to Mexico instead.

At the airport in Mexico City, Irving had himself photographed emerging from an Eastern Airlines plane. Returning to New York, he produced a notebook. In it he claimed to have recorded two meetings he said he had held with Hughes (and said that Hughes had identified himself as "Señor Octavio"). Irving claimed that the photograph of him emerging from the plane was taken by one of Hughes's men, by way of identification. Irving also brought a copy of a contract between himself and Hughes, one he had forged.

McGraw-Hill's lawyer approved the contract but asked for Hughes's signature to be notarized. This was, of course, impossible. It seemed to be the end of the "hoax," but a few days later Irving was

Another fake Hughes autobiography. George Blagowidow, president of Best Books, Inc., stands beside copies of *My Life and Opinions* "by Howard Hughes," edited by Robert P. Eaton, at Brentano's bookstore in New York, in January 1972.

informed by Beverly Loo that the signature, as it had apparently been made in Irving's presence, was acceptable without notarization.

Among the clauses of the contract stipulating complete secrecy, one read: "The money will be deposited as designated verbally or in writing by H. R. Hughes for deposit in any bank of H. R. Hughes...." Irving's wife, Edith, was a Swiss citizen and possessed a spare Swiss passport. Irving photographed her wearing a black wig, replaced the original photo in her passport, erased her signature and got her to add "H. R. Hughes." Edith flew to Zurich, where she opened an account with Crédit Suisse in that name.

When the book's forthcoming publication was announced in December, the Hughes Tool Company immediately denied that it was genuine.

Meanwhile, executives at McGraw-Hill, impressed by the high percentages that "Hughes" was demanding for subsidiary rights, had approached *Life* and negotiated $250,000 for serial publication in the magazine. Irving obtained permission to research *Life*'s files and secretly photographed more than 300 detailed but unpublished correspondents' reports on Hughes. Throughout the hot summer of 1971, he and Suskind sweated over the faking of a series of interviews with the reclusive magnate.

In late August, disaster loomed again. Beverly Loo telephoned to report that another publisher had been offered a manuscript, the autobiography of Howard Hughes, "as told to Robert Eaton." Eaton was the ex-husband of actress Lana Turner.

The two conspirators decided that the best strategy was to attack. They flew to Palm Beach (near enough for Hughes to have flown there by helicopter) and sent two telegrams to New York. The first stated that Hughes had heard of the deal with *Life* and demanded an increase in payment to $1 million. The second included a denial that the Eaton book had been authorized. In mid-September, Irving and Suskind carried 999 pages of typescript to McGraw-Hill, which then upped the offer to $750,000 "but not a penny more."

IRVING'S FORGERIES FOOL THE EXPERTS

In November, as Irving and Suskind were completing their book, Beverly Loo telephoned again, in a panic. *Ladies' Home Journal* planned to publish extracts from Eaton's work the following January. Loo needed immediate permission from Hughes to announce that McGraw-Hill was the sole publisher of an authorized version. Irving composed a long letter from "Hughes," full of wild complaints about McGraw-Hill's incompetence, which *Life* submitted to a handwriting expert. The expert compared it with a genuine letter by Hughes and announced: "It can be stated that the two handwriting specimens were written by the same person. The chances that another person could copy this handwriting even in a similar way are less than one in a million."

When the book's forthcoming publication was announced in December, the Hughes Tool Company immediately denied that it was genuine. Furthermore, that evening Hughes himself would telephone Frank McCulloch, a *Life* reporter who had interviewed him in the 1950s. The next morning, representatives of McGraw-Hill and *Life* met with Irving and McCulloch. The journalist said he had spent most of the night reading Irving's

manuscript, and "if I were placed before a court of law, I'd have to say that, to the best of my knowledge and belief, that material could only have come directly to Cliff from Howard." The publishers decided to have the "Hughes" letters examined by another group of handwriting experts, who said they were confident the letters were genuine.

In a spirit of bravado, Irving volunteered to take a polygraph test. He was due to fly back to Ibiza for Christmas with his family; after a heavy lunch, and desperately anxious that he would miss his plane, he sat for the test. His nervous condition evidently deceived the machine. The results, said the examiner, were "inconclusive."

Hughes then announced that he would give a networked press conference, his first in 15 years, by telephone to a group of journalists in a Los Angeles television studio. Irving told the press the next morning that he doubted that the voice was that of Hughes. Later the inventor of "voiceprints," Lawrence Kersta, was able to compare the tape with a recording of a speech made by Hughes 30 years earlier to a Senate subcommittee. Kersta announced that the voice was undoubtedly that of Howard Hughes.

Hughes owned a private investigation service, Intertel, which succeeded in persuading Crédit Suisse to reveal, in contravention of Swiss law, that "H. R. Hughes" was a woman. Edith Irving was soon traced to Ibiza. In February the two Irvings and Suskind were summoned to New York to appear before two grand jury

Clifford Irving, his wife, Edith, and Dick Suskind are officially booked on charges ranging from mail fraud to forgery.

hearings. Irving's last hope, that Nina van Pallandt would confirm that he had met with Hughes in Nassau, was destroyed when she testified that he had spent time only with her, and in Mexico. The conspirators now decided the time had come to confess.

On June 16, 1972, Irving was sentenced to 30 months in prison and Suskind to 6 months. Edith was sentenced to two years, with all but two months suspended, but she was subsequently sentenced to two years at a trial in Zurich. After his release Irving continued his writing career, publishing *The Hoax*, about his forgery.

THE "HITLER DIARIES"

Adolf Hitler died in the ruins of Berlin, Germany, in 1945, and many of his surviving associates were executed in Nuremberg the following year; yet there is still an international market for Nazi memorabilia. One who cashed in on this demand and nearly succeeded in the greatest document forgery of modern times was Konrad "Konni" Kujau (1938–2000).

Kujau was born at the height of the Nazi regime in Loebau, Saxony. Following the end of World War II, Loebau was in the German Democratic Republic, from 1946 through 1991; in 1957, Kujau fled across the

Nazi memorabilia continues to fascinate collectors—and inspire forgers—more than 60 years after the end of World War II.

border into West Germany. For some years he led a precarious existence. He served several short terms in jail and with his wife, Edith, set up a window-cleaning business in Stuttgart. Around 1969 he decided to deal in Nazi relics.

Through his family in East Germany, Kujau advertised, "Wanted for research: old toys, helmets, jugs, pipes, dolls, etc." To suppress any trade in objects associated with Nazis, the government of East Germany had banned the export of any such items made before 1945. Nonetheless, Kujau was soon "swamped" (as he said) with relics that had been smuggled into West Germany.

By 1974, his shop was crowded with guns and swords, a set of Nazi medals, 150 helmets, 50 uniforms, 30 large flags and more. To command high prices, he began to forge documents that authenticated his stock. For example, he took an old and rusty helmet from World War I and attached a forged label to it, supposedly signed by Rudolf Hess, Hitler's deputy. It stated that Hitler had worn the helmet in 1917.

Kujau discovered that he could fake not only Hitler's handwriting but his paintings as well. From 1975 through 1980, Fritz Stiefel, wealthy owner of an engineering firm, bought 160 drawings, oil paintings and watercolors, as well as 80 manuscript poems, speech notes and letters, all allegedly written by Hitler.

In 1978, Kujau opened a Nazi Party yearbook from 1935 and copied out a daily chronology of the Führer's appointments. He used a school notebook, one of a number he had bought in East Berlin, and made the entries using a passable copy of Hitler's handwriting. Stiefel eagerly bought it.

A journalist named Gerd Heidemann enters the story at this point. He had worked for *Stern* magazine in Hamburg, where he'd made the acquaintance of

East German-born Konni Kujau, who made a small fortune from faked Nazi relics but was eventually revealed to be the forger of the "Hitler Diaries."

former Nazis. In January 1980, he met Stiefel, who showed him the "Hitler Diary" and said he understood that another 26 volumes were in existence. Heidemann obtained the dealer's telephone number and called him in Stuttgart in January 1981. Kujau confirmed that the diaries existed, and also more paintings and manuscripts, including a third volume of *Mein Kampf* (Hitler's story of his early life) and an opera he said Hitler had written in his youth. Kujau said they were all in the possession of an old general in East Germany but could be smuggled to the West.

A 1983 issue of the German magazine *Stern* shows Kujau with one of his relics and describes him as "the man who supplied the 'Hitler Diaries.'"

Kujau discovered that he could fake not only Hitler's handwriting but his paintings as well.

belonged to Goering, which excited the dealer even more than the money. Within two weeks he had completed the forging of the next three volumes. Kujau fixed a red wax seal of a German eagle to the covers and forged a label, signed "Rudolf Hess," declaring them to be Hitler's property. He handled them roughly to make them look old and worn and sprinkled tea on some of the pages. Then Kujau flew to Hamburg and delivered them to Heidemann. The executives at Grüner & Jahr were convinced of their authenticity and swore everyone involved to secrecy.

BIG MONEY, MUNDANE DETAILS

Over the next two years Kujau forged the remaining diaries. Once he had checked his facts, it took him only a few hours to fill a volume. Much of it was a dull list of official engagements; other entries were trivial notes and comments of little historical interest. For this Grüner & Jahr were paying 200 marks a word.

Typical entries include: "Meet all the leaders of the Storm Troopers in Bavaria, give them medals,"and "Must not forget tickets for the Olympic Games for Eva."

Every few weeks Kujau would telephone Heidemann to announce that another batch of materials had been smuggled from East Germany, often inside a piano. Heidemann would collect a large sum in cash and fly to Stuttgart to pick up the volumes. But what nobody knew was that he paid Kujau only 50,000 marks for each and kept 35,000 for himself. After a while Heidemann announced that the price per volume had

Wildly excited, Heidemann enlisted the collaboration of Thomas Walde, *Stern*'s historical editor, and made an offer of 2 million marks for the remaining diaries. The men prepared a dossier detailing the discovery and presented it at a highly secret meeting with the executives of Grüner & Jahr, owners of *Stern*. The executives immediately gave authorization to pay 85,000 marks for each diary volume, plus 200,000 marks for the *Mein Kampf* manuscript, along with 500,000 marks more for the rest of Kujau's collection.

That evening Heidemann flew to Stuttgart. He handed Kujau 200,000 marks in cash and a full-dress uniform that had suddenly risen to 200,000 marks because the fictitious general needed it to pay bribes. Trapped in a spiral of greed, Grüner & Jahr authorized the increased payments.

PUBLISHING THE HOAX

At first Grüner & Jahr decided to use extracts from the diaries for publication in *Stern*, beginning in January 1983, the fiftieth anniversary of Hitler's accession to power. But then the temptation to sell syndication rights proved irresistible. In great secrecy during February 1983, they approached *Newsweek* and *Time* in the United States, *Paris Match* in France and *El Pais* in Spain.

AN EARLY CLUE

So far, little had been done about authenticating the documents. Walde had sent a few specimens to the German police's forensic department in July 1982, but it had not yet reported back on them. At the end of March 1983, however, a police examiner announced that of nine specimens he had examined, at least six contained paper whitener, which had not been in use until 1946. Heidemann telephoned Kujau, who

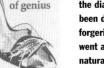
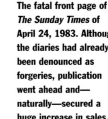

The fatal front page of *The Sunday Times* of April 24, 1983. Although the diaries had already been denounced as forgeries, publication went ahead and—naturally—secured a huge increase in sales.

was dismissive; he understood, he said, that whitener had been used since 1915. Neither Walde nor Heidemann told *Stern* of the police report.

Serialization rights in the story were offered to Times Newspapers in London. On April 1 (a significant date, as it turned out) the assistant editor of London's *Times* telephoned Hugh Trevor-Roper (Lord Dacre), one of an independent panel of directors. The distinguished author of *The Last Days of Hitler*, Trevor-Roper was asked to give his opinion on the diaries. He flew to Zurich, where the volumes were in safekeeping in a Swiss bank, and announced that he was convinced by what he saw.

Rupert Murdoch, proprietor of Times Newspapers, decided to begin publication in *The Sunday Times* on April 24. *Stern* would publish the next day, *Newsweek* on April 26 and *Paris Match* on April 27. However, inevitably, news of the forthcoming publication leaked out. David Irving, a fiercely pro-Hitler historian, appeared on BBC TV on the evening of April 22 and announced that the diaries were fakes.

Trevor-Roper was also having second thoughts and telephoned the editor of *The Times*. Murdoch, who was in the United States, was called at once. His reaction was typical: "Fuck Dacre. Publish!"

The first installments of the "Hitler Diaries" appeared in Britain, Germany, France and the United States, as planned. On May 2, however, *Stern* at last received a detailed report from the Federal Institute for Forensic Investigation in Berlin. Examiners had found traces of a synthetic textile not manufactured in quantity before 1943 and a polyester gum dating from 1953. A handwriting expert consulted by *Newsweek* strongly suspected that the diaries were forgeries.

Hearing the news, Konni Kujau fled from Stuttgart, but he surrendered to the police a week later. When he learned that Heidemann had maintained that Grüner & Jahr had paid him all the 9.3 million marks, Kujau confessed, alleging that Heidemann had known all along that the diaries were forgeries.

Kujau was charged with receiving 1.5 million marks by forgery and sentenced to four years and six months in prison. Heidemann was charged with stealing 1.7 million marks, although the prosecution stated that the amount could have been as high as 4.6 million, and was sentenced to four years and eight months. More than 5 million marks remained unaccounted for. Grüner & Jahr estimated their total loss to be 19 million marks.

Rupert Murdoch had the last word on the affair. The circulation of *The Sunday*

FORGER'S FILE
MUSSOLINI'S DIARIES

Hitler's were not the first diaries of a Fascist dictator to be offered for sale. In 1957 an Italian woman, Amalia Panvini, and her 84-year-old mother produced 30 volumes of what they claimed to be Benito Mussolini's diaries. Apparently, Mussolini's own son was deceived, along with an expert who examined them, and declared: "Thirty volumes of manuscript cannot be the work of a forger, but of a genius."

Times had risen by 60,000. "After all, we are in the entertainment business," he said. "Circulation went up, and it stayed up. We didn't lose money."

THE MORMON BOMBER

Mark Hofmann was born into a devout Mormon family in Salt Lake City in 1954. He was not a shining student at Olympus High School, being more interested in collecting old Mormon coins than in his school studies. However, shortly after graduation in 1973, he was sent as a missionary to Bristol, in southwest England. There Hofmann discovered a wealth of secondhand bookshops, and he began to buy old books about the Mormon faith.

On his return to Salt Lake City, Hofmann enrolled as a premed student at Utah State University. Some six months later, in April 1980, he showed an acquaintance a 1688 edition of the King James Bible and a folded and gummed sheet of paper Hofmann said he had found inside it. Written in much-faded ink on the outside of the paper were the words "These characters were diligently copied by my own hand from the plates of gold and given to Martin Harris.... Joseph Smith Jr."

When the gum was removed, the paper opened to reveal that it was covered with symbols and drawings. It answered the description of a paper that Martin Harris (see box) had indeed taken to New York to be inspected in 1828. Church elders declared that the document was genuine and rewarded Hofmann with a first edition of the *Book of Mormon* and old Mormon currency worth more than $20,000. He announced at once that he was dropping out of medical school and was setting himself up as a dealer in rare books.

Early in 1981, Hofmann produced two more early Mormon documents and was again rewarded by the church with items valued at over $20,000. The following year he had on offer a statement, written in pencil on lined paper, that was an account, signed by Martin Harris, of a vision in which Harris had been shown the golden plates of Moroni. Shortly after this, Hofmann said he had discovered a letter dated 1829, supposedly written by Joseph Smith's mother. In due course the church authenticated both documents, and the press began to refer to Hofmann as a "real-life Indiana Jones."

Within three years of having set up as a dealer, Hofmann was trading widely in books and autograph documents. He claimed that he had obtained many of his finds by buying letters from people who had collected them for the old postmarks but were uninterested in the contents. He flew once or twice a month to New York to attend auctions at Sotheby's or Christie's, and whenever he needed capital for his purchases, he was able to find wealthy investors among his fellow Mormons. Hofmann even claimed that he was on the track of the 116-page *Book of Mormon* that had been lost by Martin Harris. Early in 1985, Hofmann confided to a few of his close acquaintances that he had found the

Mark Hofmann in 1984, at the height of his career as a dealer and collector of Mormon literature. He holds a first edition of the *Book of Mormon*.

FORGER'S FILE
THE *BOOK OF MORMON*

Joseph Smith (1805–1844) was born the third son of an impoverished New England family that settled in Fayette, New York. In later years Smith founded the Mormon Church, also known as the Church of Jesus Christ of the Latter-day Saints. He based his church's teachings on the Bible and on the *Book of Mormon*, which he claims an angel had given him in September 1823. The angel, named Moroni, had shown Smith a number of golden plates engraved with characters in the form of hieroglyphs, hidden in a hill near the family farm. Moroni had supposedly said that the plates had been buried there for 1,400 years. Eventually, on September 22, 1827, the angel gave Smith temporary possession of the plates and two magical stones named Urim and Thummim with which to decipher them.

Joseph Smith preaching the faith of Mormonism at a camp meeting.

Smith published his *Book of Mormon* on March 26, 1830. It told how a party of Hebrews led by a prophet named Lehi had left Israel for America in about 600 B.C.E. There they had split into two opposing groups: the followers of Lehi's son Nephi, and the followers of Nephi's brother, Laman. Because of their wickedness, God cursed the Lamanites with dark skins, and for centuries they warred with the Nephites. Eventually the Nephites were wiped out in battle in the year 421, the sole survivor being Moroni, whose father had been named Mormon and who had engraved the golden plates.

The first 116 pages of the work, the *Book of Lehi*, which Smith had entrusted to his first disciple, Martin Harris, were lost, however.

most famous missing document in American history.

It was the first document printed in the American colonies, in 1639: a single, small sheet of paper, *The Oath of a Freeman*, as sworn by the first citizens of Massachusetts. Only some 50 had been printed, and all

were lost, but the text was known. Hofmann said he had bought some old papers at the Argosy Book Company on East 59th Street in New York and found the *Oath* among them. It bore a close resemblance to a later piece from the same printer, the *Bay Psalm Book* of 1640, that

Right: An apparently
successful dealer in
antique manuscripts,
Mark Hofmann stands
in front of the Mormon
Tabernacle in Salt Lake
City, Utah.

of the company. Shortly after 2:30 P.M. on October 16, Hofmann was badly injured when a third bomb exploded as he unlocked his parked car on Main Street, close to the Mormon Tabernacle.

While in the hospital with serious injuries, Hofmann appeared an innocent victim, but a host of investigators, seeking the maker of the bombs, eventually arrived at the engraving plant where the forged plate of the *Oath* had been made. The evidence was conclusive. After a preliminary hearing in May 1986, Hofmann was ordered to stand trial on charges of murder and fraud. In January 1987, he confessed to two prosecutors from the county attorney's office and on January 23 repeated his confession in court. The judge passed sentence, stipulating life imprisonment.

MORE HOFMANN FORGERIES

No one will ever be sure how many of the apparently genuine books and documents Hofmann sold were in fact forgeries. In 1997 the manuscript of a previously unknown poem by Emily Dickinson (1830–1886) was auctioned by Sotheby's and bought by the Jones Library in the poet's hometown of Amherst, Massachusetts. It turned out to be the work of Mark Hofmann.

HOW THE FORGERY WAS DETECTED

Once he had decided to forge the *Oath*, Hofmann's first step was to organize a "plant." He printed a single copy of an insignificant ballad sheet in old type on an ancient-looking scrap of paper and headed it *Oath of a Freeman;* then he priced it at $25 and slipped it into the bargain bin at the Argosy Company store. Picking out another four cheap items from the bin, he made sure he was given an itemized receipt for the $51.42 he paid. In this way he had "provenance" for the document.

Hofmann then made photocopies of

was in the New York Public Library. Hofmann offered the oath to the Library of Congress for $1 million.

Among those who had supported the purchase of Hofmann's "discoveries" for the Mormon Church were two executives of a Salt Lake City financial-planning company, Coordinated Financial Services (CFS): J. Gary Sheets and Steve Christensen. In 1985, CFS was in severe financial difficulty and filing for bankruptcy. Hofmann, too, was deeply in debt and thought up a way to distract attention from his problems.

At 7:00 on the morning of October 15, a parcel bomb exploded in the hands of Christensen in the doorway of his office. At 9:45 A.M. a similar bomb killed Sheets's wife at her home. The police assumed that the bomb had been meant for her husband. Agents of the Bureau of Alcohol, Tobacco and Firearms (ATF), noting that both targets were members of CFS, suggested that the motive was revenge for the failure

Opposite: Hofmann's
forgery of the *Oath of a
Freeman,* the first
document printed in
English in the Western
Hemisphere.

THE OATH OF A FREEMAN.

I·AB· being (by Gods providence) an Inhabitant, and Freeman, within the iurifdictiō of this Common-wealth, doe freely acknowledge my felfe to bee fubject to the governement thereof; and therefore doe heere fweare, by the great & dreadfull name of the Everliving-God, that I will be true & faithfull to the fame, & will accordingly yield affiftance & fupport therunto, with my perfon & eftate, as in equity I am bound: and will alfo truely indeavour to maintaine and preferve all the libertyes & privilidges thereof; fubmitting my felfe to the wholefome lawes, & ordres made & ftablifhed by the fame; and further, that I will not plot, nor practice any evill againft it, nor confent to any that fhall foe do, butt will timely difcover, & reveall the fame to lawefull authoritee nowe here ftablifhed, for the fpeedie preventing thereof. Moreover, I doe folemnly binde my felfe, in the fight of God, that when I fhalbe called, to give my voyce touching any fuch matter of this ftate, (in which freemen are to deale) I will give my vote & fuffrage as I fhall judge in myne owne confcience may beft conduce & tend to the publick weale of the body, without refpect of perfonnes, or favour of any man. Soe help mee God in the Lord Iefus Chrift.

several pages from a modern facsimile of the *Bay Psalm Book*, cut out individual letters and pasted them together to make the text of the *Oath*. He surrounded the text with a border made of printer's "flowers" that was also copied from the *Bay Psalm Book*.

The completed paste-up was then photocopied again, and Hofmann gave the copy to a process engraver to make a zinc letterpress-printing block. Because the original *Oath* would have been printed from individual types poorly cast in metal, Hofmann gave various letters in the block a slight irregularity by rounding off their edges or grinding down their surfaces.

To make ink, Hofmann burned a piece of seventeenth-century leather from the binding of a book so that any subsequent carbon dating would confirm that it was at least 300 years old. He mixed the ash with linseed oil and used the flyleaf from a book of the same period as the paper. To add to the appearance of age, he let fungus grow over the paper to produce the typical yellow-brown stains known as "foxing." To complete the forgery, he put the paper into a glass spark-discharge chamber, which produced ozone that oxidized and faded the ink.

After many experts on historic documents had pronounced themselves unable to determine whether or not the *Oath of a Freeman* was genuine, it was sent to the University of California at Davis for the ink to be investigated in a giant cyclotron by neutron-activation analysis. In the spring of 1986, scientists reported that they had compared the *Oath* with a genuine copy of the *Bay Psalm Book*, that the ink in both appeared to be similar, and that they could detect no indications of forgery.

William Flynn, a document analyst at the Arizona State Crime Laboratory, was asked whether any of Hofmann's written documents could be fakes. Flynn looked at the documents under a microscope and was puzzled by a slight cracking on the surface of the ink that showed up, which had not appeared in the ink on what were known to be genuine documents. There were also signs that the ink had bled into the paper, as if it had been soaked in some solution and then dried.

Flynn mixed some ink according to an old formula, but when he wrote with it, the result was smooth and black, not the faded brown of Hofmann's documents. Treatment with a dilute solution of sodium hydroxide (caustic soda) brought the writing to the correct shade, but the ink did not crack. Then Flynn tried a sample of ink to which he had added gum arabic in order to thicken it and make it dry more quickly. The ink surface cracked on

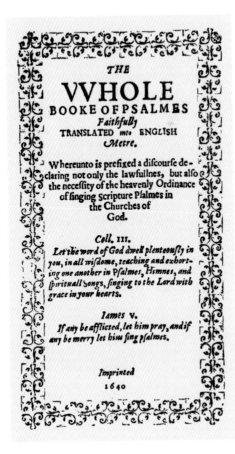

The title page of the *Bay Psalm Book*. Hofmann made photocopies from a modern facsimile as a source for the type he used in his forgery of the *Oath of a Freeman*.

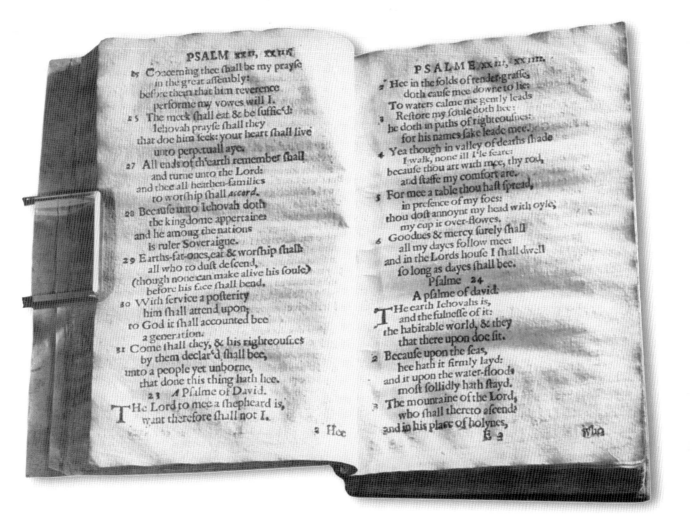

PSALM XXII, XXIII.

25 Concerning thee shall be my prayse
in the great assembly:
before them that him reverence
performe my vowes will I.
26 The meek shall eat & be suffic'd:
Iehovah prayse shall they
that doe him seek: your heart shall live
unto perpetuall aye.
27 All ends of th'earth remember shall
and turne unto the Lord:
and thee all heathen-families
to worship shall accord.
28 Because unto Iehovah doth
the kingdome appertaines
and he among the nations
is ruler Soveraigne.
29 Earths-fat-ones, eat & worship shall
all who to dust descend,
(though none can make alive his soule)
before his face shall bend.
30 With service a posterity
him shall attend upon,
to God it shall accounted bee
a generation.
31 Come shall they, & his righteousnes
by them declar'd shall bee,
unto a people yet unborne,
that done this thing hath hee.

23   A Psalme of David.

The Lord to mee a shepheard is,
want therefore shall not I.

2 Hee

PSALME XXIII, XXIIII.

2 Hee in the folds of tender-grasses
doth cause mee downe to lie:
To waters calme me gently leads
3 Restore my soule doth hee:
he doth in paths of righteousnes:
for his names sake leade mee.
4 Yea though in valley of deaths shade
I walk, none ill I'le feare:
because thou art with mee, thy rod,
and staffe my comfort are.
5 For mee a table thou hast spread,
in presence of my foes:
thou dost annoynt my head with oyle;
my cup it over-flowes.
6 Goodnes & mercy surely shall
all my dayes follow mee:
and in the Lords house I shall dwell
so long as dayes shall bee.

Psalme 24
A psalme of david.

The earth Iehovahs is,
and the fulnesse of it:
the habitable world, & they
that there upon doe sit.
2 Because upon the seas,
hee hath it firmly layd:
and it upon the water-floods
most sollidly hath stayd.
3 The mountaine of the Lord,
who shall thereto ascend?
and in his place of holynes,

B 2

Who

Two pages of the genuine *Bay Psalm Book*, showing the seventeenth-century typeface used by Hofmann in his forgery.

treatment with the sodium hydroxide. Flynn was able to report that 21 of the 79 documents sold by Hofmann to the Mormon Church were suspect.

THE KILLER MISTAKE

It was county attorney Theodore Cannon, who had spent 17 years as a letterpress printer, who finally revealed that the *Oath* must be a forgery. Each letter of type is cast on a "body," greater in height than the distance from the top of the highest character (the ascender) and the bottom of the lowest character (the descender). The descenders in one line of type therefore cannot come closer to the ascenders in the next line than the distance measured by the size of the body. In several places in Hofmann's printed documents, it could be seen with the naked eye that this was not the case.

There was also the question of the border of "flowers" around the text. Once the individual type had been assembled into text, it would have been held in place by "furniture" (long strips of metal) before the border could be set around it. Hofmann had not considered this, so there was insufficient white space between the text and the border. This proved conclusively that the *Oath* could never have been set in type.

CHAPTER 4
PHONY PREHISTORY

Making an object that appears to date from many centuries ago is tempting. As there is no previous record of its existence, its provenance is difficult to question.

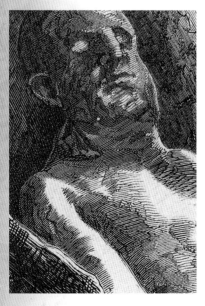

Those people who manufacture "prehistoric" fakes usually claim to have dug them up—sometimes together with other, genuine, materials. In fact, as present-day amateur archaeologists with metal detectors have shown, some of the most exciting discoveries have been made in areas where nothing previously had been suspected. Like art forgers, these fakers frequently have complex motives and are not always concerned with financial profit. In fact, as in the cases of Rouchomovsky and "Flint Jack" (see below), they may produce their fakes out of pure delight in their own skill. Some—like unsuccessful artists who turn to forgery—want to make the experts look like fools. Others gain personal prestige; still others, it seems, simply cannot resist making fakes just for the fun of it.

Opposite: The cliffs at Qumran, Israel, where the Dead Sea Scrolls were discovered. Similar scrolls, offered for sale by Moses Shapira in 1883, were condemned as forgeries.

Left: A newspaper "artist's impression" of the Cardiff Giant.

FINDING THE "MISSING LINK"

There is no more famous example of faked prehistory than the Piltdown skull. Charles Darwin (1809–1882) had published *On the Descent of Man* in 1871, a book in which he explained his theory that humankind had gradually evolved from apelike ancestors. Fifteen years previously, a human-like fossilized skeleton had been discovered in a cave in a Neanderthal gorge, not far from Düsseldorf, Germany. Two more were found at Spy, Belgium, in 1886. Other "hominid" (manlike) fossils were discovered in Java in 1891 and Germany in 1907. But none of these showed skull characteristics similar to those of modern humans, and during the early years of the twentieth century, anthropologists were obsessed with the possibility of finding the "missing link" that would prove the evolutionary theory.

In 1908 amateur geologist and lawyer Charles Dawson (1864–1916) got hold of a broken human cranium that had been dug out of a gravel pit at Piltdown in Sussex, in southeastern England. In 1912, accompanied by Arthur Smith Woodward, head of geology at the British Museum, Dawson unearthed an apelike jawbone nearby, still with its molar teeth.

The two men exhibited the skull of "Piltdown Man" at an excited meeting of the Geological Society in London in December 1912. Woodward said the cranium was definitely human; the jaw might be like an ape's, but the molars were flattened in a way that could only be human. The discoverers also found a flint ax, a bone tool and animal remains, together indicating that the find was some 500,000 years old.

Although having this "missing link" named after himself bestowed prestige on Dawson, other anthropologists were doubtful, suggesting that the two halves of the skull were from different species and different periods. Doubters were effectively silenced, however, when another similar skull was discovered two miles from Piltdown in 1915. A few months later Dawson died.

> # The flint ax had also been stained, and the bone tool showed marks of a metal instrument. It was obvious: "Piltdown Man" had never existed.

During the years that followed, other primitive skulls were discovered in various parts of the world. Some were dated much earlier than the Piltdown specimen, and one fact became quite clear. Over more than a million years hominids first developed a jaw and teeth similar to a human and only later developed a large cranium. "Piltdown Man," whatever else he might have been, was not the missing link.

NO MAN, BUT AN ORANGUTAN

In 1949, however, all was revealed. At the British Museum, Kenneth Oakley was given permission to examine the specimens to measure how much fluorine they had absorbed from their surroundings. His findings suggested that the skulls were far more recent than the animal remains found alongside them. A second run of tests showed that the jaws were even younger than the skulls. Further analysis revealed that the cranium had been stained with iron sulfate, the jaw had come from an orangutan and had been stained with potassium dichromate, and the molar teeth had been filed down. The flint ax had also been stained, and the bone tool showed marks of a metal instrument. It was obvious: "Piltdown Man" had never existed. News of the fake was duly published in 1953.

In 1959 the extent of the fake was exposed even more precisely when carbon dating revealed a more recent date for the first cranium. Rather than being a piece of prehistoric humanity, it was shown to be only some 600 years old. Further, it was known that victims of the Black Death (1348–1350) had been buried in a plague pit, just behind the existing gravel pit. It seemed very likely that "Piltdown Man" had been one of those unfortunate victims.

SO WHO EXACTLY WAS THE FAKER?
For a long time it was widely believed that Dawson had been the culprit. He had openly admitted putting some of the fragments in dichromate in the belief that this would harden them. But it did not explain the rest of the critical evidence. It may well be that Dawson was himself the first victim of the hoax. He was certainly sufficiently credulous. Dawson presented other finds that had been brought to him to local museums; they have since been shown to be transparent fakes.

The finger of suspicion has frequently been pointed at the French Jesuit priest and paleontologist, Pierre Teilhard de Chardin (1881–1955), who assisted Dawson and Woodward in 1912–1913. De Chardin was the one who had picked up a vital canine tooth that helped to confirm the human

The young French paleontologist Pierre Teilhard de Chardin (far left) and Arthur Smith Woodward (next to him) with local workmen at the Piltdown site in 1912.

nature of the Piltdown skull—and could have as easily put it where he found it. However, he had a distinguished career, both as a paleontologist and a philosopher, and his knowing involvement in a hoax of this sort seems unlikely.

It was not until the 1980s that the names of two other possible hoaxers emerged. One was the Sussex public analyst, Samuel Woodhead, who had died in 1941. The other was a professor of chemistry at London University, John Hewitt, who confessed (jokingly?) to two ladies over lunch—some 40 years after the event—that he had been responsible. Many other suspects have been named. The list even includes Sir Arthur Conan Doyle, whose novel *The Lost World*,

about surviving prehistoric creatures in the depths of the South American jungle, was first published in 1912. Some of the suspects maintained that they knew the name of the faker but kept silent.

SCRAPS OF PARCHMENT

Many doubts hang over the career of Moses Wilhelm Shapira (1830–1884). Did he knowingly deal in faked ancient pottery, or was he an innocent dupe? Did the scraps of parchment he bought come from the same source as the Dead Sea Scrolls discovered 63 years later, or were they forgeries? What has become of them?

Shapira was born into a Polish-Jewish family in what is now the Ukraine. His father relocated to Jerusalem, Palestine, and at the age of 25, Moses followed him. In Jerusalem he converted to Christianity, and in 1861 he opened a store dealing in tourist souvenirs.

In 1868 a black basalt stone a little over 3 ft. (1 m) in height was found in Dhiban, Palestine, east of the Dead Sea. Locals had broken it into several pieces in the hope of getting a good price for each, but it was repaired at the Louvre in Paris. Markings on the stone provided details of the Moabites, a people who lived in the ancient kingdom of Syria around the ninth century B.C.E. Almost the only other source of this information is found in the Bible. In addition, it enabled historians to reconstruct the Moabite alphabet and language.

This discovery roused a growing interest in the Moabites, and by 1873, Shapira was selling "Moabite" pottery—figurines, heads, vessels and erotic items— all said to have come from the same district as the stone. Some items bore inscriptions in the Moabite language. Shapira sold about 1,700 of these artifacts to the Berlin Museum and financed further excavations. However, a French scholar and diplomat, Charles Clermont-Ganneau, established that Arab potter Salim al-Kari—possibly acting on commission from Shapira—had faked the pottery. Shapira nevertheless claimed complete innocence, putting all the blame on the potter.

A REPUTATION IN RUINS

This exposure cast a shadow on what followed. According to Shapira, around 1878 he bought 15 strips of parchment measuring on average 3½ x 7 in. (8.9 x 17.8 cm), which had come from a cave in a gorge in the Dead Sea area. The Hebrew script in which they were written was a very early form, dating from before the sixth century B.C.E. Shapira decided that the text was biblical and sent the strips to a German expert for advice. But the German, remembering Shapira's involvement with the faked pottery, refused to cooperate.

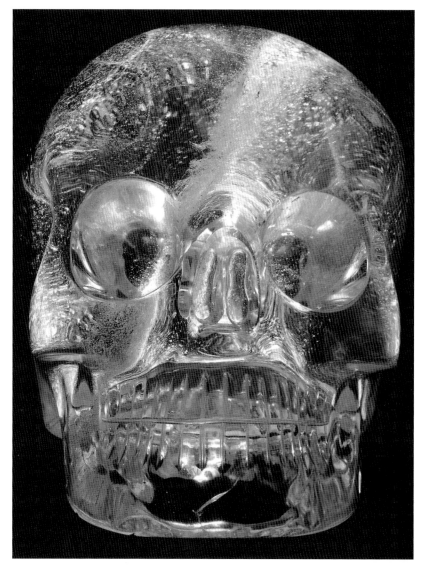

This supposedly Aztec crystal skull, owned by the British Museum, has been suspected as a fake for more than 30 years. Confirmation came in January 2005 when British experts using an electron microscope discovered that it had been polished with a jeweler's wheel.

So Shapira set to work making his own translation, which he completed in 1883. He discovered that the text was a part of the biblical book of Deuteronomy. Apparently it was 300 or 400 years older than the *Septuagint*, the Greek translation of the scriptures made in the third century B.C.E., a source that most later Bibles had followed. Although the content was similar, the scrolls differed from the *Septuagint* in many details.

THE STRIPS UNDER EXAMINATION

Shapira took the strips to London and offered them to the British Museum at a price of £1 million. While awaiting a report from their expert, Christian Ginsburg, the museum put two of the strips on display, attracting a huge crowd of visitors. Among them was Clermont-Ganneau, the Frenchman who had exposed the Moabite pottery as fake. Shapira had refused Clermont-Ganneau a closer look at the strips. Nonetheless he made a report, which appeared before Ginsburg's. Both came to the same conclusion: The parchments had been forged. All the strips had a clean-cut upper edge, and there were errors in spelling, which suggested that the text had been dictated to a scribe unfamiliar with archaic Hebrew. Clermont-Ganneau later declared that one of the pieces of parchment had been cut from a genuine Yemenite scroll that Shapira had previously sold to the museum.

Shapira was deeply in debt, and any reputation he had left was shattered. In 1884 he committed suicide in the Hotel Bloemendaal, in Rotterdam, Netherlands. Two years later Sotheby's sold the parchments at auction in London, fetching a price of ten guineas. In 1887 they were probably destroyed in a fire at the home of their owner, but there are stories that they were later heard of in Australia.

Since 1947, a considerable hoard of parchment scrolls has been discovered in

Were the Shapira strips forgeries, or has a valuable addition to biblical study been lost forever? Was an innocent man forced into the desperate act of suicide?

caves at Qumran, in the Dead Sea area. They are written in the same ancient script as the Shapira strips—and a number have one clean-cut edge. Also, like his, their texts differ in various details from the accepted version of the scriptures, but experts are confident they are authentic. So several troubling questions remain. Were the Shapira strips forgeries, or has a valuable addition to biblical study been lost forever? Was an innocent man forced into the desperate act of suicide?

THE TIARA OF SAITAPHARNES

During the nineteenth century, archaeologists began to make exciting discoveries along the northern coast of the Black Sea, in southern Russia. They found traces of a race, the Scythians, who had settled there around the seventh century B.C.E. Previously, the Scythians were thought to have been a myth, though there is evidence that Greek colonists were in the area. However, it is now known that it was Greeks who taught the Scythians how to work with gold. Centuries later, everyone who witnessed the excavation of magnificent works of art was dazzled by the expertise of Scythian goldsmiths.

In 1895 the most remarkable "find" came on the market. A richly decorated gold helmet, it was designed to be worn as a regal tiara. On its upper part were reliefs of two scenes from Homer's poem, the *Iliad*. In a lower band were scenes of hunting, the taming of horses and animal combats. An inscription in Greek characters identified it as a headdress, once offered to the Scythian king, Saitapharnes, by the inhabitants of the city of Olbia.

The owner of the tiara at the time was a Russian corn merchant named Schapshelle Gokhman. He first offered it for sale at a high price in Vienna, but skeptical archaeologists refused to authenticate it. The British Museum similarly turned down the offer. Eventually the Louvre in Paris bought the tiara for the staggering sum of 400,000 francs.

"YOU SHOULD SEE MY SARCOPHAGUS!"

Many scholars contested the tiara's authenticity. They pointed out that some relief scenes appeared to have been copied from other objects and that certain of the decorative motifs had come from different periods of antiquity. The controversy continued until 1903, when a French artist living in Montmartre, in Paris, claimed he had faked the tiara. This provoked a letter to the newspaper *Le Matin* from a Russian goldsmith living in Paris, who stated that the object had been fashioned by his good friend Israel Rouchomovsky—another Russian goldsmith, who lived in the city of Odessa on the Black Sea coast.

Rouchomovsky was brought to Paris and interrogated before a commission, chaired by the same Charles Clermont-Ganneau who had discredited Moses Shapira. However, in this case, Rouchomovsky readily admitted that he had made the tiara for Gokhman, using books and ancient fragments for inspiration. He proved his point by making a copy of part of the headdress. "The tiara is no work of art," he said. "It is crude work. You should see my sarcophagus!"

Taking due advantage of the publicity his statement had caused, Rouchomovsky then exhibited a number of his fakes at the Paris Salon and was awarded a prize for his work. Amusingly, the fakes included a drinking horn and a breastplate that had appeared on the market—allegedly genuine items—six years earlier. As for Gokhman, nothing more was heard of him.

The revelation that the Saitapharnes tiara was a modern fake provoked numerous satires such as this, with the king— wearing the tiara— rising from his grave in 1896.

THE MYSTERY OF GLOZEL

In March 1924, 17-year-old Emile Fradin was plowing one of his father's fields near the hamlet of Glozel, in the Auvergne, in central France. Suddenly the cow drawing the plow stumbled into an oval-shaped hole. When it was cleared, the hole was found to be some 9 ft. 6 in. (2.5 m) long, with a paved base. Inside were pots, tablets, bricks and lumps of glass. The bricks were covered with a thin layer that was similar to glass. It seemed probable that the cow had inadvertently revealed a medieval glass kiln, as similar kilns were known in the area. The Fradin family, however, was sure they had found the site of an ancient grave.

The news of this discovery reached Dr. Albert Morlet, a surgeon in the nearby city of Vichy and an amateur archaeologist. He bought the rights to excavate the site further, and he and Emile Fradin very soon discovered a large number of extraordinary objects. There were quantities of pots, hermaphrodite figures, handprints in clay and flint arrowheads. There were pebbles and pieces of bone carved with the images of animals, some of which had been extinct for many centuries. Most puzzling of all were clay tablets inscribed with a strange script. They contained both the letters of the modern Roman alphabet and a quantity of extra symbols, making a total of 133 characters.

ALL TOO GOOD TO BE TRUE?

The remarkable jumble of objects uncovered by Dr. Morlet and the fact that they were in the styles of widely different archaeological periods suggested that he—or someone with similar interests and access to a wide range of specimens—had "salted" the site. On the other hand, one of France's leading archaeologists, Salomon Reinach, was convinced that the clay tablets, which Dr. Morlet had calculated were 10,000 years old, were proof of his theory that writing had originated in Europe.

In 1927 the International Anthropological Congress sent a commission to examine the Glozel site. They reported that nothing there was of any great age. There were indications that steel tools had been used on the pebbles and bones and that some of the pottery was so soft that it would dissolve in water. Undaunted, Reinach organized another expedition in 1928. After three days of digging in apparently undisturbed soil, Reinach's team unearthed several objects, including another clay tablet. The fact that plant roots surrounded these was taken as evidence that they had not been buried recently. Dr. Morlet continued digging, and the Fradins opened a small museum to display his finds. Gradually, however, interest in the site died down. For 30 years after World War II, little more was heard of the controversy.

By 1974, the scientific technique of thermoluminescence had become well established in the dating of ancient pottery. Scientists from Scotland, Denmark and France conducted a series of tests on material from Glozel. They obtained a range of dates between 700 B.C.E. and 100 C.E. These were far more recent than the dating proposed by Dr. Morlet, and they accorded with carbon dating of one of the bones. Another fragment was dated at 1200–1350 B.C.E., but this was possibly a piece of brick from the kiln.

In 1983 a new excavation was made in Glozel, some 550 yards (500 m) distant from the original and under conditions of strict security. Only a few pieces were found, but strangely, several had been inscribed with the mystery script. To this day the puzzle remains unsolved.

The subsidence in the field at Glozel in which the first fragments were found.

FORGER'S FILE
THE ELEMENTS OF THE GLOZEL ENIGMA

- The "pro-Glozellians" claim the thermoluminescence figures as vindication, proof that the finds are truly ancient.
- However, if the datings are correct, how could bones be inscribed with pictures of long-extinct animals?
- Dr. Morlet was an amateur archaeologist and no doubt had access to a variety of specimens from different periods.
- The first Glozel digs were, literally, a "free for all." There was no supervision, and anybody could claim to have unearthed a find—even someone who had brought it to the site.

THE PRINCE OF FABRICATORS

He had many nicknames, among them "Fossil Willy," "Shirtless," "Snake Billy" and "Bones." But the one he was best known by was "Flint Jack." His real name was Edward Simpson. He was born in 1815 in the village of Sleights, near the port of Whitby, in Yorkshire, England.

When Simpson was 14, an amateur geologist and historian, Dr. George Young, took him on fossil-hunting expeditions. Later Simpson worked as assistant to a local physician who was also interested in fossils. When this man died, "Jack" started collecting fossils himself, selling them to dealers. In 1843 one of these dealers showed him a flint arrowhead and asked if he could copy it. Jack, it seems, had a natural understanding of how flints were flaked to make arrowheads. His copy was so good he was immediately tempted into making many more. They sold like hotcakes.

Soon Jack widened his activities. He began making "ancient urns," which he said he had unearthed in burial mounds on the high moors. He carved an inscription on a "Roman" milestone, which he then buried in a field, digging it up later and carrying it off in a wheelbarrow to sell. An article appeared in an 1867 archaeological journal, in which a close acquaintance wrote a description of Jack. He called him "the very prince of fabricators—flints of every form, celts [chisels], stone hammers, ancient pottery, inscribed stones, fibulae [clasp pins], querns [grinding stones], armor and every conceivable thing—whose productions have fooled the most learned and are to be found in the cabinets of collectors everywhere."

However, from 1846 onward, Jack began to drink heavily and took to wandering the length and breadth of England like a tramp. He made his way to London, where he sold both genuine fossils and fake flint implements. Asked whether he had fooled the British Museum, Jack replied: "Why, of course I did! They have lots of my things—and good things they are, too."

A WANDR'ING FRAUDSTER

Returning to the north, Jack worked in York for the city museum but soon was off again. In 1852 he returned to London, where he made sets of educational specimens for James Tennant, professor of geology at King's College. But he had to keep moving, selling his wares everywhere to buy drink. It was 1861 when he got back to London, and on January 6, 1862, the audience at a Geological Society meeting was surprised when "a weather-beaten man of about 45 years of age…in dirty tattered clothes and heavy navvy's boots" appeared on the platform. They were, perhaps, even more surprised when Jack spent more than an hour demonstrating his skill in the making of flint implements.

At last, in order to buy beer, Jack was reduced to theft and in 1867 was sentenced to a year in Bedford prison. But his skills were beginning to fail, he was an incurable drunk, and he spent at least one more term in prison before dying in the workhouse some years later.

Nearly a century after the time of his greatest fame, a writer on archaeology hailed Flint Jack as ideally qualified for the work of a modern museum assistant. "If there had been no current interest in antiquities, he might never have realized and developed his own particular genius; and in turn, his intentions would not have been misunderstood, nor his talents misused, if the attitude of most antiquaries had been different."

GIANTS IN THE EARTH

In the spring of 1868, a bluff cigarmaker from Binghamton, New York, named George Hull was on a visit to his sister in Ackley, Iowa. One evening he heard a fire-and-brimstone preacher quote from the Bible, Genesis 6:4: "And there were giants in the earth at that time." As he later described, that sentence kept Hull awake for most of the night. He had hit upon a brilliant idea.

GENERATING A GIANT

At a quarry near Fort Dodge, Hull found a block of solid gypsum, 12 ft. long by 4 ft. wide and 22 in. thick (365 x 120 x 55 cm). It weighed more than 2 tons, but Hull

"Flint Jack" as he appeared at a meeting in London of the Geological Society in January 1862: "a weather-beaten man…in dirty tattered clothes and heavy navvy's boots."

eventually managed to transport it to Chicago—leaving several broken wagons and damaged bridges along the way. On the premises of Edward Burghardt, a stonecutter, the gypsum was transformed into the statue of a giant man, bald-headed, but otherwise intact. The figure was twisted as if he had died in great agony, and Hull himself posed for the head. Dark streaks in the gypsum looked like human veins, and beating the statue with steel needles hammered into wooden blocks simulated the pores of the skin.

Hull then treated the statue with sulfuric acid to age it before transporting it to the farm of a cousin, William "Stubby" Newell. The farm was outside the village of Cardiff, some 13 miles from Syracuse, New York, and Newell had been fighting a losing battle with it for some years. He and Hull, with help from two others they swore to secrecy, buried the giant in a shallow grave behind the barn,

covered it over and left it for nearly a year.

The plan was for Newell to bring workers to his farm to dig for a well and to allow them to discover the "body"; but even before he did this, another lucky find was made nearby. A farmer less than a mile away unearthed some bones while plowing; these were pronounced genuine fossils by scientists from Cornell University. The scene was set for the emergence of the Cardiff Giant.

On Friday, October 15, 1869, workers digging the well found and uncovered the statue. The news spread rapidly through the area. Newell at once erected a tent over the "grave," charging sightseers an entry fee of 50 cents to view the figure. Within a week crowds were arriving from as far away as New York City, and the price of entrance had risen to $1. Newell exchanged his farm overalls for a morning coat and began to give lectures on the discovery of the giant.

A SPELLBOUND CROWD

"As one looked upon it," wrote a newspaper reporter, "he could not help feeling that he was in the presence of a great and superior being. The crowd as they gathered round it seemed almost spellbound. There was no levity."

After a month the giant was moved to Syracuse and placed on exhibition. Eminent scientists argued over whether this was an ancient statue or a fossilized human. Dr. Andrew D. White, first president of Cornell, had a fragment analyzed; he learned that the figure had been made of plain gypsum, but White did not make his discovery public.

> ## "As one looked upon it, he could not help feeling that he was in the presence of a great and superior being."
> —NEWSPAPER REPORT ON THE CARDIFF GIANT

A FAKE OF A FAKE

A celebrated sculptor from New York, Erasmus Dow Palmer, had no doubts: "Fraud!" he declared. His verdict reached the ears of showman Phineas T. Barnum, who was running a museum and menagerie

The body of the Cardiff Giant was put on display at the Farmers' Museum, Cooperstown, New York, in May 1948. It lies in an earth "grave," exactly as it was excavated.

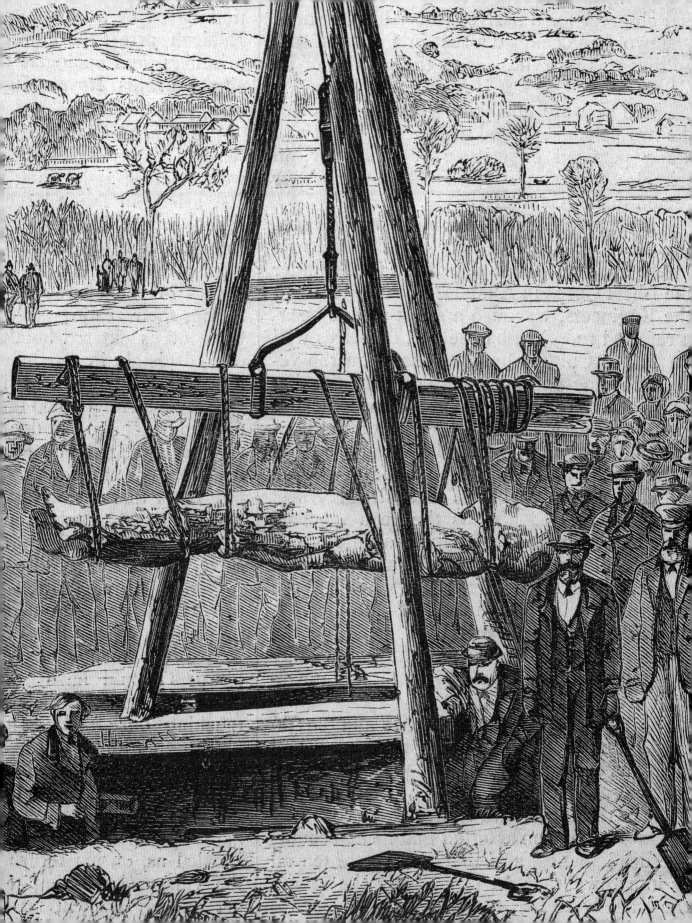

The size and weight of
the Cardiff Giant are
apparent from this
illustration of the raising
of the statue from
William Newell's field
in August 1869.

FORGER'S FILE
RETURNED TO
A SHALLOW GRAVE

"Old Hoaxey" was the name newspapers gave the statue after its history was uncovered. As Old Hoaxey, it appeared year after year at fairs and carnivals. In 1901 it became an attraction at the Pan-American Exposition in Buffalo, New York. In 1934 it was seen at the New York State Fair in Syracuse. Finally, in 1948 the New York State Historical Association purchased the figure and placed it on view in the Farmers' Museum, Cooperstown—lying in a shallow grave, even as it had been found 81 years before.

on Broadway and who decided that a fake of a fake was just what he needed. When the Cardiff Giant was brought from Syracuse to New York City for the Christmas shopping season, a replica was already standing in Barnum's museum. However, the presence of two giants only two blocks apart turned out to be very good business for both.

In January the original statue was taken to Boston, where the renowned essayist Ralph Waldo Emerson pronounced it "astonishing...undoubtedly a bona fide, petrified human being." However, Dr. Oliver Wendell Holmes, the eminent Boston anatomist, did something that nobody else had thought of doing. He bored a hole behind the giant's left ear, revealing nothing but solid stone and no trace of a fossilized brain.

The Cardiff Giant continued on its travels. It was no longer regarded as a fossil but was still considered a statue of great antiquity. Then the press began to look more carefully into its history and followed its trail all the way back to Chicago. Confronted with the facts, George Hull laughed and admitted everything.

With a small fortune at his disposal and encouraged by the credulity of the public the first time around, Hull decided to improve on his first effort. He had a figure sculpted from a mix of ground stone, clay, bones, blood and meat, which was then fired in a kiln for several weeks. With the help of a man named William Conant, the figure was buried close to the village of Beulah, near Pueblo, Colorado, in 1877. Several months later Conant and his son "discovered" a foot sticking from the ground and unearthed a petrified body about 7 ft. 6 in. (2.7 m) long. It had a rather small simianlike head and unusually long arms. Newspapers soon nicknamed it "Solid Muldoon," after a famous strongman of the time.

"There can be no question about the genuineness of this piece of statuary," reported the *Daily Times* of Denver. "The stone shows the effects of time, and the circumstances of the discovery are such as to preclude anything like a repetition of the clumsy Cardiff Giant fraud." How wrong they were would be revealed only five months later, when the figure was displayed in New York City. A man to whom Hull owed money told his story to the *New York Tribune*, and that was the end of Solid Muldoon.

CHAPTER 5
BOGUS IDENTITY

History is full of people who assumed alternate identities. Indeed, one of the oldest stories in the Bible tells of how Isaac deceived his father, Abraham, by pretending to be his own brother, Esau.

An impostor can have many different motives. He may find he can only enter the profession of his choice by faking credentials or claiming to be of the opposite sex. Discharged criminals who are anxious to go straight or fraudsters who want to cover their tracks may assume other personas. Still others may see a way of making lots of money through confidence trickery. Someone who is often mistaken for someone else may realize he can use the error to their advantage. And sometimes tricksters just do it for the pleasure of fooling others. It is more often women who choose or are forced by circumstances to adopt a change of gender. There are many stories of young women who served in the navy or army without arousing

Opposite: A forged passport and counterfeit money, hidden inside a hollowed-out book—the ingenuity of criminals is legendary.

Left: Who was "Kaspar Hauser"? He appeared as an adolescent boy, almost speechless, in the streets of Nuremberg, Germany, in May 1828. Wild rumor linked him with the royal house of Baden.

The young "Dr. James Barry." In fact, a remarkably precocious girl, she enlisted as a qualified physician in the British army at the age of only 14.

suspicion, but one of the most fascinating is that of "James Barry" (1799–1865). As a six-year-old child, she arrived in London from Ireland accompanied by her mother, whom she always described as "my aunt." Brilliantly precocious, Barry dressed as a boy and enrolled as a medical student at Edinburgh University, Scotland, graduating at the age of 12.

After working for a leading surgeon in a London hospital, "Dr. Barry" enlisted as a

professional medic in the British army in 1813. She was posted to South Africa in 1816 and appointed personal physician to the governor of the Cape. She worked tirelessly to improve the conditions of military hospital patients, even as Florence Nightingale was to do years later. The two women eventually met during the Crimean War (1854–1856). Miss Nightingale later described how "Dr. Barry" had harangued her from horseback. "I should say she was the most hardened creature I ever met throughout the army."

Barry was promoted to Army Medical Inspector in 1822, but her assumed personality won her many enemies. There was malicious gossip about her gender, but it was detected only once in her life. During the 1840s, she fell asleep uncovered and woke to find two brother officers at her bedside. Both had to be sworn to secrecy.

Her final military posting was to Canada, as Inspector General of Hospitals. When she died in London in 1865, an army surgeon-major certified her death as a

"Her hands and arms seem not to have participated of the change of sexes, but are fitter to carry a chair than a fan."

—HORACE WALPOLE (1717–1797)
ENGLISH WRITER

fellow officer. It was a woman brought in to lay out the body who exclaimed: "The devil a General—it's a woman!"

THE TRANSVESTITE SPY

An unusual case of a man who successfully passed himself off as a woman is that of the Chevalier d'Eon (1728–1810). He was born Charles Geneviève Louis André d'Eon de Beaumont in Tonnerre, France, the son of an attorney. During much of his childhood, his mother would dress d'Eon in his sister's clothes, which suited his slender body, soft fair hair and blue eyes. As a student at the College Mazarin in Paris, d'Eon excelled at languages, then became a secretary in the Paris finance department.

D'Eon made a successful bet with his friends that he could convince Madame de Pompadour, mistress of King Louis XV, that he was a woman. The king himself was equally fooled. Impressed, Louis recruited d'Eon to join his personal network of spies.

In 1755, Louis was eager to establish friendly relations with Russia and determined to contact the czarina, the future Catherine the Great. Very soon, two people arrived at the Russian court: a certain Chevalier Douglass, who said he had come from Sweden to investigate mining prospects, and his "niece," pretty little Lia de Beaumont. "She" carried a handsomely bound copy of Montesquieu's *L'Esprit des Lois*, but hidden in its binding was a letter addressed to the czarina. D'Eon (for it was he) was able to gather useful information by gossiping with the maids of

Left: Barry photographed shortly before her death, at the age of 66. It was only after this death that her true sex was discovered.

"She appeared to me a man in women's clothes."

—JAMES BOSWELL (1740–1795)

the court and succeeded in charming the czarina herself. As a result of this visit, relations with France were restored and a threatened treaty between Russia and England was left unsigned.

Louis XV named d'Eon a chevalier as a reward, appointed him a captain in the elite Dragoons and, in 1763, sent him to London as first secretary at the French embassy. There d'Eon spied against the British. However, he fell out with a newly appointed ambassador, tried to blackmail the new French king, Louis XVI, with threats concerning the secret files he held, and finally was forced to agree to a condition that he should dress as a woman for the rest of his life.

By now all London was buzzing with tales about the true nature of the Chevalier. The *Morning Post* of November 11, 1775, reported: "The City is about to issue a new policy on the sex of the Chevalier d'Eon; the odds are seven to four for woman against man, and a gentleman well known in these sort of negotiations has undertaken to resolve this question before the expiry of fifteen days." But neither this gentleman nor any other was able to settle the matter in the Chevalier's lifetime.

In 1777, d'Eon returned to France, where he spent much of the time with his mother until in 1785 he left again for England. He was a first-class swordsman, and to earn money, he gave fencing exhibitions posing as a woman, sometimes dressed as Joan of Arc. Eventually, as his skill declined, he was wounded in a bout and could fence no longer. A near-penniless man of 83, he died in London on May 21,

Opposite: The Chevalier d'Eon in middle age, wearing the medal of his order but compelled by the French king to dress in women's clothing for the rest of his life.

FORGER'S FILE
POPE JOAN

The story of Pope Joan was first recorded in the thirteenth century and was widely believed in Europe for more than 400 years. It was said that she had been born in Germany of English parents and later appeared in Rome dressed as a monk, calling herself Johannes Anglicus. She gained a reputation for deep learning and was eventually elected to the papacy as Pope John VIII. According to the story, her true gender was revealed only when she died in childbirth during a religious procession. In 1647 the Protestant scholar David Blondel declared that the story was a myth, and in 1863 it was finally proven to be no more than a popular legend.

The legend of Pope Joan is perpetuated in *La Papesse*, the second in the traditional pack of Tarot playing cards.

1810. At last, a doctor was able to declare that d'Eon was neither a woman nor a hermaphrodite but a genuine male. He has been hailed as "the patron saint of transvestites."

FALSE CREDENTIALS

One of the most audacious rogues of the twentieth century, who adopted a wide range of fake identities, was "Stanley Clifford Weyman" (see pages 190–93). On several occasions he impersonated officers of the United States armed forces and also represented himself as an attorney and a journalist. But Weyman particularly enjoyed using his forged credentials to play the part of a qualified physician. Another

The "Great Impostor," Fernand Demara, at the age of 30, wearing the uniform of the Royal Canadian Navy, as he posed as surgeon-lieutenant Dr. Joseph Cyr.

trickster who posed as a doctor—and nearly was decorated as a Canadian national hero—was Fernand Waldo Demara. He achieved international fame in 1961, when the story of his career was made into a movie, *The Great Impostor*, starring Tony Curtis in the lead role.

Demara was born in Lawrence, Massachusetts, in December 1921. From his early school years he felt drawn to the Roman Catholic faith, and as a teenager, he entered a Trappist monastery as a novice. The austere regime of the Trappists, however, was too much for a lively youngster; after two years Demara was recommended to the Brothers of Charity in Boston for training as a priest. But once again he rebelled against even their relatively easygoing discipline. Expelled from the brotherhood, he enlisted in the United States Army.

At the age of 19, however, Demara's footloose wandering had become the pattern of his life. He stole all the personal records and mementos of a fellow soldier and entered another Trappist monastery as Anthony Ingolia. Unfortunately, his reputation soon caught up with him, and this time—the United States having just entered World War II in December 1941—he joined the navy as Fred W. Demara.

Demara had no intention of being posted to a ship, so he immediately applied for training at a hospital school. He passed the basic course successfully but was turned down for advanced training, on the grounds that his background education was insufficient. Instead, Demara was sent as a medical corpsman to a marine battalion near Norfolk, Virginia. There he stole a stack of official stationery. Picking the name of a suitably qualified medical man from the yearbook of Iowa State University, he wrote in that person's name for copies of his credentials. When they duly arrived, he inserted his

In 1963, Demara (left) surrendered to Los Angeles County D.A. Manley Bowler, to answer a charge of stealing a car from a California boys' camp.

own details, made photocopies and applied for a naval commission.

MULTIPLE IDENTITIES

In the weeks before a decision could come through, Demara realized that he had discovered an easy way of obtaining false credentials; soon he had papers identifying him as Robert Linton French, a Ph.D. in psychology from Stanford and a former research fellow at Yale. While on leave back home in Lawrence, he stole a pile of blank papers from his parish priest and others from the office of Cardinal O'Connor in Boston.

When Demara returned to Norfolk, he was told he would be commissioned—as soon as a security check could be made on his background. "I could see that my usefulness to the service was over," he later

admitted. He went out to the end of the docks that night and left his naval uniform in a pile with a note that said: "I have made a fool of myself. This is the only way out. Forgive me."

Now a deserter from both the army and the navy, he appeared at the Abbey of Our Lady of Gethsemani in Kentucky as Dr. Robert French and entered the novitiate. But once again he quickly found the demanding Trappist discipline unbearable, and he was recommended to a Benedictine abbey at Subiaco, in the Ozark Mountains of Arkansas.

Here he badly overplayed his hand. He presented, among other papers, a forged letter from Cardinal O'Connor and a forged confirmation certificate signed by the Right Reverend (later Cardinal) Francis J. Spellman. Within weeks, letters arrived

PURSUED BY HIS OWN IDENTITY

After his exposure Demara sold his story to *Life* magazine for $2,500, then tried to lose himself in near anonymity. He worked for a time in a Massachusetts institute for child guidance, and after this—as Ben W. Jones—first as a bookkeeper and then as a guard captain at a prison in Huntsville, Texas. But his photograph in *Life* kept catching up with him, and each time, he was forced to leave in a hurry. As Frank Kingston, he cared for children with Down's syndrome; as Jefferson Baird Thorne, he taught English, French and Latin at a school in Winchendon, Massachusetts; and as Martin Godgart, he was a school assistant on a tiny island off the coast of Maine. He ended his career under his own name, as a minister to the sick and dying in a hospital in Anaheim, California, where he died of a heart attack at the age of 61.

from Boston denouncing the forgeries, and once more Dr. French was on the road.

PIOUS PSYCHOLOGY

He taught psychology for a year at a church school in Chicago, spent a few weeks at another Catholic monastery in Milwaukee and was then appointed Dean of the School of Philosophy at Gannon College in Erie, Pennsylvania. He had plans to establish "a society of pious laymen for the instruction of Catholic youth," to be named the Pious Society of St. Mark. However, a quarrel with his superior affronted his dignity, so he left.

In Olympia, Washington—about as far away as he could get—Demara established a "student psychological center" at a Benedictine abbey and set about making himself known to all the prominent citizens of the town. Soon he was made an honorary deputy sheriff, a notary public, and had applied to become a justice of the peace. Then, as always, the paper trail he had left behind caught up with him. He was arrested by the FBI, sent to the naval barracks as a deserter and sentenced to six years in prison.

DUPLICITOUS DOCTORS

Released on parole after 18 months for good behavior, Demara became Dr. C. B. Hamman, a zoologist with a specialty in cancer research, working at a Catholic school in Maine. While there he contrived to steal all the credentials of an acquaintance, Dr. Joseph Cyr. Then came another affront to his assumed dignity and yet another furious departure.

As "Dr. Joseph Cyr," Demara went north to St. John, New Brunswick, and obtained a commission as a surgeon-lieutenant in the Royal Canadian Navy. Then he fell in love. He planned, as soon as he had served his time, to get married and settle down as a local physician in some out-of-the-way corner of Canada. But the Korean War (1950–1953) was then raging, and Demara was posted to the destroyer *Cayuga*, which sailed for Korean waters in June 1951.

At first the surgeon-lieutenant was required only to extract a tooth or treat colds and other infections. Then, one day, a junk carrying wounded South Korean soldiers came alongside the *Cayuga*. Three had been seriously injured and one had a bullet lodged near his heart. Without any knowledge of surgery, Demara had no alternative but to operate. Miraculously, he succeeded, and the Korean soldier recovered within days. The other two were also dealt with successfully.

The Canadian navy's public-information service issued a detailed story about "Dr. Cyr," and his commanding officer put his name forward for a citation. The real Dr. Joseph Cyr heard about it, however, and Demara's medical career came to an end—as did his hopes of marrying and settling down.

"CATCH ME IF YOU CAN"

Probably the most audacious of modern impostors was Frank W. Abagnale, whose

Always heavy set, Demara put on a great deal of weight in his later years. He found final fulfillment as a minister to the sick and dying in a California hospital.

early life was described in the book *Catch Me If You Can* (1980) and immortalized in the recent movie with the same title. He was born in Bronxville, New York, in 1948, and began his criminal career by raising money on his father's charge card. At the age of 16, already giving the appearance of a full-grown adult, he left home, changed the birth date on his driver's license to 1938 and decided to masquerade as a PanAm pilot. Simply by telephoning the airline, he got the address of the tailoring company that made the uniforms and obtained the necessary dark blue suit. Then he went to the PanAm commissary at Kennedy Airport and, with a tale that his two-year-old had hidden his insignia, got himself a pair of wings and a badge for his hat.

Now Abagnale needed to know more about the company's activities and also procure himself an ID card and a pilot's license. He fulfilled the first requirement by extensive research in the public library and by quizzing a flight captain in the role of a reporter for a high-school magazine. He obtained a passable ID card, complete with his photo, and added the PanAm logo from decals provided with a model aircraft kit. As for the license, he found a firm in Milwaukee that would engrave a plaque in silver, using a standard FAA format and inserting the relevant personal details. With this plaque in hand, Abagnale had it photocopied to a smaller size on a suitable sheet of paper. Now, as "Frank Williams," he was a full-fledged pilot in all but experience.

For some time, Abagnale hung out at La Guardia Airport, picking up airline jargon, and learned all about "deadheading" in the flight-deck jump seat. He opened a bank account in his new name and found that while in uniform, he had no difficulty cashing bad checks at airline counters. From then on, he flew for free all over the United States as a pilot heading for another airport to pick up a plane. He stayed at hotels frequented by aircrews, charged his overnights to PanAm and left behind a profusion of bad checks that would take months to be discovered.

THERE'S A PEDIATRICIAN IN MY CLOSET!

After two years of this vagrant life, Abagnale felt the need for a rest and rented an apartment in Atlanta, Georgia, identifying himself as a pediatrician. All went well until a new neighbor turned out to be chief resident pediatrician at Smithers Hospital in nearby Marietta. It was not long before "Dr. Williams" was invited to visit the hospital and soon became well

His career as an international trickster long behind him, Frank W. Abagnale Jr. is now a respected professional adviser on financial security. But in his youth he was known to the police in 26 countries as the "Skywayman."

known there. Eventually he was asked if he would temporarily take over supervision of the night shift in the pediatrics ward.

Abagnale rose to the challenge. Like Stanley Weyman, who impersonated a physician, (see page 192), he survived by allowing real doctors to make diagnoses, then concurring with them; he also hid in a linen closet to avoid being called.

Then it was once more time to move on. As "Robert E. Conrad," a law graduate from Harvard, he took the bar examination in a southern state and joined the staff of the attorney general. But then a genuine Harvard law graduate arrived, and Abagnale had to move away in a hurry.

As "Frank Adams," an ex-TWA pilot with a Ph.D. in sociology from Columbia University, New York, he taught summer school at Brigham Young University in Provo, Utah. After this, on his way to San Francisco, he stopped off in Eureka, California. Although in his previous three incarnations he had earned good money and had no need to pass bad checks, Adams was struck by the number of banks in the city, so he decided to begin forging PanAm paychecks.

GETTING AWAY WITH IT

The great problem facing a check forger is that the forgery may be detected very

Leonardo DiCaprio played the 20-year-old Frank Abagnale in the movie *Catch Me If You Can.* In this scene he has assembled his team of pretty coeds, leading them to believe that they are about to begin training as stewardesses.

> ## "Frank Abagnale could write a check on toilet paper, drawn on the Confederate States Treasury, sign it "U. R. Hooked," and cash it at any bank in town, using a Hong Kong driver's license for identification."
>
> —FORMER HOUSTON POLICE CHIEF

Opposite: In October 1906, Wilhelm Voigt (1849–1922), a former shoemaker, appeared in the town of Köpernick, Germany, dressed in the uniform of a captain of the 1st Prussian Guards. Ordering some soldiers to follow him, he arrested the town's secretary and mayor, and sent them under escort to the capital. He was soon arrested and imprisoned but was pardoned 18 months later. Here he is pictured in London during a succesful theater tour.

quickly. To avoid this, Frank Abagnale exploited his knowledge of details not known to the ordinary bank teller. As an example, he explained, the series of numbers printed in the bottom-left-hand corner of a check is coded, such as with 1130 0119 546 085. There are 12 Federal Reserve Districts; the figure "11" denotes the eleventh, which includes Texas. The "3" shows that the check was printed in Houston, and the "0" indicates the immediate availability of credit. In the second series of figures, "0" identifies the Houston clearinghouse, and "119" represents the identification of the individual bank. The remaining figures comprise the account number.

When a check reaches the clearinghouse—often the same night—it is sorted by computer and, in this case, rejected because the account number represents San Francisco. It is then sent to San Francisco, where it is rejected by computer again, picked up by a bank clerk and returned to Houston. A week may have passed before such a counterfeit is detected, by which time the forger is usually far away.

A LOVE AFFAIR ENDS IN TROUBLE
Within a short while Abagnale had amassed some $75,000-worth of genuine bills and had fallen in love with a girl in San Francisco. Then, foolishly, he

confessed his true identity to her, and she informed the police. He fled once more, this time to Las Vegas, where he briefly picked up a girl who was a graphic designer for a company that printed checks. She told Abagnale all he needed to know. Next day he bought a camera and a small offset press, installed them in a rented warehouse and printed 500 genuine-looking PanAm paychecks.

THE LONG ARM OF THE LAW
And so it went on. Abagnale opened bank accounts in the name of Frank Adams all over the country, and he now claims that by 1967 (when he was still only 19!), he had acquired illicit cash assets of nearly $500,000. He spent time in Mexico, then flew to Paris, where he persuaded a local printer to duplicate a genuine PanAm check. But Abagnale did not know that an inspector from the FBI had been on his case for nearly a year, and when he turned up in Boston, he was arrested. However, the police had been told only to hold him for questioning, and he succeeded in being released on bail before an FBI investigator could arrive.

Everyone assumed that Abagnale would have taken the first flight to Miami, but he remained in Boston. The next morning he acquired the uniform of a bank security guard, and that night he stood in front of the night safe depository, upon which he placed a notice that all deposits were to be handed to him. With the cash he flew to Tel Aviv, to Istanbul, then to Athens, wearing his PanAm uniform only when checking in and out of a hotel or cadging a free flight. But he soon became aware that a lone pilot, without a surrounding crew, would arouse suspicion. He needed a crew.

His plan was simple. Abagnale represented himself as a PanAm officer assigned the job of finding university girls who wanted to become stewardesses.

Recruiting eight of the prettiest and most outgoing of such coeds, he had them fitted with uniforms made by a Hollywood company and took them on a summer tour of Europe. Everywhere, he signed accounts on behalf of PanAm or used one of his counterfeit checks.

ARRESTED AT LAST

Feeling in need of another rest, Abagnale retired to Montpellier, in southern France. There he was found by the French police and arrested. There were extradition warrants out for him in 26 countries, but France claimed the first trial; Abagnale was

detective, Martin Knopf, to make inquiries. Knopf confidently announced that he had identified "Anastasia" as Franziska Schanzkowska, a Polish factory worker who had disappeared in Berlin in 1920.

But there were many—including "Anastasia" herself—who refused to accept this. In 1928, Princess Georgievna, the real Anastasia's second cousin, invited her to the United States. The two women soon quarreled, however, and the famous Russian composer and pianist, Sergei Rachmaninov,

The young woman who claimed to be Anastasia appeared in Berlin, Germany, in February 1920. In the following years she was hospitalized several times, and is photographed here in a Berlin infirmary in 1925. In 1928 she adopted the pseudonym "Anna Anderson."

arranged for "Anastasia" to stay for four months at a hotel on Long Island. There, to avoid publicity, she was registered as "Anna Anderson"—the name by which she came to be known for the next 40 years.

For more than 60 years the arguments continued. Much of the interest in the case turned upon an unsubstantiated report that a vast fortune in Russian gold was being held in the Bank of England. But Anna, who had returned to Germany in 1931, claimed that she was entitled to only a share of the czar's assets within Germany, which amounted to no more than $10,000 in present-day value. The legal arguments dragged on until 1970, at which point the German court found itself unable to confirm or deny Anna's claim.

DNA analysis established the identity of the bones of the czarina and czar—and finally solved the mystery of Anna Anderson.

A movie, *Anastasia*, with Ingrid Bergman in the title role, was made in Hollywood in 1956; another, titled *Is Anna Anderson Anastasia?* starring Lilli Palmer, was produced in Germany in 1957. In 1969, Anna Anderson married a retired American professor, Dr. John Manahan, so that she could live legally in the United States; in 1984 she died, and her body was cremated.

THE MYSTERY IS SOLVED
In 1989 a Russian moviemaker, Gely Ryabov, announced that he had found bones and scraps of clothing at a site 5 miles (8 kilometers) away from the mine shaft in which Sokolov had reported the Romanovs were buried. Two years later Soviet president Boris Yeltsin gave

permission for an excavation to be carried out. The bones and skulls recovered were assembled into four male and five female skeletons. Whose were the two that were missing? Russian scientists decided that they were those of Alexei and Maria, but an invited team of American experts, headed by Dr. William Maples of the University of Florida, came to the conclusion that one missing skull was that of Anastasia.

DNA analysis established the identity of the bones of the czarina and czar—and finally solved the mystery of Anna Anderson. Although her body had been cremated, it turned out that an American hospital had stored a tissue sample after an operation. In 1994 analysis proved that she was not one of the imperial Russian family, and samples provided by the Schanzkowska family in Poland established that she was indeed the missing Franziska.

THE "RED BARON" OF ARIZONA
Making a false claim to a country's throne is seldom successful, but assuming a fake title of nobility is often a sure way to acquire a veil of respectability. Art forger Elmyr de Hory (see pages 78–84) was happy to be known as "Baron" de Hory during his time in Hollywood, and "Count" Victor Lustig (see pages 202–209) graduated from petty cardsharp to one of the biggest confidence men of the twentieth century. Arthur Orton, however, who claimed the title of Twelfth Baronet Titchborne in England, was less fortunate (see pages 186–190).

Another "Baron," who laid claim to vast tracts of what was at that time the Territory of Arizona, was James Addison Reavis (1843–1914), a former streetcar conductor from St. Louis. The area of land he claimed was equal to half that of the state of Indiana; it included the city of Phoenix and six towns. It covered the right-of-way of the Southern Pacific Railroad, the rich Silver

King mine and millions of dollars' worth of unmined ores.

Following the war with Mexico (1846–1848), New Mexico Territory, which included all of Arizona north of the Gila River, was ceded to the United States, and the area south of the Gila was purchased in 1853. Under the peace terms any land grant that had been made by Spain, while Mexico was still a Spanish colony, was to be honored. In 1884, Reavis — "Don Jayme, Baron Peralta de Arizonac and Caballero de los Colorados" — made his appearance.

"GET OFF MY LAND!"

Reavis had all the documents to substantiate his claim. Many were undoubtedly forged, but he said he had bought the title from a young doctor, George Willing, who had himself bought it from a penniless Mexican, Miguel Peralta, for $1,000. Reavis put up posters everywhere, warning those on "his" land that they were trespassing, and had his claims against Southern Pacific and Silver King legally confirmed. The economy of Arizona was thrown into turmoil.

In 1887, Reavis arrived in style in Tucson, accompanied by his wife, "Baroness Sofia Loreta Micaela Peralta." He had discovered her — in reality, a servant named Carmelita — in the home of rancher John Slaughter and immediately identified her as the missing Peralta heiress. Reavis produced a host of documents, including her grandfather's will, to prove it.

From his settlements with Southern Pacific and Silver King, and by selling quit-claims to established tenants, Reavis became a wealthy man. He was still reviled in the press for his grandiose pretensions, but local businessmen and even major national companies were happy to cooperate with him. Meanwhile, the territory surveyor-general and claims assessor, Royal Johnson, was looking into Reavis's claims in detail. It

Reavis had planted forged documents and had later had them certified. Lawyers found parchments where erasures and substitutions could be detected and paper that was not quite of the right sort.

took him until 1890 to make his report. Although it did not accuse Reavis of fraud, it noted certain inconsistencies in the documents and did not recommend the claims for the government's approval.

FORGED DOCUMENTS SIGNAL HIS DOWNFALL

In 1891 a Court of Private Land Grant Claims with far greater powers than Johnson's was set up to deal with all claims to former Spanish land. Among the lawyers who looked into Reavis's background was Severo Mallet-Prevost, who spoke excellent Spanish. Between 1893 and 1895, he followed the trail of the "Baron" through the southwest. He also went to Spain and searched through archives in Seville and Madrid. There Mallet-Provost found plenty of evidence that Reavis had planted forged documents and had later had them certified. He found parchments where erasures and substitutions could be detected and paper that was not quite of the right sort.

In certain documents the first and last few pages were genuine, but the ones in between were clearly more modern. Instead of iron ink, an ink containing dogwood dye had been used, and there were traces of a steel pen, whereas the originals had been written with a quill. The dogwood ink was removed with chemicals, to reveal the very different details that had been erased.

His claim disallowed, Reavis was

indicted and brought to trial in January 1895 and upon conviction was sentenced to six years in the penitentiary at Santa Fe. The "Baroness," who was considered to be an innocent dupe, divorced him several years after he was paroled. According to a Phoenix citizen who knew him in his last years, Reavis spent his days in the city library, reading, over and over again, the newspaper stories of his days of grandeur.

FROM BOOTLEGGING TO DRUGS
Wall Street suffered a severe shock in the first week of December 1938. Frank Donald Coster, president of McKesson & Robbins Inc.—a highly reputable drug company

When the British magazine *Wide World* appeared in 1898, it bore on its cover the legend "Truth Is Stranger Than Fiction." But its serialization of the adventures of "Louis de Rougemont" (pictured) was soon exposed as pure fiction. De Rougemont was said to be French, born in 1844. He claimed an astonishing career, including more than 20 years as leader of a cannibal tribe of aborigines in Australia. But all that is known of his true Australian experiences is that he worked as a butler.

with assets of $80 million and annual sales of about $160 million—had been accused of fraud. At least $18 million could not be accounted for.

Coster lived quietly with his family in Fairfield, Connecticut, and was known as a successful businessman. He was a director of three trust companies, a member of the Bankers' Club and the New York Yacht Club, and a prominent Methodist. It seemed incredible that such a respectable member of the community, always seen in an old-fashioned suit, spats and round glasses, could have committed fraud.

FBI inquiries, however, soon uncovered a number of surprising facts. Coster was, in reality, Philip Musica, born in Naples, Italy, in 1877. He had moved with his family to America when he was six. Three senior executives of McKesson & Robbins were also unmasked: "George Dietrich" was his brother Giorgio Musica, "Robert Dietrich" his brother Roberto, and "George Venard" was his brother Arturo.

Gradually the story of Philip Musica was revealed. His father, Antonio, a New York barber, had been persuaded by his son to go into the business of buying human hair for the making of wigs and hairpieces. The enterprise flourished. Philip began to lead the life of a prosperous playboy, but the money for this came from loans that he raised against warehouse stocks that did not exist. In March 1913 he applied for a loan of $370,000 against 216 cases of first-quality hair, but bank investigators who visited the warehouse found only a few boxes with a total value of $213. That night the entire Musica family disappeared from the city and were discovered a few days later in New Orleans, aboard a boat about to sail for Costa Rica.

PHILIP DOES A DEAL

Antonio, Philip, Giorgio and Arturo were charged with fraud, but Philip did a deal with the New York district attorney, pleading guilty and informing on business associates and close friends. He proved so useful as an informer that he escaped imprisonment and was, in fact, hired as an investigator for the D.A. under the name of William Johnson.

Philip Musica next emerged, under the name of "Costa," in 1919. Following the passing of the Volstead Act, enforcing Prohibition, he set up the Adelphi Pharmaceutical Manufacturing Corporation. Under law the company was allowed to purchase 5,000 gallons (19,000 l) of alcohol per month, but Musica immediately sold it on to bootleggers. Within a few years

In 1956, Cyril Henry Hoskins, the son of a plumber from Devonshire, renamed himself Lobsang Rampa and claimed to be a Tibetan lama. He published a book, *The Third Eye*, that became an international success. He was exposed as a fraud, but Hoskins went on to write 16 more books.

FORGER'S FILE
CARNEGIE'S DAUGHTER?

Cassie Chadwick, better known as "Betsy Bigley," had a career that rivals that of Thérèse Humbert (see page 199). She was born Elizabeth Bigley in Ontario, Canada, in the late 1850s but relocated to the United States, where she established herself as a successful clairvoyant, employing private detectives to provide her with information about her clients. In 1897 (by then known as "Mrs. Connie Hoover") she married Dr. Leroy Chadwick in Cleveland, Ohio, and prepared her most daring confidence trick. She made the acquaintance of lawyer James Dillon and persuaded him that she was the illegitimate daughter of Andrew Carnegie, with forged promissory notes from the rich man to prove it. With these—and the "confidential" rumors about her wealth spread by Dillon, a notorious gossip—she was able to live the high life for seven years until a banker asked for repayment of a loan. In November 1904 she was exposed and, in March 1905, was convicted on seven counts of fraud and sentenced to 14 years in prison. She died two years later while still in custody at the age of 48.

The only known image of Betsy Bigley.

"F. Donald Coster" was a seemingly respectable broker in the house of Clark & Hubbard and proprietor of another pharmaceutical firm, the Girard Company, with "George and Robert Dietrich" as partners. Using "George Venard" (brother Arturo) as an intermediary, this company also sold its alcohol allocation to bootleggers.

A CROOKED BUSINESSMAN

With the help of a Wall Street investor named Julian Thompson, "Coster" bought a controlling interest in McKesson & Robbins, merging the Girard Company with it and appointing Thompson treasurer. The company did well, and Coster nursed it through the 1929 stock market crash and the subsequent Depression. But he managed this by pretending that he had warehouses full of raw drugs, bought cheaply and now valued at $2 million.

In 1937, faced with a brief trade recession, McKesson & Robbins's board of directors voted to realize these assets, and Coster faced detection. He managed to prevaricate until the fall of 1938, when, after a row with Thompson, he carried out his wild threat to petition for receivership.

FORGER'S FILE
BORROWING AN IDENTITY
FROM BEYOND THE GRAVE

Criminals were quick to detect a loophole in the system of issuing passports. Search a few country cemeteries, and you will soon find the grave of a young child who was born close to the date of your own birthday. Represent yourself, perhaps, as an amateur genealogist researching family history, and ask at the county records office for a copy of the child's birth certificate. This, accompanied by a genuine, certified photograph of you, has usually been sufficient documentation for the issue of a passport.

On December 6, trading in McKesson & Robbins's shares was suspended, and an army of investigators—from the SEC, the FBI, the Attorney General's office and the New York D.A.—began inquiries.

On the morning of December 16, even as two FBI agents were on their way to arrest him, Philip Musica shot himself through the head. He had kept his true identity secret for nearly 20 years, and there was one last twist in his death. Everybody in Fairfield knew him as a Methodist, but when the police examined his body, they found a small leather pouch containing a crucifix. Engraved on the back were the words "I am a Catholic. In case of accident, notify a priest."

Fortunately, McKesson & Robbins was such an important part of the drug industry that other companies made every effort to keep it going. It was placed in capable hands and continued to expand. The amount stolen by Musica was calculated at $2,900,000, and only $51,000—the value of his yacht and a piece of real estate—was ever recovered.

IDENTITY THEFT

Falsely assuming the identity of another person, as these stories illustrate, has gone on throughout the history of humankind. Most of these cases have involved the individual's attempt to become someone more eminent and possibly richer. Nowadays, however, any person—no matter how obscure and retiring—faces the threat of having his or her identity adopted by a criminal, reputation ruined and finances plundered.

When every citizen became entitled to a passport, this identity document seemed an ideal way of preventing a wanted criminal from passing from one country to another and for keeping track of would-be immigrants. Of course, hundreds of thousands of passports have been forged, and inspection procedures are generally superficial. Immigration officials rely far more on their instincts in spotting doubtful characters passing before them. Many forgeries are also relatively crude, and sophisticated details in the design of genuine passports make them increasingly difficult to forge. Far easier is using a genuine passport containing a false name.

In *Catch Me If You Can*, Frank Abagnale described how he obtained a passport in the name of a dead child, as did the fictional assassin in Frederick Forsyth's

According to Scotland Yard, identity theft is replacing drug trafficking as the crime of choice for underworld operators and terrorist cells.

novel, *The Day of the Jackal.* There were still easier methods. Edward Bunker, the reformed jailbird who played "Mr. Blue" in the movie *Reservoir Dogs*, relates in his autobiography how, while on the run, he crossed over into Canada and obtained a Canadian passport without difficulty.

Since September 11, 2001, and particularly with the passing of antiterrorism acts in many countries, the ease of obtaining a passport in such a way has decreased but is still not impossible.

STEALING PERSONAL DATA

The growing use of computerized data storage and transmission has opened up a wide number of ways to steal identities. According to Scotland Yard, identity theft is replacing drug trafficking as the crime of choice for underworld operators and terrorist cells.

Using hackers and other means, criminals target people who are customers or contacts of legitimate companies in order to steal personal data. For example, an e-mail from a bogus credit card company announced that a refund had been deposited in the target's bank account. To release the money, the victim

Despite the many precautions taken by credit card companies to improve security, a card can be "cloned" very quickly by a crooked storekeeper or restaurant proprietor. Only later does the unsuspecting holder of the card discover unauthorized charges on his or her account.

Even while he was in prison, awaiting his trial for fraud, Harry Domela was commissioned to write about his exploits. When he was released, he found himself a best-selling author.

of the local barracks and demanded the suppression of all newspaper reports about him. After all,
he said, he hoped to spend a few more days in Erfurt as a private individual.

From Erfurt, Domela went to Weimar, where again he requested the suppression of all reports of his arrival. The news leaked out, however, and once more local bigwigs feted him. Nevertheless, he decided it was time to become penniless Harry Domela again before he was unmasked, so he bought the cheapest ticket for a train ride to Berlin.

But even as Domela's train crawled slowly to the German capital in January 1927, newspapers were aware that police inquiries had revealed that the real Prince Wilhelm had been nowhere near Erfurt or Weimar in the past year. Domela emerged from the train to be greeted by newsboys waving papers with huge headlines:

FALSE HOHENZOLLERN PRINCE FOOLS DIE-HARD MONARCHISTS.
WHERE IS "PRINCE WILHELM"?
ALL GERMANY IS LOOKING FOR THE PRINCE OF IMPOSTORS.
OUR REPUBLIC—ONCE AGAIN THE WORLD'S LAUGHING STOCK.

THE "PRINCE" IS APPREHENDED

Everywhere in the city, people were amused by Domela's deception, but his photograph was in the papers and he would soon be recognized. He leapt onto another train, headed for the French border, where he saw a recruiting poster for the Foreign Legion.

Desperate to escape Germany before he was detected, Domela immediately signed on— and was already being marched away when two detectives arrested him. He was brought to trial in Cologne in July, where witness after witness testified that he had not cheated them. On the contrary, "His Highness" had brought increased revenue to hotels and restaurants, record receipts for charities and generally increased prosperity.

Domela was sentenced to seven months in prison—in fact, exactly the time he had

already spent awaiting trial, and so he was released. Even while he was in prison, a Berlin publisher had offered Domela 25,000 marks to write of his experiences, and the book quickly sold 70,000 copies. Domela appeared onstage in a successful comedy, *Alt-Heidelberg*, and the royalties from his book made him a rich man. He bought a small cinema in Berlin, which opened in 1930 with a movie entitled *The False Prince*.

The subsequent fate of Harry Domela is unknown. One report states that he died in

The real Prince Wilhelm von Hohenzollern at a reception, not long after Harry Domela had opened his Berlin cinema with the movie *The False Prince*.

a Nazi concentration camp; another, that he imigrated to South America when the Nazis came to power.

MEETING THE FAMILY

In the 1950s the aged ex-Crown Princess Cecilie, the true Wilhelm's mother, recalled how Domela had turned up at her home in the late summer of 1927, after his release from prison. "I could hardly turn him away, could I? He did us no harm.... When the Crown Prince and I heard about his exploits, we were convulsed with laughter. So I invited him to tea. A charming young man, with excellent manners. He said he could not rest until he had met his 'mama' in the flesh. It was a most amusing tea party. But there was one thing that puzzled me: How on earth could anyone have mistaken him for Wilhelm?"

The tumbledown shack at Wagga Wagga in Australia, in which local butcher Thomas Castro lived with his wife and children.

THE TICHBORNE CASE

Roger Tichborne was the eldest son of James, brother of the tenth baronet Tichborne, with extensive estates in Hampshire, southern England. Roger was born in 1829, educated at Stonyhurst—the exclusive Catholic boarding school in Yorkshire—and commissioned into the Sixth Dragoon Guards at the age of 20.

The tenth baronet died without issue, and his successor was a cousin, Sir Edward Doughty, who also had no heirs. On Doughty's death it appeared that the baronet's nephew Roger would succeed to the title. In 1852 he fell in love with Sir Edward's daughter Katherine. The Catholic Church, however, forbade first cousins to marry, and Sir Edward decreed that the couple should not see each other for three years. If they still wished to marry at the end

The Roger Tichborne who had disappeared in 1852 had been slim, with a long, melancholy face. Castro, allegedly age 37, was tubby and appeared middle-aged.

of that time, he would seek a dispensation from the church.

Roger, in true Victorian fashion, resigned his commission and sailed away to South America. After ten months he took a passage from Rio de Janeiro, Brazil, to New York, aboard a small British ship, the *Bella*. But the *Bella* sank in a violent storm, and no trace was ever recovered except her logbook, found floating 400 miles (645 km) from land.

In 1855 the British court pronounced Roger Tichborne dead, and when Sir Edward died, Roger's younger brother, Alfred, inherited the estates. Alfred lived only for a few years, however, leaving his baby son, Henry, to be named as the twelfth baronet.

THE BUTCHER FROM WAGGA WAGGA

Roger's mother, Henriette, refused to believe he was dead and began to advertise in newspapers for information. In 1865 she received a letter from a lawyer in the small Australian town of Wagga Wagga. The letter said that Roger was living close by, under the name of Thomas Castro. Castro was the local butcher in Wagga Wagga, poorly educated, and with an illiterate wife. He wrote to Henriette in January 1866, addressing her as "My Dear Mother," and she replied, telling "Roger" that his father and younger brother were dead. No doubt Castro had at first intended only to embezzle money from her, but this news fired his ambition. He visited a retired family servant who by chance was

now living in Sydney and readily persuaded the old man to identify him as Roger Tichborne.

With this confirmation Henriette immediately sent money, and Castro boarded a ship with his family for England. He journeyed on to Paris, where Henriette lived. She must have been surprised at his appearance. The Roger Tichborne who had disappeared in 1852 had been slim, with a long, melancholy face. Castro, allegedly age 37, was tubby and appeared middle-aged. But she accepted him as her son.

Thomas Castro, the butcher from Wagga Wagga, who claimed the title of twelfth baronet Tichborne.

To raise money to finance his claim on the Tichborne estate, Castro sold mortgage debentures—in the name of "Roger Charles Doughty Tichborne"—at £100 apiece. All those who bought them were destined to lose their investment.

With a yearly allowance of £1,000 from his "mother," Castro returned to England and set about claiming the Tichborne title. He learned all he could about Roger's family and successfully duped a number of his acquaintances into accepting his assumed identity. He said he had been rescued from the *Bella* by a ship that was on its way to Australia and had failed to write to his family, due to "carelessness and neglect." He also blackened the name of Katherine Doughty, saying she had been pregnant when he left England.

WHERE'S THE TATTOO?

It took four years for the claim to be heard by the Chancery Division of the High Court in London. In the meantime Castro raised more money by issuing mortgage debentures on the Tichborne estate, which sold for £100 apiece. At the hearing, 90 witnesses, including the family governess and former officers of the Sixth Dragoons, testified to Castro's true identity as Roger Tichborne. However, others insisted that he was really Arthur Orton, who had been born in the East End of London in 1834. The final testimony against Castro/Orton was that the real Roger had his initials tattooed on his arm, something that Castro/Orton lacked. After a hearing lasting more than three months, the court denied his claim.

Castro was immediately arrested on 23 counts of perjury but then released on bail. Over the next year he traveled throughout England as "Sir Roger Tichborne," speaking at public meetings and raising a subscription fund for his defense. He became a popular hero, and during his trial,

Good men and true, the jury sits to hear the evidence in the Chancery Division of the High Court in London. After a hearing lasting more than three months, Castro's claim was denied.

EXTRACTS FROM CASTRO'S NOTEBOOK

All Castro could do was protest weakly that the notebook produced in evidence against him at his trial had been a forgery. His own scribblings contributed to his downfall.

"Thomas Castro...Roger Charles Tichborne, Bart, some day, I hope."

"Some men has plenty money and no brains, and some men has plenty brains and no money. Surely men with plenty money and no brains were made for men with plenty brains and no money."

prosecuting counsel were booed in the street and often needed police protection.

The trial of Thomas Castro was one of the longest criminal hearings in British legal history, taking up a total of 188 days. His defense counsel made an opening address lasting 21 days and a closing plea that lasted 23. The Lord Chief Justice, in summing up, took 20 days. For the crown 210 witnesses were called; the claimant produced 300 for his defense.

However, the weight of evidence against Castro was overwhelming, particularly when some of his witnesses were shown to be lying. He was found guilty, and the Lord Chief Justice, "taking into account the heinous nature of the claimant's perjuries," sentenced him to two consecutive seven-year terms in prison.

Arthur Orton was released in 1884. He sold his supposed "confessions" to a newspaper, then later disavowed them. He appeared on the vaudeville stage to maintain his claim, but the public had lost interest. He declined steadily and died in a cheap lodging house at age 64, in 1898. To the very end he called himself "Sir Roger Tichborne," and that was the name inscribed on his coffin.

"I LIVED MANY LIVES"

"Stanley Clifford Weyman" (1890–1960) was born Stanley Jacob Weinberg in Brooklyn, New York. His parents were too poor to give him a college education, so his first job was in a local countinghouse. But at the age of 21 he appeared in Manhattan, resplendent in a uniform of purple, and declared himself the U.S. Consul Delegate to Morocco. He ran up bills in expensive restaurants; but then, to raise money, he stole a camera and ended up in a reformatory for a year.

Out on parole, Weyman took on two roles at once—as a Serbian military attaché and a lieutenant in the United States Navy. But he was soon unmasked and served two years more in prison. Again released on parole, he became a "lieutenant-commander in the Romanian army," and "Romanian Consul-General" in New York. He fitted himself out in an eye-catching bright blue uniform decorated with gold braid and in 1915 made an official inspection of the battleship USS *Wyoming*, then lying at anchor in the Hudson River.

When the visit was over, Weyman invited all the ship's officers to a banquet at the

Weyman fitted himself out in an eye-catching bright blue uniform decorated with gold braid and in 1915 made an official inspection of the battleship USS *Wyoming*.

Astor Hotel. Unfortunately, the event had been publicized. A New York detective read about it, and two officers arrived at the hotel to escort Weyman back to jail for violating his parole. Said Weyman: "They could have waited until dessert."

ANOTHER IDENTITY

When the United States entered World War I in 1917, Weyman appeared as "Royal St. Cyr," a lieutenant in the Army Air Corps. One day he turned up at the 47th Regiment Armory in Brooklyn and announced that he had come to make a formal inspection. But the tailor who had made Weyman's uniform had become suspicious and informed the police. Weyman was once more arrested, even as he was conducting his inspection.

In 1920, out of jail and again working in a countinghouse, Weyman read an advertisement seeking a physician to go to Lima, Peru, to supervise sanitation installations for an American construction company. He quickly forged false medical credentials and was accepted.

In Lima, the supposed "Dr." Stanley Weyman rented a palatial residence, hired house servants and imported two American cars. He held lavish parties and sent all the bills to the construction company. In his

A passport is readily accepted as an identity document in most parts of the world, and it remains a means of tracking the movements of both nationals and foreigners. However, it is still possible to obtain a passport in a false name, as many criminals have demonstrated.

In July 1917, fleeing a failed revolution in Russia, Lenin shaved his beard and wore a wig to hide his baldness. But his wig often fell off, and he was easily recognized. He fled, hiding first in a haystack outside St. Petersburg and then using this passport to escape to Finland.

role as sanitation consultant, Weyman merely nodded wisely at the suggestions of the local expert. The volume of his expenses, however, worried the company back in the United States. They reexamined his credentials and dismissed him.

Once again in New York in 1921, Weyman presented himself to the visiting Princess Fatima of Afghanistan as Under-secretary Stanley Clifford Weyman of the State Department. He told her the United States could officially recognize her visit, but there was just one minor matter. A small sum (he discreetly suggested $10,000) would be needed for "gifts." He then took her in a private railroad car to Washington, and—now decked out in the summer whites of a lieutenant-commander in the U.S. Navy—presented her to Secretary of State Charles Evans Hughes. He even arranged an interview with President Warren G. Harding.

In 1922, Dr. Adolf Lorenz, a renowned Austrian chiropractor, visited the United States and was greeted aboard his incoming ship by "Dr. Clifford Weyman from the New York Health Commissioners." When Lorenz set up a clinic in the Hospital for Joint Diseases, Weyman was with him, dressed in surgical garb and overseeing everything.

However, once again Weyman's impostures caught up with him. It soon became obvious that he was no surgeon and his behavior as a naval officer in Washington aroused suspicion. Two men from naval intelligence arrived, and soon Weyman was back in jail for two years, this time for impersonating a federal officer.

"One man's life is a boring thing. I lived many lives. I'm never bored."

—FRANK WEYMAN

In 1926 the famous movie star Rudolf Valentino died in a New York hospital. Weyman called on Valentino's grief-stricken lover, actress Pola Negri, and appointed himself her personal physician. "Rudy would have wanted me to take care of you," he said. Weyman escorted Negri to the funeral and even set up an emergency first-aid station outside the funeral home.

IN AND OUT OF JAIL
Later Weyman posed as an attorney, opening an office on Broadway. All went well until a bar association investigator

asked to see his license; then he once more found himself in jail. Little is known about his subsequent activities until early 1942, after the United States had entered World War II. He opened a consulting office in midtown New York, where he gave advice to draft dodgers on how to feign medical conditions. But it was not long before he was again arrested and this time sentenced to seven years.

Emerging from jail in 1948, Weyman forged another set of credentials and got himself appointed an accredited journalist to the newly established United Nations. He lasted two years, ingratiating himself with the delegates, before he made a serious mistake. The Thai delegation invited him to be their diplomatically accredited press officer, so he wrote to the State Department to ask whether this would affect his U.S. citizenship. He was only too well known in their files.

In 1954, Weyman applied for an $8,000 home-improvement loan. But the house did not exist, and once more he was in court, where he failed to convince the judge that he was insane. However, Weyman died a hero's death in August 1960, when he was shot trying to prevent a robbery in the hotel where he worked as a night porter. As he once said: "One man's life is a boring thing. I lived many lives. I'm never bored."

CHAPTER 6
THE CONFIDENCE TRICKSTERS

The most audacious of all fakers and fraudsters are, without a doubt, confidence tricksters.

W hatever secret enjoyment they may gain from their activities—and their careers show every sign of the delight they derive—confidence tricksters are in the business solely for personal profit. As the following stories exemplify, the motive confidence men exploit is greed—not their own, but that of

their victims. What they always propose to their potential targets is a sure way of making money, perhaps not entirely legally but too tempting to be missed. Con men are hard workers. They may spend months, and often considerable sums of money, in "softening up" their intended victims. They may set up complicated "front" organizations, designed to lure the victims ever deeper into the net that has been spread out for them. At last, when the time is ripe, they close the net and the target is left much poorer—and scarcely wiser.

Opposite: On his way to jail after 20 years of fleecing his victims, "Count" Victor Lustig, closely escorted by three grim-faced federal agents.

Left: Joseph "Yellow Kid" Weil was credited with having made some $8 million by his swindles.

THE MAN WHO FLEECED JAY GOULD

The family of Gordon is one of the most eminent in Scotland, having played a prominent part in the history of the country for many centuries. So, when "Lord Gordon-Gordon" arrived in Minneapolis, Minnesota, in 1871, and deposited the sum of $40,000 in a local bank, local citizens were delighted.

But who was he, truly? There are two conflicting theories. Was he the illegitimate child of a clergyman's son and the family maid, or was he the well-brought-up son of an apparently respectable married couple—who, in fact, were engaged in smuggling on the island of Jersey? Gordon's first recorded appearance was in 1868, when he made purchases from the Edinburgh jewel merchants Marshall & Son, under the name of "Lord Glencairn." He let it be known that he was heir to the Glencairn fortune, which he would later inherit in March 1870 at the age of 27. It seems probable, therefore, that Gordon was born in 1843.

After raising credit at Marshall & Son for a year or more, "Glencairn" vanished. Arriving in Minneapolis, "Lord Gordon-Gordon" announced that he intended to bring over a number of his tenant families from Scotland and settle them on a huge tract of land he proposed to buy. The news of this venture reached Colonel John Loomis, land commissioner of the Northern Pacific Railroad, which was then badly in need of capital. Loomis immediately arranged an extravagant expedition for the lord to survey the land to the west and stake out the sites of proposed towns.

CONTROLLING THE ERIE RAILROAD

After this expedition Gordon-Gordon moved to New York, carrying a letter of introduction to Horace Greeley, who was delighted to meet someone who had followed his dictum "Go West, young

The 1870s saw railroad companies frantically engaged in the raising of capital to build competing routes across the North American continent. In this 1870 cartoon "Commodore" Cornelius Vanderbilt challenges James Fisk of the Erie Railroad—which Jay Gould precariously controlled.

THE GREAT RACE FOR THE WESTERN STAKES 1870

Horace Greeley, editor, politician and founder of the *New York Tribune,* was one of those taken in by "Lord Gordon-Gordon" and his supposed aristocratic connections.

man." It was then February 1872, and financier Jay Gould was engaged in a struggle with fellow stockholders over control of the Erie Railroad. Gordon-Gordon announced that he was holding 60,000 shares of Erie stock, with which he was able to threaten Gould's presidency.

Eventually it required the personal intervention of President Ulysses S. Grant and Canadian Prime Minister Sir John A. Macdonald to restore international calm.

Gould panicked and was persuaded to hand over 20,000 shares valued at $35 each, plus $200,000 in cash, in exchange for Gordon-Gordon's cooperation. But Gould soon discovered that the securities were being sold and he was therefore losing control of Erie. He demanded his money back. Greeley persuaded Gordon-Gordon to return the securities and cash, but Gould found he had been shortchanged by $150,000, and he brought the case to court.

The trial began in May 1872, and at first Gordon-Gordon was a model witness, freely providing the names and addresses of his Scottish family and lawyers. Gould, however, immediately cabled them all, and by the next morning he had confirmation that no such lord existed. But Gordon-Gordon had meanwhile taken the midnight train to Montreal, leaving his bondsmen to pay his $37,000 bail.

A MANITOBA SOJOURN

From Montreal, Gordon-Gordon continued on to what is now Winnipeg, Manitoba, which was then a Hudson Bay Company's trading post known as Fort Garry. He spent a leisurely time there, enjoying frequent hunting expeditions. However, news of such a distinguished British gentleman in such a remote place reached Minneapolis in June 1873. On July 2 a party of seven Minnesotans seized Gordon-Gordon and attempted to abduct him to the United States. They were caught the next day, only 100 yards short of the border, and arrested. They had no legal authority to be in Canada.

FORGER'S FILE
JAY GOULD

One of the most flamboyant wheeler-dealers of the nineteenth century, Jay Gould (1836–1892) was born in Roxbury, New York. After making a small fortune in lumbering, he became, by the age of 21, principal shareholder in a Pennsylvania bank. Gould set himself up as a broker in New York in 1859, began to buy railroad bonds, and by clever manipulation of shares, seized control of the Erie Railroad Company for four years (1868–1872). He then attempted to corner the gold market, resulting in the "Black Friday" stock market crash of September 1869. He died—"unlamented" according to Chambers Biographical Dictionary—worth around $100 million.

For the rest of the summer, courts in Manitoba and Minnesota, together with Canadian, American and British authorities, wrangled over the case; eventually it required the personal intervention of President Ulysses S. Grant and Canadian Prime Minister Sir John A. Macdonald to restore international calm. Gordon-Gordon remained in Fort Garry, confident that existing extradition treaties did not cover crimes such as embezzlement.

Edinburgh jewel merchants, however, learned of the case and sent their clerk, Thomas Smith, to identify "Glencairn" in Fort Garry. A warrant was issued for his arrest. On August 1, 1874, at the home of the lady with whom he was boarding, Gordon-Gordon shot himself through the head and died immediately. His true name went with him to his grave and will never now be known.

LA GRANDE THÉRÈSE

Most fraudsters represent themselves as someone else, particularly when there is a will to be contested. One famous Frenchwoman did the opposite; she invented a succession of wills in her favor.

She was plain, dumpy and worked as a laundry maid in the household of Gustave Humbert, a successful lawyer and aspiring politician in a town not far from Toulouse, in southwestern France. Her name was

Thérèse Aurignac (1860–1917), and she captured the interest of Humbert's son Frédéric with the tale she had to tell. As a child, so she said, Thérèse had attracted the attention of a Mlle. de Marcotte. The rich old lady, who was childless, had taken a fancy to Thérèse and had made a will bequeathing her a château, the estate and a

Jay Gould made millions of dollars in stock dealing but was uncharacteristically swindled by "Lord Gordon-Gordon."

Above: "La Grande Thérèse" in all her finery, at the height of her infamous career.

Opposite: Asked at her trial where she lived, Mme. Humbert replied, "In prison."

AN AMERICAN MILLIONAIRE TO THE RESCUE

Gustave Humbert had risen rapidly in politics and had just been appointed Minister of Justice in the government. When his son told him of his problems, Humbert was forced to pay the couple's debts to avoid a scandal. Thérèse spent a long time in private conversation with him and confessed that the story of Mlle. de Marcotte was a lie. But, she said, it was an innocent fiction, because the truth was more complicated and almost unbelievable. Some two years earlier, while she was aboard a train near Nice, she had saved the life of an elderly American who had suffered a heart attack. Now she had received a letter from the executors of the late Robert Henry Crawford, a millionaire, the man whose life she had saved.

Mr. Crawford had left two interconnected wills. His fortune was to be divided between his two nephews and Thérèse's young sister, Marie, and the entire estate invested in France. The income from the investment was to provide Mme. Humbert with an annual income of nearly $100,000, but the capital was not to be touched until Marie's twenty-first birthday. Even then, distribution of the estate could not take place until she was married to one of the nephews. All bonds and securities were to be assigned to the Humberts and kept in a specially sealed safe.

The Humberts took over a grand Parisian house, and Thérèse installed the necessary fireproof safe in her bedroom. She fetched a magistrate from a provincial town—one easily impressed—to act as notary and had him notarize the list of bundled "securities" that she had placed in the safe. He confirmed that they had a total value of 100 million francs. Then Thérèse locked the safe and placed impressive wax seals over the door.

With this fortune under lock and key in her possession, Thérèse found it easy to

vast fortune. Mlle. de Marcotte would die very soon; then Thérèse would be rich. Frédéric believed every word.

Despite his father's opposition, Frédéric married Thérèse as soon as he had graduated from law school, and the couple set off for Paris. This was at a time when the city earned its reputation of "Gay Paree," and the Humberts, enjoying life to the full, were soon deeply in debt. They kept their creditors at bay with promises of the inheritance that was due any day; but some of these creditors investigated and discovered that "Mlle. de Marcotte" did not exist.

raise huge loans from willing bankers. Her bill for hats and dresses alone was said to run into five figures annually, and it was calculated that in the course of her extravagant career, she had borrowed a total of some 64 million francs. The Humberts appeared at every important social event and dined in the best restaurants. Thérèse, in her finery, was known everywhere as *"la grande Thérèse."* If ever doubts were expressed about her ability to pay off her debts, she would invite the doubter to her bedroom. Then, swearing him to secrecy, she would slip a hot knife blade below the seals on the safe and show him the "securities."

BEWARE OF BANKERS FROM LYON

But one banker, a man from Lyon named Delatte, was on a visit to the United States, where he inquired about the existence of the late Mr. Crawford and his nephews. Nobody had heard of them. To divert attention from the gossip that began to circulate, Thérèse now announced that the nephews were disputing the conditions of the will. Frédéric assembled a formidable team of advocates for what promised to be a long legal dispute.

But Marie's 21st birthday was near at hand, and Thérèse quickly thought up another diversionary tactic. Her two brothers, Emile and Romain, set up a business that specialized in *rente viagère*, a kind of life annuity. They offered very good rates and paid promptly. But nobody outside the family knew that none of the sums deposited had been invested. The annuities were paid out of incoming payments.

Eventually a suspicious official of the Banque de France looked closely into the affairs of the company and reported his findings to the French prime minister, Pierre Waldeck-Rousseau. Only too aware of the effect of financial scandals on French politics, Waldeck-Rousseau arranged for details to be leaked to the newspaper *Le Matin*. Thérèse was forced

to threaten proceedings for libel. Her lawyer, Maître du Buit, announced that he would refute the accusations by opening the famous safe himself, in the presence of principal creditors.

THE FLAMES OF JUSTICE

On May 8, 1902, a mysterious fire broke out in Thérèse's bedroom. That, she declared, was too much. She and Frédéric, her two brothers, and Marie disappeared by train. Two days later de Buit led a group of creditors into the bedroom. Amid the ashes stood the safe, its wax seals melted but otherwise untouched. Inside was nothing but a single brick.

Seven months later the Spanish police discovered the family in a lodging house in Madrid. They were extradited and—except for Marie—stood trial in Paris on August 8, 1903, on 257 charges of forgery and fraud. Newspapers from all over the world reported the sensational case. It was on the last day of the trial that Thérèse told her final lie. The safe had once held banknotes for millions of francs, she said. But they were the former property of Marshal Bazaine—a soldier who had been condemned as a traitor—and she had burned them all "out of patriotism." One of the judges leaned forward politely and asked: "Then why the brick?"

Thérèse and Frédéric were each sentenced to five years' imprisonment, Romain to three, and Emile to two. Madame Humbert served three-and-a-half years before being released for good conduct, and the last seen of her was a newspaper photograph of a stout woman in black, boarding a train that carried her into obscurity.

THE MAN WHO SOLD THE EIFFEL TOWER—TWICE

Victor Lustig (1890–1947) was the son of the respected mayor of Hostinne, a town in Bohemia (now part of the Czech Republic).

He was sent to school in Dresden, Germany, where the only subjects in which he excelled were languages. He spoke German, English, French and Italian, and was chosen to continue his studies in Paris. For some time Victor's father believed that his son had been a student at the Sorbonne. But after discovering the excitements of the city before World War I, young Lustig had found ways of financing a more luxurious lifestyle.

THE CHARMING COUNT VON LUSTIG

He took up gambling: bridge and poker, but particularly billiards, which he played

No longer quite the dapper, distinguished foreign aristocrat, but still smartly dressed: the 45-year-old Victor Lustig, photographed at the time of his final arrest.

For some time Victor's father believed that his son had been a student at the Sorbonne. But after discovering the excitements of Paris, young Lustig had found ways of financing a more luxurious lifestyle.

very well. Many newly rich Americans were making the fashionable trip to Europe and became easy prey for card sharks who were "working the boats" aboard the transatlantic liners. Lustig joined them and, calling himself "Count" von Lustig, employed his inherent Czech charm to great effect.

Nicky Arnstein, a notorious trickster, spotted Lustig and took him on as a partner. Arnstein taught him the skills of the confidence man: how to identify a suitable "mark" and work on his vanity and greed, to know the right moment to go for the kill, and how to extricate himself unscathed.

WHAT TO DO WITH ALL THESE BONDS?

At the end of World War I, Lustig and Arnstein moved to the United States. After a series of successful operations, Lustig found himself in possession of $25,000 worth of genuine government bonds. It seemed a shame just to cash them. One day in 1924, a banker named Green, in a small town in Kansas, was visited by a distinguished foreigner, dressed in striped trousers and spats and wearing a monocle. He introduced himself as Count von Lustig; having been driven from his Austrian estates by the war, he had sold his family heirlooms and now had $50,000 in U.S. Government bonds with which to buy

property in the area. Handed two bundles, each apparently of $25,000, the banker accepted one for the sale of a property and gave Lustig $25,000 in cash for the other. But, of course, half of each bundle was made up of neatly cut sheets of paper.

In 1925, Lustig returned to Paris in the company of a partner known as "Dapper Dan" Collins. They stayed at a high-class hotel, and Lustig introduced Collins as his private secretary. One morning the pair were having coffee together in the Champs Elysée when Lustig stared out at the Eiffel Tower and announced: "I think it is time for us to go into the scrap iron business."

LUSTIG GOES INTO GOVERNMENT

He knew that, faced with a huge bill for essential repairs, the French government was seriously considering demolishing the Eiffel Tower. A week later five representatives of the scrap iron trade were summoned by letter to a meeting on behalf of the "Deputy Director of the Ministère des Postes et des Telegraphes." Lustig—for it was he—invited them to submit sealed tenders for the dismantling of the tower. He and Collins soon spotted their mark, André Poisson, and the next day Collins called on Poisson to tell him that his bid was acceptable. The dealer, however, appeared uneasy at the news. Perhaps, suggested Collins, he was unsure that the two tricksters were really government employees?

"I shall prove it to him," said Lustig. He arranged a secret meeting with Poisson at the hotel and complained bitterly about the inadequacy of his salary. Poisson understood immediately and pressed a substantial sum of cash into Lustig's hands. The first installment of his payment for the Eiffel Tower arrived a few days later. Lustig and Collins had already packed; within minutes they had cashed the check at the Banque de France and left by car for Austria.

Returning to the United States, Lustig found many gullible dupes for his activities in Miami and also across the channel in Havana, Cuba. Then, picking up a pretty 18-year-old actress, he represented himself as a successful Broadway producer who was preparing a new musical. He found his victim in a starstruck manufacturer from Rhode Island, who willingly handed over $34,000 in cash for a share in the production.

Lustig, of course, immediately left for Europe; back in Paris, he managed to sell the Eiffel Tower once more, in exactly the same way. But this time his victim informed the police, and the "Count" was forced to exit in a hurry.

THE "ROMANIAN BOX" TRICK

Once more in the United States, Lustig settled in Palm Beach, Florida, and set about making the acquaintance of rich men who arrived there in their yachts. One of these was a prominent man in the automobile business named Hermann Loller. By discreet inquiry, Lustig discovered that Loller's business was having difficulties, so he decided to make use of the old, well-established "Romanian box" trick.

Here's how it worked: Lustig told Loller—in the strictest confidence—that he possessed a machine, invented by a brilliant Romanian scientist, that would reproduce banknotes. It was a wooden box with a beautiful finish, covered with dials and knobs and with a slot at either end. Lustig took a genuine $1,000 bill, together with a blank sheet of paper, and fed both into one of the slots. He explained that a complex photographic process inside the box took several hours to complete; when he and Loller returned, out from the second slot came two identical bills.

Lustig encouraged Loller to take the bills to be inspected by banks, knowing that the forgery could not be detected. "But not both to the same bank," said Lustig, "because they would notice that each note had the same serial number." Both, in fact, were genuine. On one Lustig had changed two 3s into 8s so that they appeared identical.

FORGER'S FILE
USING DISHONESTY HONESTLY

In Chicago, Lustig achieved his bravest confidence trick, even though it gained him relatively little. Dressed impeccably, as always, he was escorted before Al Capone. Lustig told him that he was engaged in a scheme on Wall Street that was guaranteed to double investors' money in two months. Capone handed over $50,000, growling menacingly: "You know enough about me to know that when I go into business, I don't fool around."

Lustig found no way of raising another $50,000; so when the two months were up, he returned to Chicago. He told Capone that the scheme had failed and then, to the gangster's great surprise, handed back 50 $1,000 bills. Capone remarked that Lustig seemed an honest man. "You in a fix?" With a self-deprecating smile, Lustig admitted that he was just a penniless aristocrat. "Here," said Capone, peeling off a small handful, "take five."

Handcuffed to the detective on his right, Lustig leaves court to serve a 20-year sentence in Alcatraz.

Loller agreed to buy the box for $25,000 and took it off to his yacht. There, following Lustig's instructions, he fed a $1,000 bill into the slot. But after six hours, all that had emerged was the same bill he had inserted. Furiously, he tried again and again, and at last broke open the box. Inside were a pair of rubber rollers and some sheets of blank paper. He was enraged, but there was no way he could inform the authorities that he had bought a machine with which to counterfeit money.

NO ONE WILL ADMIT HE'S BEEN DUPED

By now the FBI held a fat file on Lustig. He had been brought in for questioning many times, but his victims were always unwilling to admit they had been fooled. In 1934 the U.S. Treasury discovered a flood of counterfeit $100 bills, which they calculated were being distributed at a rate of $100,000 a month. They believed the bills were the work of William Watts. A former pharmacist, Watts was known to have engraved labels for bootleg whiskey bottles; officials suspected Lustig knew him.

When Lustig was eventually found and brought in for exhaustive questioning, he led FBI agents to a locker containing three sets of counterfeit plates and $50,000 in forged bills. He had hoped in this way to negotiate his release, but instead Lustig was charged with conspiracy and held in the Manhattan House of Detention.

A few days later passersby saw a man with a large white cloth, cleaning windows on an upper story of the prison. The cloth

Loller was enraged, but there was no way he could inform the authorities that he had bought a machine with which to counterfeit money.

unfolded into a rope of bedsheets, down which Lustig slid to the sidewalk. He bowed to the bystanders and calmly bustled away. It was three months before he was recaptured in Pittsburgh, Pennsylvania, while living under the name of Robert Miller.

Lustig and Watts were tried in New York City in December 1935. Watts was sentenced to 15 years in prison and Lustig to 20, in Alcatraz. There he found several acquaintances from his days as a confidence trickster. One, who had been convicted of tax fraud, worked in the prison laundry: his name was Al Capone.

In 1947, at only 57, the "Count" fell ill. He was transferred to the Medical Center for Federal Prisoners in Springfield, Missouri, and died shortly thereafter.

DAPPER DAN

The career of the man known as "Dapper Dan" Collins began long before he met Victor Lustig. He was born in France as Robert Arthur Tourbillon in 1885. His first employment, in his teens, was with a French circus; in an act known as the "Circle of Death," Collins rode a bicycle through a group of lions. A handsome man—at least in his earlier years—he soon turned to crime, exploiting his wit and charm. He was known in criminal circles as the "Rat," an acronym of his initials. In 1908 he immigrated to the United States, where he carried on successfully until 1916, when he was sentenced to four years in prison. He later said that he had been

convicted of "white slavery," a polite term for pimping.

FROM WEALTHY WIDOWS TO NEW JERSEY FARMERS

On his release, Tourbillon adopted the name of Collins and returned to France, where he employed his good looks to attract a succession of rich widows and adopted a hedonistic lifestyle. However, he was identified by a couple of detectives—who happened, in fact, to be on the trail of another man—and extradited to the United States aboard the liner *France*. Certain that he would be going to jail, Collins spent lavishly on board, throwing wild parties. But when he came to trial, under his real name of Tourbillon, he was amazed—and discomfited—when all the charges against him were dropped.

It was not long, however, before he was charged with defrauding a New Jersey farmer of $30,000 and sent to prison for two years. He served 16 months and announced on his release that he was returning to France. That was the last that was ever heard of him.

THE MAN WHO (NEARLY) SOLD THE STATUE OF LIBERTY

A man who could rival Victor Lustig was Scotsman Arthur Furguson. He was playing minor roles with a touring company when, one day in 1925, he chanced to be in Trafalgar Square, London. Staring up at Nelson's Column at that moment was a tourist. The statue on top of the column, so Furguson told him in a moment of idle mischief, was of England's greatest naval hero; what a pity it had to be taken down and sold to repay Britain's national debt. The tourist was visibly upset, and further conversation revealed that he was a very rich man from Iowa.

It was then that Furguson had his brilliant idea. He told the American that

Opposite: In one of his most ambitious and seemingly incredible schemes, Victor Lustig succeeded in persuading a Parisian scrap metal dealer that he was able to sell him the Eiffel Tower. Pocketing the first installment of the money, Lustig escaped— only to pull off the same scam a second time.

he was, in fact, the official from the Ministry of Works who had been ordered to arrange the sale. There was, he said, already a long list of potential buyers, but… The Iowan took the hook. He had the money; couldn't he jump to the top of the list? He said he would undertake to reerect the column in Iowa.

Furguson agreed to telephone his superiors and returned within a few minutes to say that the monument was the man's, in exchange for an immediate check for £6,000. He handed over a receipt, together with the address and telephone number of a demolition company, and vanished.

But it was not to be for long. Soon the police received a complaint from another rich American. He had put up money to purchase Buckingham Palace, but the guards had refused to allow him through the gates. A third victim protested that he had paid £1,000—a real bargain—for the clock tower of the Houses of Parliament, popularly known as Big Ben.

LIBERTY FOR SALE

Surprised at the ease with which these wealthy men had been tricked, Furguson decided he could best make use of his talents in the United States. There he persuaded a Texas rancher to take a 99-year lease on the White House at $100,000 a year, the first year's rent to be paid in advance.

In Manhattan the Scotsman encountered a visitor from Sydney, Australia. He told him that there was a plan to widen the Hudson River; unfortunately, this meant that the Statue of Liberty had to be removed. Wouldn't it look fine, erected in the middle of Sydney Harbor? He was the city official in charge, so he said, and the price was a mere $100,000. The excited Australian was given a guided tour of the statue by Furguson, then asked another visitor to photograph him standing below it.

Unhappily for Furguson, he also appeared in the photograph. When the Australian called the New York branch of his bank to arrange the financing, suspicions were at once aroused; the Aussie was advised to check with the police department. He showed the police his photograph, and "city official" Furguson was soon serving a five-year sentence. On his release he relocated to Los Angeles, where he bought himself a luxurious home with his ill-gotten gains.

Scottish con man Arthur Furguson was caught when he arranged to sell the Statue of Liberty to an unsuspecting Australian.

FORGER'S FILE
"YELLOW KID" WEIL AND THE WIRE

Joseph Weil (died 1976) was born in Chicago and earned his nickname from his fondness for the cartoon character the Yellow Kid, who had first appeared in the *New York World* in 1896. Weil is famous for the many profitable confidence schemes he pulled off. "That Yellow Kid would tear himself off if he could," said one of his associates. He may well have been the inventor of the con known as "the wire," which formed the plot of the 1973 movie *The Sting*.

At the beginning of the twentieth century, bookmaking was legal in the United States; it was usually conducted in poolrooms, and horse race results were phoned there by wire from Western Union headquarters. Weil would persuade his rich victim (the mark) that he had a hold over the Western Union operator, who would delay calling a result for a couple of minutes, meanwhile sending a coded signal naming the winner. This would give the mark time to place a sure winning bet.

Weil organized everything down to the smallest detail. He rented the banqueting suite of a Chicago hotel and fitted it out as a fully equipped betting establishment. He not only

"Yellow Kid" Weil told his story to writer W. T. Brannon in 1947.

hired a number of con men acquaintances as "stooges," but also brought in about 100 actors who had been told they were auditioning for a new play. All went as planned; the coded message came through, and the mark rushed to place his bet—but was prevented by a staged row that broke out in front of the betting window.

But now the "Western Union operator" needed to be paid off, also the operator in New York whom he said he had bribed. Weil insisted that he, too, should be compensated for the mark's failure. The mark had to pay out three times what he had intended to bet, but "Can we try again?" he would usually ask.

Furguson was able to perpetrate some lesser confidence tricks without attracting the attentions of the California police, and he died there in 1938.

SELLING THE EIFFEL TOWER—AGAIN

Twenty years after Lustig's most famous exploit, the story of the "sale" of the Eiffel Tower had faded from most people's memories. A wealthy Texan was most certainly unaware of it when he encountered Englishman Stanley Lowe in Paris shortly after the end of World War II. Lowe told him, untruthfully, that the Eiffel Tower had been badly damaged during the war and would have to be taken down and sold as scrap for a paltry $40,000. But happily for the Texan, the intended fraud was discovered in time, and Lowe spent nine months in jail.

This was only one of many of Lowe's confidence games. Neatly dressed in clerical garb, he once persuaded an unsuspecting Japanese tourist in London to donate $100,000 to a "fund" being raised to restore St. Paul's Cathedral, which had indeed been badly damaged by bombs during the war. Posing as Oscar-winning Hollywood producer "Mark Sheridan," Lowe found investors for a forthcoming movie. As "Group Captain

FORGER'S FILE
THE CONFIDENCE TRICKSTERS' VOCABULARY

BIG CON: A con game, involving large amounts of money, that includes the payoff, the rag and the wire.

BIG STORE: The fake establishment—poolroom or broker's office—set up for the big con.

BLOW OFF: To get rid of the mark after he has been fleeced.

GRIFTER: One who lives by his wits.

MARK: The victim, upon being spotted.

THE PAYOFF: A big con game in which a wealthy mark is persuaded to believe he or she has been allowed into a scheme to swindle a large racing syndicate.

THE RAG: A big con similar to the payoff, but one using stocks instead of races. It is run from a fake broker's office.

ROPER: An outside man who brings the mark to the big store.

SHILL: An accomplice who plays a confidence game so that the mark sees him winning.

STING: The successful confidence trick.

SHORT CON: A small con game in which the mark is fleeced only of what he has with him.

THE WIRE: A big con game involving a fake Western Union operator, who undertakes to delay reporting a horse race result so that the mark can place a sure winning bet.

Rivers Bogle Bland," a former RAF pilot now working on an ultra-secret project for the British government, he contrived to deprive other victims of their money.

Lowe's last big trick was to get himself hired as a footman in Marlborough House in London, residence of the dowager Queen Mary. His plan was to make off with as many of her jewels and small works of art as he could. However, he gave himself away by arriving for work one day in a new Jaguar he had just stolen. The police were alerted, and Stanley Lowe was soon back in prison. After his release all his audacity was gone, and he ended his life in a small, cheap room.

On his release from jail, Stanley Lowe returned with a bouquet of flowers for the prison governor. It was to say "thank you" for the governor's help in getting him to "go straight."

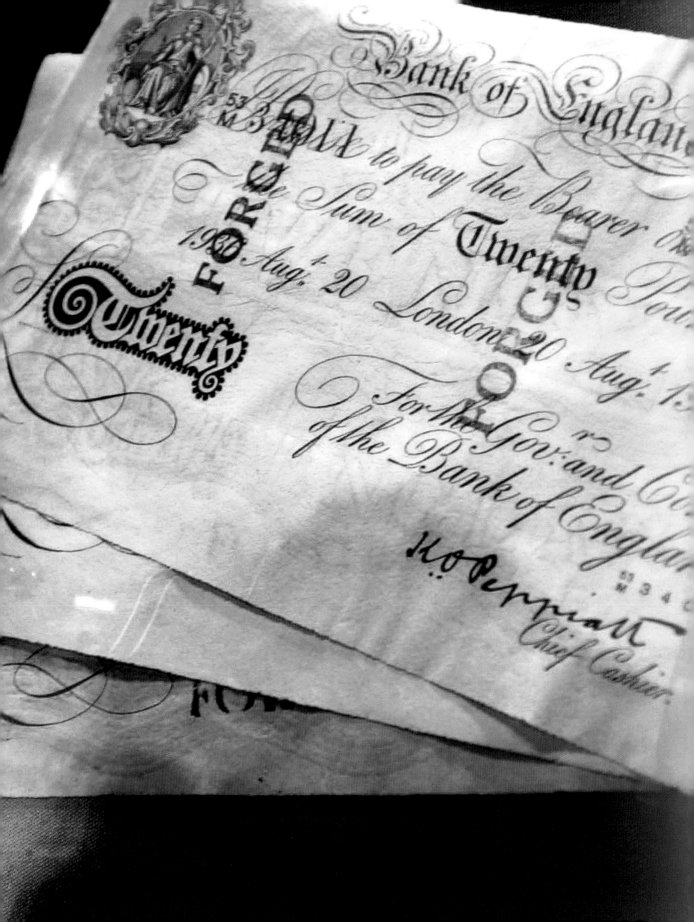

CHAPTER 7
FAKING FOR A CAUSE

Not all fakes and forgeries are made for profit, or even for fun. Some are made deliberately to support a cause or a belief.

n certain cases, such as with propaganda directed against an enemy in wartime, the motive for the forgery can be considered legitimate, even praiseworthy. During two world wars, for example, the opposing sides produced all sorts of forged documents: Some were to protect agents working undercover in enemy territory; others were aimed at undermining enemy morale. Many religious and mystical movements have also had their share of fakes; eager believers are prepared to accept what can easily be shown to be false. As a case in point, it has been noted that the number of "fragments of the true cross" scattered throughout the world would, if reassembled, make up enough timber for several crosses.

Opposite: Some of the British banknotes forged by SS Major Bernhard Krüger during World War II. They were recovered from the Toplitzsee in Austria in 1959.

Left: Young Frances Griffiths, with the fairies photographed by her cousin Elsie Wright.

FORGER'S FILE
THE POISONOUS PROTOCOLS

One of the most infamous political forgeries of the twentieth century was the so-called "Protocols of the Learned Elders of Zion." They first appeared in the Russian newspaper Znamia in 1903, next in a book by Sergei Nilus in 1905. Nilus said that the Protocols had been taken from the minutes of a meeting in France of the first Zionist Congress in 1897. In fact, the congress had been held in Basle, Switzerland, and conducted in German. The texts were violently inflammatory, describing plans by the Jews, together with the Freemasons, to corrupt Christian civilization and establish a world state.

Anti-Semitic feeling ran high in Russia in the early years of the 20th century, and the Protocols were read aloud in Moscow's churches. They were translated into German, French, English and other languages and became the most widely read anti-Semitic literature of all time.

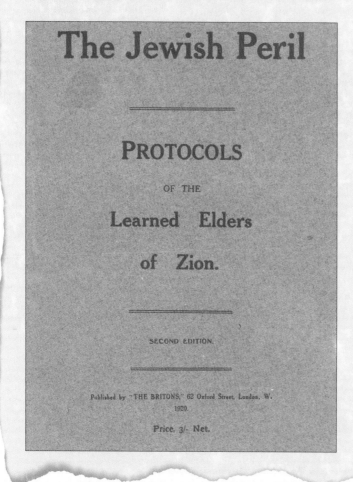

The title page of the second edition of the Protocols, titled "The Jewish Peril," published in London in 1920.

Philip Graves, a newspaper correspondent for the *Times* of London, revealed the Protocols as a forgery. He pointed out their close similarity to a satire written in 1864 by the French lawyer Maurice Joly. It took the form of a dialogue in hell between the eighteenth-century French political philosopher Montesquieu and the cynical fifteenth-century Italian writer Niccolò Machiavelli. Montesquieu spoke for liberalism, and Machiavelli was a thinly disguised representation of the ruling French emperor, Napoleon III.

The source of the Protocols turned out to be Pyotr Ruchkovsky, head of the foreign branch of the Russian secret police. A committee of American historians appraised the forged document in 1942. They stated categorically that the Protocols had no claim to authenticity.

GOVERNMENT WARTIME FORGERIES

No government will ever officially admit to having committed forgery. For obvious reasons this applies particularly to the counterfeiting of fiscal material, such as banknotes and postage stamps. Nevertheless, evidence has emerged over the years that certainly throughout two world wars and possibly at other times, many warring nations have produced forgeries in the name of propaganda. During World War I, both the British and Germans printed forged postage stamps, but it was during World War II that forgery became an important part of propaganda campaigns.

THE BLACK GAME

Richard Crossman (1907–74) was a British government minister from 1964 through 1970, but during World War II he was involved with psychological warfare (nowadays known as "psywar") for three years with the British Political Warfare Executive (PWE) and later with U.S. forces.

In 1973, in a letter concerning the Watergate scandal, he wrote to the *Times* newspaper: "Inner government is, of course, a necessary apparatus of total war; and the best paid and most attractive of its departments are those which deal with covert operations in which we British have always excelled...subversive operations and black propaganda were the only aspects of war at which we achieved real pre-eminence. We trained a small army of gifted amateurs for all the dirtiest tricks, from lying, bugging, forging and embezzlement to sheer murder—all, of course, in the name of preserving the democratic way of life. The Americans adored subversion, but they were too heavy-handed and never learned from us to play it as a game...."

The British did indeed regard psywar as a game. One of those involved has said that only a nation that understood the rules of cricket and could also solve the cryptic crosswords found in the principal national newspapers was capable of the subtle acts of subversion carried out during the war. In fact, prospective recruits to the Enigma program, which consistently broke the encoded messages of the German forces, were given a crossword from the *Daily Telegraph* to solve as part of their assessment.

Official World War II propaganda relied largely upon the broadcasts of the BBC, together with the distribution of leaflets dropped by aircraft and the

The Cunard liner *Lusitania* was sunk by a German U-boat on May 7, 1915. Soon afterward this medal was struck in Germany. Although it appears to celebrate the sinking, its creator insisted that his intention was to condemn Cunard for allowing civilians to sail in a vessel carrying armaments. However, British propagandists soon commissioned 250,000 counterfeit medals, which were distributed worldwide to bolster the anti-German cause.

Two versions of *Krankheit rettet (The Malingerer's Book)*, a fake handbook dropped into Germany and aimed at undermining German morale and fighting strength. It contained details on how a soldier could simulate a variety of illnesses that might get him a few days off duty, a stay in the hospital, or even a discharge.

publication of bulletins in neutral countries. This was known as "white" propaganda. "Black" propaganda, which was never officially admitted to, was left in the hands, as Crossman said, of "a small army of gifted amateurs."

FAKE RADIO STATIONS

Black propaganda took two principal forms. Under the direction of former newspaperman Sefton Delmer (1904–1979), small secret radio stations beamed programs of news and entertainment in German, identifying themselves by such names as *Kurzwellensender Atlantik* and *Soldatensender Calais*. A separate unit, run by Ellic Howe (1910–1991), was devoted to the production of forged documents of many different kinds.

Howe, who left Oxford University in 1930, spent three years in Europe, becoming fluent in French, German and Italian. In

1934 he decided to train in the printing industry in England, where he learned every aspect of typesetting and collected a vast range of printing specimens from France, Germany, Belgium and Holland.

In 1938, a year before the outbreak of World War II, Howe enlisted in an antiaircraft unit and by 1941 was a sergeant major. One day in September of that year, while on leave, he paid a visit to the Monotype Corporation in Surrey, in southeastern England, which manufactured typefaces for printers. While there, he idly inspected the records of German *Fraktur* (Gothic) types that had been cut by the company and discovered that none had ever been delivered to a British printing company, and so could not be traced back to Britain. He was immediately struck by the possibility that these could be used to forge false documents for circulation in Germany.

THE POWER OF PRINT

Howe wrote a paper, "Political Warfare and the Printed Word: A Psychological Study," and submitted it to his commanding officer. Within a few weeks he was returned to civilian status, and he reported to PWE. His first important assignment was to forge the German identity card that was needed by the Special Operations Executive (SOE) for their agents abroad. Howe's wide contacts in various branches of the printing industry now proved invaluable. The Monotype Corporation offered him the extended loan of any *Fraktur* matrices (the molds from which type was then cast) he might ask for, and paper makers undertook the production of suitable paper with forged watermarks. In one case, when a forgery of the *Reichsbank* letterhead was needed in a hurry, a paper company employee quickly discovered that the paper used for bottle labels of a famous brand of beer would be just right.

The next stage was the forging of French postage stamps. The firm of Waterlow & Sons (see pages 31–32), which had been printing stamps for half a century, undertook the task. In July 1942 a secret report to the British Foreign Secretary read: "A special black leaflet…has been prepared for distribution inside Vichy France. Two thousand copies, ready for posting, in forged envelopes and with forged stamps, will be smuggled across the Pyrenees through the existing chain of couriers…."

WINNING NEUTRAL HEARTS AND MINDS

This was only one of dozens of documents that Howe printed; those intended for distribution in German territory had a text supplied by Delmer. Among the first was *Europa in Gefahr (Europe in Peril)*, a little booklet allegedly derived from a report written by the Nazi Party representative in Shanghai, China, detailing the atrocities committed by the Japanese in Hong Kong

and implying that Japan intended to conquer the world. Others included a "Manual for Candidates for the SS," which contained fictitious information about the privileges enjoyed by the SS, including details of a horrific rape performed with evident pleasure by drunken SS men. These documents were circulated in neutral countries, smuggled into Nazi-occupied Europe and dropped from aircraft over Germany.

With practice the forgeries became still more ingenious. There was a scientific

In 1917 press baron Lord Northcliffe owned, among other newspapers, the *Daily Mail*, and was a member of a government committee formed to encourage the assistance of the United States in WW I. Germany produced this crude forgery, *The Great Anti-Northcliffe Mail*, in an effort to "eliminate the Northcliffe Press from the part it is playing in the war."

treatise, stating that current methods of milling German flour were liable to cause serious damage to health, including causing male impotence. A bogus postage stamp featured the face of Heinrich Himmler, instead of that of Hitler, suggesting that the head of the SS was about to take over. A little booklet (see page 218) described how soldiers could fake illness and injury and thus avoid active service. These were disguised with innocent-looking slipcovers identifying them, for instance, as French phrase books.

CALLING UP NOSTRADAMUS

Two productions from "Mr. Howe's unit," as it became known, were particularly clever. One was *Nostradamus Predicts the Course of the War*, a 124-page booklet in which some 100 verses written by the sixteenth-century French astrologer were translated into German, with accompanying commentaries suggesting that Hitler's demise was near. The other was *Der Zenit*, a bogus astrological magazine that included genuine-looking commercial advertisements and that pointed out, among other matters, that U-boats should not be allowed to leave port on "unfavorable days."

With the D-day landings on the continent of Europe in June 1944, the activities of "Mr. Howe's unit" and of Delmer's clandestine radio stations contributed in no small measure to a decline in the morale of the German troops.

OFFICIAL DENIALS

It should be stressed that the British government has never admitted to these forgeries, and most pertinent records were destroyed in 1945. It was nearly 20 years after the war that Delmer's *Black Boomerang* reminiscences were published, and nearly 40 before Howe was able to assemble sufficient material for his book *The Black Game*. Other major nations

> # "If it's printed, it's true, and if one can find a plausible excuse for using or faking a rubber stamp impression on the printed document, then it must be doubly true!"
>
> —ELLIC HOWE

engaged in World War II, including the Soviet Union and the United States, have continued to deny the production of counterfeit documents.

Nevertheless, the issue of *Soviet War News* dated January 7, 1942, reported that Russian planes had dropped millions of packages behind German lines, containing postcards with stamps, ready for posting. One picture showed a field of wooden crosses, with one abandoned helmet and the caption *Lebensraum in Osten* (*Living space in the East*)—Hitler's justification for the invasion of the Soviet Union.

As for the United States, stamp collectors well know of a variety of postage stamps that were produced as propaganda during World War II. Like the British-produced stamp of Himmler, these are not strictly forgeries, as they are not reproductions of official German issues; but they are sufficiently similar to escape notice in a postal sorting office. Probably the most successful were produced in "Operation Cornflakes," designed to ruin the breakfasts of German families who received them in the mail. They carry the usual portrait of Hitler, but changed into a death's head.

The CIA still denies the existence of these stamps. However, its predecessor, the Office of Strategic Services (OSS), reported in 1945 the production of a total of 1,138,500 "Hitler heads," which included

The Nazis tried to ruin the British economy during World War II by forging millions of pounds worth of banknotes. Many of the notes were sunk in a remote Austrian lake at the end of the war. In 1959 so many notes were recovered from the lake bed that they had to be carried away by wheelbarrow.

726,550 individual stamps, 70,000 "sex cards and envelopes," and 6,500 "numbered stamps." Despite the public denials, behind closed doors at CIA headquarters in Langley, Virginia, there is still a display case of these stamps, postcards and even a forged newspaper, *Das Neue Deutschland*, produced by the OSS.

OPERATION BERNHARD

Early in World War II the Nazis decided to ruin the British economy by printing millions of forged Bank of England notes and dropping them over Britain from the air. However, the project was delayed several times by what is commonly regarded as typical German thoroughness. For example, some of the early banknotes were offered for authentication to foreign banks and even to the Bank of England, as a test. But after six were identified as forgeries and the man offering them was imprisoned, the operation was temporarily held up.

In charge of the operation, which was named after him, was SS Major Bernhard Krüger (born 1904), who ran the workshop producing forged documents for German

A German forgery of a British twopenny stamp issued in the Bahamas. The overprinting is meant to suggest that the British Empire is being liquidated after the defeat of the Allies— an attempt to destroy British morale.

agents abroad. First they had to make a linen paper based on flax. Experiments with German flax were unsuccessful, and Turkish flax, though better, still did not give the right appearance. It was only when someone suggested that the linen rags from which the paper was made should be washed first that a satisfactory result was obtained. The SS commandeered a paper mill, and by May 1943, "Operation Bernhard" was at last in full swing.

A team of some 30 concentration camp inmates at Sachsenhausen produced the forgeries. They were housed in a separate block and given extra food and other privileges. The principal engraver was a convicted Bulgarian Jewish counterfeiter, Solly Smolianov, who was transferred from prison to Sachsenhausen. The unit produced notes of every denomination from £1 to £1,000; however, when the Bank of England withdrew the issue of large denominations, about half the notes produced were £5 notes.

PERPETRATING POSTAGE PROPAGANDA

Then the head of the SS, Heinrich Himmler, came up with a new propaganda proposal: postage stamps, which he intended should become valuable collectors' items after the war. These were copies of genuine British issues but with subversive changes. The imperial orb on the crown above the head of King George VI was replaced by a six-pointed star of David, with the "D" representing pennies by the Russian hammer and sickle. The Coronation issue of 1937 included several other modifications. In place of the usual "Postage...Revenue" was "SSSR... Britannia," the star of David replaced other devices, and the head of Russian leader Joseph Stalin replaced that of Queen Mary. In addition, the date of the Coronation was replaced by "Teheran

British stamps forged in Sachsenhausen concentration camp. The star of David on the crown above the head of King George VI and the replacement of the "D" by a hammer and sickle (far left) are typical of these issues. Stalin's head is shown in place of that of Queen Mary, (left), meant to imply that Britain's alliance with the Soviets was a step towards being absorbed into the USSR. A curious error was made by the engraver of the fake 1935 Jubilee stamp, (bottom), which reads "This war is a Jewsh war."

28 11 1943," the date of an important conference in Iran at which Winston Churchill, Franklin D. Roosevelt and Stalin had discussed the forthcoming liberation of Europe.

Similar alterations were made to the stamp issued in 1935 that celebrated the Silver Jubilee of King George V: Stalin's head replaced that of the king. But Himmler, still expecting to make peace with Britain, had given orders that George VI's head on the other stamps was not to be altered. Unfortunately, a curious mistake was made in the engraving of the Jubilee stamp. Replacing the words "Silver Jubilee" and "Halfpenny," it read, "This war is a Jewsh war." It has been suggested that this had been deliberate sabotage, but Krüger confirmed many years after the war that it was a genuine error.

Late in the war, "Operation Bernhard" also forged dollar bills, but the production of Bank of England notes remained their major output. It has been calculated that nine million notes with a face value of over £134 million were printed; however, only some £12 million were ever distributed.

In the closing days of the war in 1945, several truckloads of counterfeits and their plates were sunk in rivers and lakes in Austria, and the printing plant itself was destroyed. One load of cases reached a secret German naval research establishment on a remote Austrian lake called Toplitzsee, where it was sunk to a depth of 260 ft. (78 m). Teams of British and American divers attempted to find it, without success, and for 14 years the treasure in the lake remained nothing but a legend.

In July 1959 the German magazine

Stern decided to mount a search expedition. It was equipped with an underwater television camera, a powerful searchlight and a mechanical grab, and on July 27 the first £5 notes were brought to the surface. Gradually, before ranks of news photographers and television cameras, case after case was hauled up. Among the millions of counterfeit notes, there were the account books of "Operation Bernhard," meticulously kept.

THE COTTINGLEY FAIRIES

When a person really wants to believe in something, he can too easily be fooled by fake evidence. Sir Arthur Conan Doyle (1859–1930) was the creator of Sherlock Holmes, the brilliant detective who was never diverted from his search for the truth. Yet Conan Doyle himself became convinced of the existence of fairies.

It all began when 10-year-old Frances Griffiths sent a letter to a friend in 1918. This read, in part: "I am sending two photos… one of me…with some fairies up the beck [small stream]." Frances was living with the family of her cousin, 15-year-old Elsie Wright, in Cottingley, on the edge of the city of Bradford, Yorkshire, in northern England. Elsie had borrowed her father's quarter-plate box camera some months before and had taken the photograph of Frances.

Mr. Wright developed the plate and was unimpressed with what he saw: Frances's head with a number of indeterminate white shapes ranged before her. Nevertheless, the two girls insisted that they had regularly played with fairies "up the beck" and to prove it produced another photograph, this time taken by Frances, of Elsie with a "gnome." It was underexposed and unclear, and Frances's parents remained convinced that the girls had been playing tricks.

However, in 1919, Mrs. Wright attended a meeting of the Theosophical Society in Bradford, at which a talk was given on "fairy life," and mentioned the photographs. Early in 1920 two rough prints reached the hands of leading theosophist Edward Gardner. He passed them to a commercial photographer, with instructions to make new negatives from the prints and "sharpen them up." The improved prints clearly revealed several winged fairies in draperies dancing in front of Elsie, and Frances with an ugly-faced gnome before her; and Gardner became convinced of their authenticity.

Conan Doyle, who had become a fanatical exponent of spiritualism following the death of his son, also believed the photos were authentic. He showed the photographs to several experts, who were suspicious but could not say how they had been faked. So Conan Doyle published them with an article he had written for the December 1920 issue of *Strand* magazine.

Sir Arthur Conan Doyle was the creator of Sherlock Holmes, the brilliant detective who was never diverted from his search for the truth. Yet Conan Doyle himself became convinced of the existence of fairies.

Meanwhile, prompted by Gardner, the girls had produced three more photographs, which were published in *Strand* in March 1921 and subsequently in Conan Doyle's book *The Coming of the Fairies* in 1922.

ARE THERE FAIRIES AT THE BOTTOM OF YOUR GARDEN?

The press seized upon the story, and the young photographers became the subject of intense curiosity, so much so that Elsie immigrated to the United States in 1926.

Opposite: In 1959, a scuba-diver surfaces as the first notes are brought up from the bottom of the Toplitzsee, 14 years after they were sunk there during the last days of World War II.

However, she found that her fame had gone before her. For over 50 years the story of the "Cottingley fairies" was repeated in newspapers and books, either expressing belief in their existence or questioning how the photographs had been faked.

Investigators discovered that Elsie had worked for a short time at a local photographer's and also had artistic talent. Indeed, she had done a competent painting of "fairies by a stream." In 1978 an American illusionist, "The Amazing Randi," pointed out the similarity between the figures in the first photograph and those in *Princess Mary's Gift Book*, published in 1914. There was also a close resemblance to dancing fairies in a contemporary advertisement for Price's Night Lights. A

team from *New Scientist* magazine subjected the photographs to computer enhancement and claimed to detect strings attached to some of the fairy figures.

In 1971 the elderly Elsie, who had managed to avoid publicity for years, was persuaded to give a television interview. While admitting to a good sense of fun, she refused to say whether or not the photographs were fakes. Five years later both ladies were interviewed on television. Again, both refused to admit complicity. "You tell us how she could do it," demanded Frances. But the broadcast concluded with a shot of the interviewer sitting behind a row of dancing fairies. "Simple cardboard cut-outs," he declared, "mounted on wire frames."

Above: Elsie Wright, 68 years old, with one of the photographs taken by Frances. Appearing on television in 1971, she refused to say whether the photographs were a trick.

Opposite: Frances Griffiths, photographed by her cousin Elsie. According to the two girls' account, the fairy was "leaping." It leapt so high that Frances flung her head back.

FORGER'S FILE
THE FOX SISTERS

The modern spiritualist movement is said to have begun in the United States in 1848, shortly after the Fox family had moved into a new home in Hydesville, New York. There were two sisters: Margaretta (Maggie) was 14, and Catherine (Katie) was 11. Soon rapping sounds in the night disturbed the family.

Maggie and Katie discovered that if they clapped their hands, the raps echoed back the same number and would also answer questions with "yes" or "no." When the girls' supposed powers created a local sensation, Mrs. Fox took the two girls to stay with her married daughter, Leah, in nearby Rochester. Leah, realizing the potential, took charge of the girls, and they gave their first public demonstration in Rochester in 1849, following this with a tour of towns in eastern states. P. T. Barnum took the Fox sisters to New York City, where they impressed many eminent citizens despite the opinion expressed by three professors from Buffalo University that the sounds were produced by simple movement of the knee joints.

"Spirit rapping" rapidly became a craze in the United States, and a woman from Boston, a Mrs. Hayden, carried the new "Spiritualism" to Britain. The Fox sisters, however, soon became victims of their own fame. By 1855 both had become alcoholics. Maggie converted to Catholicism, while Katie continued to perform intermittently. It was not until 1888 that the sisters made a public appearance together in New York City, at which Maggie denounced Spiritualism as a fraud. She demonstrated how she had produced the rapping sounds with her toes and revealed that Leah had given them the necessary cues by body language during their performances.

THE PRIORY OF SION

In 2003–2004, Dan Brown's thriller *The Da Vinci Code* became one of the greatest best-sellers of all time. The first page of the text is headed "Fact" and continues: "The Priory of Sion—a European secret society founded in 1099—is a real organization. In 1975 Paris's Bibliothèque Nationale discovered parchments, known as *Les Dossiers Secrets*, identifying numerous members of the Priory of Sion...."

The library's "parchments" are a loose collection of news clippings, typewritten sheets of paper, genealogies and printed pamphlets, all held in a card folder. The contents of the folder have in fact changed from time to time, indicating that someone has withdrawn it from the library and made alterations. The "author" of most of these documents is listed as "Henri Lobineau"—a pseudonym. Other related documents in the library's collection are privately printed pamphlets, usually typewritten and reproduced on an office duplicator. The existence of these has been known since the 1960s. All are concerned, to a greater or lesser degree, with the "mystery of Rennes-le-chateau."

During the early years of the twentieth century, the priest of this village in southern France was found guilty of selling Masses. On receipt of money from persons all over Europe, he undertook to perform a Mass for their deceased loved ones. But his unexplained wealth led the inhabitants of the village to gossip that he had found a "treasure" in the church.

A VILLAGE MYTH OR SOLOMON'S TREASURE?

In 1955 a man named Noël Corbu opened a hotel and restaurant in the former home of the priest. But business was poor, so he made a tape recording of the story of the treasure in the hope of attracting customers. The story was picked up by a local newspaper, and a journalist from *Ici Paris*, Gerard de Sède, incorporated it in a book, *l'Or de Rennes (The Gold of Rennes)*, in 1967. De Sède suggested that the treasure was the lost menorah from Solomon's temple in Jerusalem. The journalist had obtained information for a previous book from a certain Pierre Plantard; whether Plantard had also been involved in *l'Or de Rennes* is not known, but Plantard quickly elaborated on the legend. It is also highly likely that Plantard was responsible for the "Henri Lobineau" documents.

The supposed importance of Rennes-le-chateau in early Christian history was growing. In 1969, English scriptwriter Henry Lincoln read de Sède's book and with the writer's assistance set out to make a BBC television documentary, "The Lost Treasure of Jerusalem." In due course he was put in touch with Plantard, who told him of the continuing existence of the "Priory of Sion." He even suggested that he, Plantard, was a descendant of the ancient Merovingian dynasty that had ruled in southern France for three centuries and that they in turn were descended from a child whom Christ had fathered with Mary Magdalene.

A NONEXISTENT TOMBSTONE

Lincoln put all this into the best-seller *The Holy Blood and the Holy Grail* (1982), which he wrote in collaboration with Michael Baigent and Richard Leigh. This book sparked a flood of other interpretations of the "mystery." Much of the investigation was based upon reproductions of the inscription on a tombstone, said to have been in the churchyard at Rennes-le-chateau, and of two parchments allegedly discovered by the priest. No trace of the original tombstone has been found, and the reproduction of the engraving has been declared a forgery. Plantard had a collaborator, a dissolute Marquis Philippe de Cherisey, who at one time played guitar in various London clubs. A reproduction of one of the parchments carries a

An illustration to a story by the young English poet Alfred Noyes, "A Spell for a Fairy," in *Princess Mary's Gift Book (1914)*. The theme of the story was how to make fairies visible, and the figures of fairies bear a close resemblance to those in the Cottingley photographs.

notation, in Plantard's handwriting: "This is the original document faked by Philippe de Cherisey which Gerard de Sède reproduced in his book...."

Whether the Priory of Sion ever existed in the eleventh and twelfth centuries remains in doubt. Plantard registered *Le Prieuré de Sion* in 1956 as a "Chivalry of Catholic Rules and Institutions of the Independent and Traditionalist Union," naming himself as secretary-general. It was an extreme right-wing organization, successor to Alpha Galantes, a proto-Nazi group established by Plantard during World War II and expressly devoted to "renewing France through the principles of chivalry."

However, the Rennes-le-chateau "industry" has flourished without

Whether the Priory of Sion ever existed in the eleventh and twelfth centuries remains in doubt.

restraint. Every so often permission is obtained to dig for the "treasure," always without success. Mystical movements have arisen, and two British writers, in *The Tomb of God* (1996), have gone so far as to identify a hill across the valley from Rennes as the burial place of Christ. Another writer claims that the whole of the landscape visible from the village is a vast Egyptian temple. All this is predicated on the basis of Plantard's word and on the documents forged by de Cherisey.

THE SHROUD OF TURIN

Few church relics have aroused such interest and controversy in recent times as the "Turin shroud." Some details of its earliest known history are revealing.
- April 1349: Geoffrey de Charny builds a church at Lirey, not far from Troyes,

France, to hold a shroud that he is said to have brought from Constantinople.
- 1355: The shroud is first exhibited at Lirey, and pilgrims travel to view it.
- 1389: French king Charles VI orders the bailiff of Troyes to seize the shroud, but it is left in Geoffrey de Charny's hands.
- The bishop of Troyes, in a letter to Pope Clement VII, describes the cloth as bearing the double imprint of a crucified man, and claims that it is the true shroud in which the body of Jesus was wrapped.
- May 1398: Geoffrey de Charny dies. His widow, Margaret, marries Humbert de la Roche (1418).
- 1438: Humbert dies; during the following twelve years, until her death, Margaret exhibits the shroud at various places in northern France.
- 1464: The shroud is recorded in the possession of Duke Louis of Savoy, who begins building a chapel at Chambéry.
- June 6, 1483: Priests at Chambéry describe the shroud as "enveloped in a red silk drape and kept in a case covered with crimson velours, decorated with silver-gilt nails and locked with a golden key."
- April 14, 1503: A Savoy courtier reports that the authenticity of the shroud has been confirmed by fire, boiling in oil, and many launderings, but "it was not possible to efface or remove the imprint and image." Signs of the trial by fire are visible in a painting made in 1516.
- 1509: A new silver casket is made.
- December 4, 1532: Fire breaks out in the chapel and flames melt the casket, while the shroud is burned and develops holes in several places.
- April 1534: Nuns repair the fire damage, attaching a backing cloth and sewing patches over the major damage.
- 1536: François Rabelais, in his novel *Gargantua*, alleges that "the Holy Shroud of Chambéry...caught fire so that not a

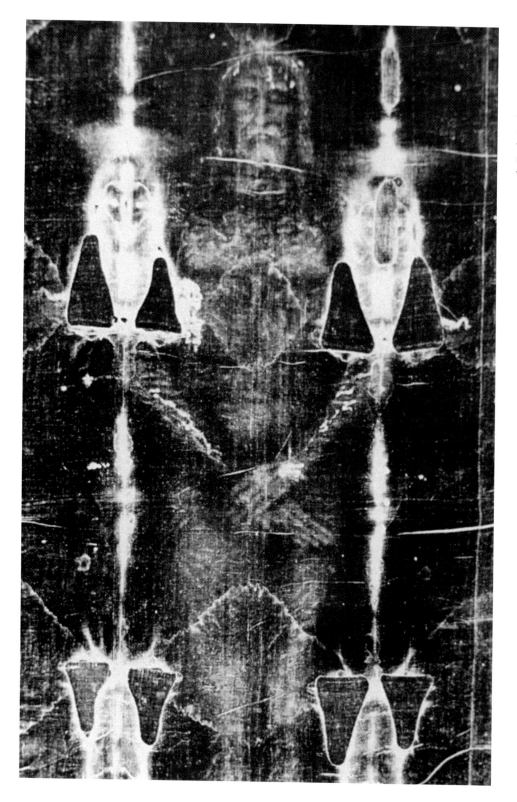

A negative image of the front of the figure on the Turin shroud, very similar to the portrayal of Christ in medieval paintings. The damage to the cloth over the centuries and some of the patches applied by nuns in 1534 are clearly visible.

single scrap could be saved."

- September 14, 1578: After being exhibited in many places, the shroud of Chambéry arrives in Turin, Italy.

THE SHROUD IN MODERN TIMES

From that time on, apart from a period during World War II, when it was taken for safety to an abbey outside Naples, the shroud remained in Turin, where it was occasionally displayed to huge crowds of pilgrims. In 1898 an Italian amateur photographer took the first photograph. More photographs were taken in 1931.

What is beyond dispute is that the cloth,

The face of the figure as it appears on the Turin shroud.

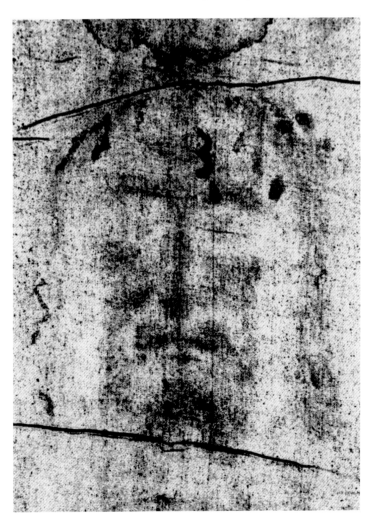

some 13 ft. 6 in. (410 cm) long and 4 ft. 6 in. (140 cm) wide, carries the ghostly image of a long-haired, bearded man, both his front and back. His hands are folded in front, and there is a suggestion of a wound in the right wrist. The image on the cloth is faint, but a negative image made from it reveals a portrait of the crucified Christ, similar to paintings made during the Middle Ages.

The authenticity of the shroud had been questioned many times during its history, but it was only in the twentieth century that scientists began to take an interest in the subject. In 1931, Dr. Pierre Barbet of the French Academy reported: "I saw that the images of the wounds were of a color quite different from that of the rest of the body, and this color was that of dried blood which had sunk into the stuff.... It is difficult for one unversed in painting to define the exact color, but the foundation was red, diluted more or less according to the wounds."

A SCIENTIFIC EXAMINATION

The church was naturally reluctant to allow more than a superficial examination of the relic. However, in November 1973 the shroud was exhibited for the first time on television and in color. At that time, small samples of the cloth were taken, together with two short lengths of thread. A Swiss forensic scientist was allowed to take 12 samples of dust, using adhesive tape, from the extreme frontal end of the cloth.

In October 1978, during a public exhibition of the shroud, threads from a "bloodstain" on the back of the image were taken, together with another 32 adhesive tape samples lifted from the cloth. These were delivered to Dr. Walter McCrone, an American expert in microscopy and microchemistry. In 1979 he reported that forensic tests did not indicate any evidence of blood and that the image revealed the use of two pigments, red ocher and

vermilion. He said, "Anybody who is emotionally wrapped up in the shroud should start to consider the possibility that he better relax his emotions."

SCORCHED BY RADIATION?

Finally, after years of argument and delay, in 1988 three laboratories, in Arizona, Oxford (England) and Zurich (Switzerland), submitted samples of the cloth to radiocarbon dating. In October of that year, the Roman Catholic Church officially announced the results: They indicated an approximate date of 1325 and certainly between 1260 and 1390. There seems little doubt that the shroud carries the residue of a painting by a medieval artist, made around the time it was first known to be in the possession of Geoffrey de Charny.

However, in January 2005, Raymond Rogers, a retired chemist from the Los Alamos National Laboratory, New Mexico, protested that the shroud was much older. He claimed that the carbon-dating was carried out only on the pieces of cloth used to patch the shroud in 1534, and that

chemical analysis suggested that the main fabric was 1,300 to 3,000 years old.

Only one thing is certain. Wrapping it around Christ's body could not have produced the image on the shroud. Viewed fully frontally—as in a portrait—the average apparent width of the human face is some six inches. But the surface distance from ear to ear is ten inches or more. British artist Robert Hunt demonstrated this very simply. He covered his young daughter's body and face with poster paint and wrapped her in a sheet. The resultant print of an extremely fat girl was, as he said, "completely unrecognizable." And the ghostly image on the Turin shroud is, if anything, even narrower than average.

In answer to this criticism, some enthusiasts have proposed that the shroud was not wrapped around Christ's body but in some way was stretched horizontally above and below it and that a sudden flash of intense radiation produced the image like a scorch mark. However, this does not explain how the top of the head, on the frontal image, is almost touching the head of the image of the back.

Some 140,000 people filed through San Giovanni Cathedral in Turin when the shroud was put on public display in September 1978. Threads and other samples were taken at this time for scientific analysis. It can be seen that the front and back body images touch at the head—impossible if they had been produced while the shroud was wrapped over a body.

CHAPTER 8
SUSPECT SCIENCE

For many centuries charlatans have flourished on the fringes of the medical profession, promising expensive "miracle cures" for a variety of common diseases.

Nearly everybody is concerned about the state of his or her health, and many people can be easily persuaded by a soft-spoken physician in a white coat. Many fake doctors, from snake-oil merchants at country fairs to seemingly reputable physicians, have profited by the credulity of their victims. With the development of legitimate science, they have adopted a smattering of technical terms that can confuse and persuade the man on the street to accept even the most outrageous claims. More serious, however, is when a qualified scientist fakes the results of his experiments for professional or financial gain.

Opposite: A male midwife toad—actually a species of frog. It carries the fertilized eggs between its hind legs.

Left: Paul Kammerer, who committed suicide after it was revealed that he had faked the results of his experiments with the toad.

Dr. Franz Anton Mesmer, whose concept of "animal magnetism" was dismissed by an investigating commission that included Benjamin Franklin.

found new followers among "alternative health" practitioners. Mesmer was also responsible almost accidentally for what was at first called "mesmerism" and is today known as hypnotism.

Born in southern Germany, Dr. Mesmer earned his degree in Vienna in 1766. He established a medical practice, but marriage to a rich widow gave him plenty of time for experiments. He began treating patients with physical problems, using two large magnets, one above and one below the afflicted body part. His original theory was that a magnetic field could, in some way, "harmonize" with the natural flow of the body.

BIZARRE METHODS

Mesmer continued his experiments. He used all kinds of objects that he believed to be magnetized in some way, even clothing and beds. He invented the *baquet*, a tub filled with iron filings and powdered glass. Iron rods protruding from the lid of the tub were bent at right angles so that a number of patients could place the rods against painful areas while holding hands to complete the flow of the "magnetic fluid."

Mesmer then discovered that magnetized objects were unnecessary. He could achieve the same results by gently stroking the patient, following the direction of the nerves. He called this "animal magnetism" and wrote: "It is not a secret remedy, and I wish to train medical men in my methods."

But Mesmer was derided by the medical establishment in Vienna—as was Franz Joseph Gall (1758–1828), a contemporary of Mesmer's who invented phrenology—and left for Paris. There, too, conventional physicians were antagonistic, but Mesmer

MAGNETS AND MESMER

Electricity and magnetism became a popular obsession toward the end of the eighteenth century. Franz Anton Mesmer (1733–1815) was one of the first to apply the new discoveries to medicine. The theories he proposed to explain his treatments do not stand up to scrutiny, and even in his own time Mesmer was regarded by the medical profession as a fraud. However, magnetic therapy has recently gained a popular following. Unfortunately, his sense of drama overwhelmed his sense of propriety, and he began to hold healing sessions dressed in a flowing magician's robe. The government decided to appoint a commission to look into his claims. The panel included Benjamin Franklin (a pioneer in the study of electricity), Antoine Lavoisier (France's leading chemist) and Dr. Joseph Guillotin, after whom the guillotine had been named. They reported that Mesmer had undoubtedly effected many cures, but they dismissed the concept of animal magnetism.

As a result, Mesmer lost his flourishing practice. When the French Revolution broke out in 1789, he left France and retired to Switzerland. In 1814 he moved to a village near his birthplace and died there the following year.

Hypnotism, as we now know it, was discovered by one of Mesmer's followers, the Marquis de Puysgur. Attempting a treatment by animal magnetism, he stroked a young boy's head and was surprised to find that the boy fell into a trance—a trance in which he would still obey commands. The same technique has proved of considerable value in modern psychological treatment.

ELECTRIC MEDICINE

Childless couples make easy targets for quacks who promise a sure treatment for infertility. They are even more likely to be persuaded if assured that the children will be "beings rational and far stronger and more beautiful in mental, as well as bodily, endowment than the present puny, feeble and nonsensical race."

This was the claim of James Graham (1745–1794), who enjoyed fame and fortune for only a few years with his "electric medicine." He was born in Edinburgh, Scotland, where he went to medical school. No record exists of his having graduated, but Graham called himself "Doctor" for the rest of his life.

During the early 1770s, Graham went to America, where he met Benjamin Franklin and learned of his experiments with electricity. Returning to Britain in 1774, Graham set himself up, initially in the west of England, and began to advertise his miraculous cures. He soon attracted a

Mesmer's *baquet* (tub), which provided a fashionable method of curing ailments in late-eighteenth-century Vienna. One man, supported by his crutch, can be seen placing his leg against one of the protruding iron rods.

wealthy and famous clientele and in 1779 relocated to London, where he opened an opulent "Temple of Health." Here Graham installed his "magnetic throne" and "electrical bathtub," and dispensed his "famous aetherial and balsamic medicine."

For a fee of two guineas, prospective patients and idle visitors could stroll through ten richly decorated and furnished salons, inspect Graham's electrical apparatus and listen to his lectures. To the constant sound of music, scantily clad young women posed among the classical sculptures. It has been alleged that one was Emma Lyon, later the notorious wife of Sir William Hamilton and the lover of Admiral Horatio Nelson.

THE CELESTIAL BED

A separate door led to a lavish chamber, designed to look like a Turkish harem, in which Graham installed his Grand Celestial Bed. It was 12 ft. (3.6 m) long and 9 ft. (2.7 m) wide and supported by 40 pillars of colored glass. Graham advertised that couples who spent the night—for a fee of at least £50—would be "blessed with progeny."

> **For a fee of two guineas, prospective patients and idle visitors could stroll through ten richly decorated and furnished salons, inspect Graham's electrical apparatus and listen to his lectures.**

The air was sweet with perfume, mechanical players made music and a huge mirror above the bed reflected the activities below.

The mattress was "filled with sweet new wheat or oat straw, mingled with balm, rose leaves, and lavender flowers"; or, alternatively, with "the strongest, most

springy hair, procured at vast expense from the tails of English stallions." The bed was linked to three-quarters of a ton of magnets, wired together, and the message "Be fruitful. Multiply and Replenish the Earth" was inscribed on the headboard.

IMPROPER DISCUSSIONS

For a time the Temple of Health was a resounding success. Then, for some reason—possibly declining income—Graham moved to nearby Pall Mall and opened a Temple of Hymen, at which prices were lower. By 1782, however, he was deeply in debt, and he returned to Edinburgh the following year. His plainspoken lectures "On the means of exciting and rendering permanent the rational, temperate and serene pleasures of the married state" caused a scandal, and magistrates fined him for "improper discussions."

Graham now abandoned his electrical theories and declared that people could obtain all the nutrients they needed by taking "earth baths," which would allow them to live for 150 years. He also preached abstention from meat and alcohol, extolled the virtues of cold baths and open windows and refused to wear woolen clothing. At last Graham "got religion," founded the New Jerusalem Church—of which he was the only member—and began signing his letters "Servant of the Lord. O.W.L." [Oh, Wonderful Love]. He died of a burst blood vessel in 1794.

THE POWER OF THE ETHER

In the second half of the nineteenth century, physicists accepted that light was wave motion, but they believed that the waves—like waves in water or sound—had to be transmitted through a medium of some kind. This was named the "luminiferous ether," and numerous experiments were devised in an attempt to detect its existence. It was not until the early years of the twentieth

century—in particular, following the publication of Einstein's theory of relativity—that it was finally agreed that the "ether" did not exist and was unnecessary for the propagation of light waves.

In 1872, therefore, when John Worrell Keely (1837–1896) announced that he had discovered a way of exploiting "etheric energy," there were many who believed him. A Philadelphia jobbing carpenter and mechanic, he launched the Keely Motor Company in New York and soon raised $1 million worth of capital from wealthy financiers. In 1874, Keely demonstrated his "etheric generator" to astounded audiences in Philadelphia. He poured five gallons (19 l) of water into the machine, and very soon a pressure gauge read 10,000 lb. per sq. in. The water, said Keely, had been converted into ether, generating power that would supersede all other known forms of power. A quart of water could propel a steam train from Philadelphia to San Francisco and back; a gallon was sufficient to send a steamship to and from Liverpool. "A bucket of water has enough of this vapor to produce a power sufficient to move the world out of its course."

A spectator reported: "Great ropes were torn apart, iron bars broken in two or twisted out of shape, bullets discharged through 12-inch planks, by a force which could not be determined."

SYMPATHETIC EQUILIBRIUM

Keely maintained that musical frequencies could resonate with atoms or with the ether itself. His "hydro-pneumatic pulsating vacuo-engine" was attached to a "liberator," a complex of brass wires, tubing and tuning forks. He frequently used a musical instrument—a violin, harmonica or zither—to set it in motion. He spoke of "sympathetic equilibrium," "quadrupole negative

After returning to his hometown of Edinburgh in 1783, James Graham (second from left) introduced the use of "earth baths" for curative and rejuvenative treatments.

John Worrell Keely (seated) with the only part of his "etheric generator" that he allowed the public to see. It was not until after his death that an investigation revealed the true source of its power.

harmonics" and "etheric disintegration."

Keely wrote: "With our present knowledge, no definition can be given of the latent force that, possessing all the conditions of attraction and repulsion associated with it, is free of magnetism. If it is a condition of electricity, robbed of all electrical phenomena or a magnetic force repellent to the phenomena associated with magnetic development, the only conclusion I can arrive at is that this indefinable element is the soul of matter."

However, as Keely continued with adjustments and refinements of his apparatus, investors gradually lost interest. He was nearly bankrupt when the wealthy widow of a Philadelphia paper manufacturer, Mrs. Clara Bloomfield-Moore, offered him support. Keely reluctantly agreed to let experts observe his demonstrations, in which his machine lifted great weights or fired his "vaporic gun," but he refused to allow them detailed examination.

In March 1884, Keely announced that the development of his motor was nearly completed. But it remained unfinished. When he died in 1898, it had already been dismantled by others who had hoped to discover its secrets, but nobody could make it work. Finally, the building in which it had been housed was torn apart. In false ceilings and walls, investigators found drive belts linked to a silent motor in the basement and controlled by pneumatic switches under the floor. A system of pipes was found inside false beams, and in the basement there was also a three-ton sphere, a reservoir for compressed air. This was obviously the source of Keely's "etheric power." His fraud was revealed.

What is remarkable is that there are still people who believe that Keely had made a revolutionary discovery. An Internet site called KeelyNet is devoted to promulgating his theories, and many other sites discuss his "sympathetic vibratory physics."

MAGIC BLACK BOXES

With the discovery of the wave motion of light—soon followed by radio waves, X-rays and early theories about the structure of the atom—quite a number of people began to suggest, as had Keely, that all matter had a natural vibration that could be "tuned into." Dr. Albert Abrams (1863–1924) made a considerable fortune by exploiting this belief.

Born in San Francisco, California, Abrams earned his first degree at the University of Heidelberg, Germany, in 1882, and later studied in Berlin, Vienna, London and Paris. Returning to the United States,

Dr. Albert Abrams in 1921, with some of the equipment he assembled in developing the "electronic reaction of Abrams." In the foreground is his Dynamizer, and the metronome is presumably necessary for tuning the Oscilloclast.

Sir Peter Medawar (1917–1987) won the Nobel Prize in 1960 for work on immunological tolerance to skin and organ transplants. He once wrote: "Among scientists are collectors, classifiers, and compulsive tidiers-up; many are detectives and many are explorers. There are poet-scientists and philosopher-scientists, and even a few mystics." Later he remarked that he was sorry he had not added "...and a few crooks."

he was appointed head of the medical clinic at Cooper Medical College in his home city and for more than 20 years led the life of a well-respected physician.

In 1910, Dr. Abrams came up with a new treatment that he called "spondylotherapy." It consisted of tapping the spine and was really no more than a combination of existing chiropractic and osteopathy; but Abrams was able to tour the country giving instruction courses at $200 apiece, and he published a profitable book on the subject.

STRIP TO THE WAIST
AND FACE WEST

With this success behind him, Abrams announced the development of an apparatus, the "Dynamizer," that would enable him to diagnose patients anywhere in the world—without moving from his office in California. All he required was a drop of the patient's blood on blotting paper. Abrams explained this by saying that every disease had its characteristic "vibratory rate," which his equipment could identify.

Diagnosis required a healthy volunteer, one who stood stripped to the waist facing west in a dim light. A wire from Abrams's apparatus led to a metal plate on the volunteer's forehead. After the blood sample had been placed in the machine, the doctor tapped the healthy person's abdomen, searching for "areas of dullness" that indicated the disease from which the patient was suffering. In due course Abrams decided that even a blood sample was unnecessary; the patient's signature would do.

Around 1920 he announced the discovery of ERA—the "electronic reaction of Abrams." Disease, he said, came from a disharmony of electronic oscillation; "specific drugs must have the same vibratory rate as the diseases against which they are effective. That is why they cure." He had invented a machine that would produce the necessary vibration for any disease, without the need for drugs. He called it the "Oscilloclast."

THE ABRAMS ELECTRONIC
ASSEMBLY

Quite a few reputable physicians, as well as many quacks, invested in the Abrams Electronic Assembly. The equipment was not sold but leased, each item at $250 a year. The working parts were in a sealed box, and the lessee had to sign an agreement never to open it. By 1923, Abrams had distributed an estimated 3,500 dynamizers and Oscilloclasts. A lessee could take in up to $2,000 a week for treatments, and Abrams's personal fortune was calculated to have grown to more than $2 million.

For some time the American Medical Association (AMA) had been viewing these developments with disquiet. One day Dr. Abrams received a blood sample from a physician in Chesaning, Michigan, with a request for a diagnosis. He reported that the patient was suffering from diabetes, malaria, cancer and two social diseases. The Chesaning physician sent this diagnosis to the AMA; the "patient," he explained, was a healthy Young Plymouth Rock rooster. Another skeptic sent two separate samples of blood from a single male guinea pig; "Miss Bell" learned that she had cancer and a sinus infection; a "Mrs. Jones" had a skin ailment and stomach trouble.

Dr. Abrams at work with his Dynamizer. By tapping the volunteer's abdomen, Abrams claimed to be able to diagnose the diseases from which another patient was suffering.

In the fall of 1923, the magazine *Scientific American* gathered a panel of experts and arranged for one of the Oscilloclast boxes to be opened. It contained a condenser, a rheostat, an ohmmeter and a magnetic interrupter, all neatly wired up but without any apparent function. "At its best," the panel concluded, "it is all an illusion. At worst, it is a colossal fraud."

Only a few months after this, Dr. Abrams fell ill with pneumonia. The Oscilloclast could do nothing for him, and he died.

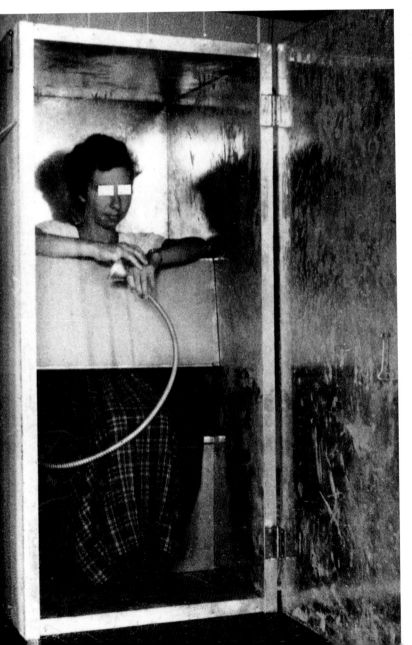

William Reich's Orgone Energy Accumulator. The wooden casing absorbed "orgone" from the air, and the metal lining radiated it onto the person sitting inside.

40107? YOU'RE SUFFERING FROM UNREQUITED LOVE!

Some 20 years later a British civil engineer, George de la Warr (1905–1969), took up the idea of the Abrams Electronic Assembly and modified it. His black box was covered in artificial leather, with chrome trim; along its front was a row of Bakelite dials, and there were two wells for samples of the blood or hair of the patient. It differed from the Dynamizer in that there was no tapping of the abdomen. Instead, the operator slid his or her finger over a rubber diaphragm until it finally stuck at some point. Inside the box there was nothing except a wire running from dial to dial and finally to the sample wells.

> "At its best, it [Abrams's Oscilloclast] is all an illusion. At worst, it is a colossal fraud."
> —*SCIENTIFIC AMERICAN*, 1923

The stated function of the dials was to alter the effective length of the wire. The operator moved each in turn, noting the setting at which the "stick" was reached. A *Guide to Clinical Condition* was provided with each box sold so that a diagnosis could be made. A setting of 907, for example, denoted a fracture, and 80799, a bruise. Poison was indicated by 700457, a virus by 97964 and "pericardial effusion" by 60682587. Psychological conditions could also be diagnosed: "vanity" at 50413, "thoughtfulness" at 40421 and "unrequited love" at 40107!

De la Warr followed up this diagnostic box with a slightly smaller treatment box, which was similar in appearance and had no apparent source of power. Having arrived at a diagnosis, the operator looked up the

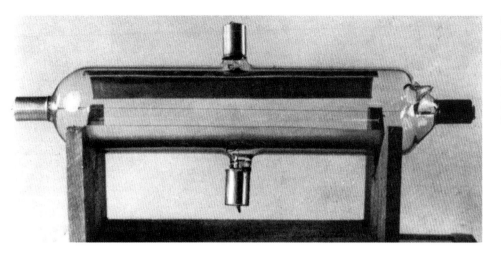

ailment's "broadcast treatment rate" and set the dials appropriately. That was all. It was not even necessary to tell the patient that he or she was being cured by this "treatment."

During the 1950s, hundreds of these "radionic" boxes were sold at £100 apiece, not only in Britain but throughout the world. In addition, de la Warr and his wife carried on a lucrative private diagnostic practice. Then, in June 1960, a case was brought before the high court in London.

CHARGES AGAINST DE LA WARR
The plaintiff charged that George de la Warr was "an exponent of and practitioner in the pseudoscience of radionics and that in 1956 he fraudulently represented that there were associated substances, distinctive waves, vibrations or radiations capable of affecting a device of the defendant called a 'Delawarr Diagnostic Instrument.'"

In summing up at the end of the hearing, the judge pointed out that no witnesses for the defense had attempted to claim that they knew how the box worked, only that it sometimes worked. He was satisfied that de la Warr honestly believed in his invention and had had no fraudulent intention. He therefore found for the defendant.

However, the de la Warrs had to pay the costs of their defense. The judge's other comments made it clear that he had grave doubts about the working of the de la Warr apparatus, and these reservations did not encourage investors to finance further development. The result hit the de la Warrs very hard, and by the time of George's death in 1969, manufacture of the instruments had almost ceased.

THE ORGONE ACCUMULATOR
After he graduated with a medical degree in Vienna in 1922, Austrian-born Wilhelm Reich (1897–1957) was considered one of the most brilliant pupils of psychoanalyst Sigmund Freud (1856–1939). Reich was convinced of the importance of intense sexual activity. His books *The Function of the Orgasm* (1927) and *The Mass Psychology of Fascism* (1933) provoked an interest in the connection between sexual liberation and politics.

Escaping from the Nazis to the United States in 1939, Reich announced that he had discovered an electrochemical substance essential to sexual energy; he named it "orgone." It came originally from the sun and was present in the air, water and all organic matter. Orgone, he said, was blue; this explained why sitting in the sun under a blue sky produced a feeling of well-being.

Reich, however, realized that this was a

"**W**hatever you have done to me or will do to me in the future, whether you glorify me as a genius or put me in a mental institution, whether you adore me as your savior or hang me as a spy, sooner or later necessity will force you to understand that I have discovered the laws of the living." —Wilhelm Reich, *Little Man* (1949)

The aging Wilhelm Reich, who died in prison in 1957.

slow way of absorbing orgone, so he invented his Orgone Accumulator. This was a box, about 3 ft. (90 cm) square, with an outer casing of wood and an inner layer of sheet metal. The organic material supposedly absorbed orgone from the air, after which it was radiated by the metal lining to a person sitting inside the box. Reich's Institute of Orgonomy also developed an orgone blanket—made of alternate layers of wool and steel—for the bedridden, and miniature devices called "shooters," which could be placed against areas of the body suffering pain.

THE FDA TAKES NOTICE

While manufacturing and selling his Orgone Accumulators, Reich discovered the existence of "bions," microscopic "life essence" particles of the same size as bacteria—although he and his followers were the only ones able to detect them. This claim attracted the attention of the Food and Drug Administration (FDA), which in 1954 carried out an investigation. It concluded that orgone did not exist and that the accumulators were useless in the treatment of disease.

An injunction was issued against Reich, forbidding him to ship his boxes or literature across state lines. In keeping with his combative character, Reich ignored the injunction, and in May 1956 he stood trial in Portland, Maine. He received a two-year sentence and was fined $10,000. Reich appealed and was released on bail, and at once set about developing an orgone rainmaker and an orgone energy motor. However, the appeal failed, and he entered the Federal Penitentiary at Lewisburg, Pennsylvania, where, after less than a year, he died.

FAKING THE RESULTS

Many of the "scientific" inventions brought to the market can be laughable when they are properly investigated. It is much more serious, however, when a qualified scientist deliberately fakes the results of his experiments.

THE CONFLICTING THEORIES OF LAMARCK AND DARWIN

Why is there such diversity among living species? The French naturalist Jean Baptiste Lamarck (1744–1829) put forward a theory that explained this. Many generations ago a giraffe, for example, had a short neck like other animals. Reaching upward to graze on the higher leaves of trees, it stretched its neck—and its offspring inherited this characteristic. Progressively, generation after generation, the giraffe's neck became longer and longer. It was an attractive theory, and many people believed in it for a century.

The implications are disturbing. If you are a weight lifter, for example, your children will have well-developed muscles. So, if the Lamarckian theory of inherited characteristics were true, it would be possible to breed a race of superhumans.

The opposing theory of evolution put forward by Charles Darwin (1809–1882) seemed to put an end to Lamarckism. Darwin's theory implied that the emergence of a species occurred solely as the result of a genetic accident. If a genetic characteristic proved to be advantageous, it was transmitted to succeeding generations by the "survival of the fittest," but only from an accidental cause. For want of a better term, Darwin called this "natural selection." Further research and refinement of

Darwin's theory have since swept aside the theories of Lamarck.

THE MIDWIFE TOAD

Paul Kammerer was born in Vienna in 1880. He intended to take up a musical career but instead earned a doctorate in biology in 1904. However, he became notorious for faking the results of scientific experiments with the so-called midwife toad.

Kammerer's experiments began with two species of salamander. The black salamander comes from the Alps and gives birth on land to two fully formed offspring. The spotted salamander lives in damp lowlands; it gives birth in water to up to 50 tadpoles, which later develop into adults.

Kammerer forced the black species to breed in warm, moist conditions and the spotted species in cold and dry. After several

Austrian scientist Dr. Paul Kammerer. He performed experiments intended to demonstrate the validity of Lamarck's theories.

unsuccessful births the black salamanders produced tadpoles in water, and the spotted salamanders gave birth to two fully developed young. Kammerer then bred from these and demonstrated that the offspring seemed to have inherited from their parents the characteristic of giving birth to fully developed young.

Later he turned his attention to the midwife toad (see below). He kept his specimens in a tank of water, forcing them to mate in the wet and, after several generations, claimed they had developed a rough pigmented area on their hands, typical of other frogs. His experiments caused controversy in scientific circles around the world. Doubts were raised. One of his laboratory assistants admitted that his records were fragmentary. Alma Mahler (widow of Austrian composer Gustav Mahler), who had been hired by Kammerer after her husband's death in 1911, said he would have preferred "slightly less exact records, with positive results" than those she had made.

"SUCCESS WHERE DARWIN MET FAILURE!"

During World War I, Kammerer was forced to give up his laboratory work. He set out on a lecture circuit, with just one dead specimen of toad to display. In America the press hailed him as a genius: "Scientist tells of success where Darwin met failure!" However, in August 1926, Dr. G. Kingsley Noble, curator of reptiles at the American Museum of Natural History, published a paper in the British scientific journal *Nature*. He announced that examination of the dark pad revealed that it contained India ink. It was not naturally rough, but seemed to have been artificially altered to appear so—perhaps by transplanting skin from another species.

FORGER'S FILE
WHAT MADE KAMMERER'S MIDWIFE TOAD SO SPECIAL?

The midwife toad is really a member of the frog family, but its behavior is very different from that of other frogs. Mating takes place on dry land, with the male holding the female with his front legs. He winds the fertilized eggs around his hind legs and incubates them. When they are ready to hatch, he enters the water and waits there until all the tadpoles have emerged. Hence the frog's name. Other species of frogs mate in water and have a rough, dark area on the palm of the hand so they can grasp the slippery female. The midwife toad's palm is smooth.

Kammerer protested that this was not his doing, but his reputation was ruined. On September 22, 1926, he wrote that he hoped to summon up "enough courage and strength to put an end to my wrecked life." The next morning, on a hillside outside Vienna, he put a bullet through his head.

MARXIST MYTH

Shortly before his death, Kammerer had been offered a post as head of a biology department at Moscow University. Lamarckism fitted in with Marxist philosophy, in particular the belief that improvement of the social environment would improve the human breed. Trofim Denisovich Lysenko (1898–1976) followed in Kammerer's footsteps, with the approval of Russian dictator Joseph Stalin. Russian agriculturists had already experimented with "vernalization," which consisted of soaking and chilling the seeds of winter wheat so that they could be planted in the spring rather than the fall, and so give a higher yield. Lysenko applied this method to other crops and soon rose to be head of the Moscow Institute of Genetics.

Ironically, he denied the existence of genes. He spoke of "the unity of the organism with its environment" and later claimed that wheat plants raised in the right conditions would yield seeds of rye. Those who opposed his theories soon found themselves in prison. For more than 30 years Lysenko was a dictator in his own field.

A LOAD OF BULL

After Stalin's death in 1953, Nikita Khrushchev emerged as Russian leader and continued official support for Lysenko. Khrushchev was deposed in 1964, and in 1965 an official inquiry team investigated the most recent of Lysenko's claims. At an experimental farm large domestic cows were being crossed with Jersey bulls, which Lysenko maintained resulted in a dramatic increase in butterfat in the milk of their offspring. Investigators discovered that the results had been deliberately falsified. The cows had been specially selected and given a rich diet. But while their milk was certainly high in butterfat,

The Russian crop and animal breeder Trofim Denisovich Lysenko, whose Lamarckian theories gained the full support of dictator Joseph Stalin and were not finally discredited until 1965.

they produced less milk than normal cows.

Orthodox geneticists greeted the report's publication with delight all over the world, and Lysenko was finally discredited.

OF MOUSE AND MAN

In the years following World War II, many researchers turned their attention to the problems of grafting skin and transplanting organs. Because the function of the body's immune system is to detect and destroy foreign cells of any kind, it will reject tissue other than its own or that of a closely related donor. In 1970, Dr. William T.

After serving for two years in the U.S. Army's burn treatment unit, Dr. William Summerlin undertook research in dermatology at Stanford University in California. Here, colleagues watch as a piece of skin for grafting is removed from nutrient solution.

Summerlin (born 1938) believed he had found a way to overcome this. His story is similar to that of Paul Kammerer.

After graduating and serving his internship, Summerlin spent two years in the U.S. Army's burn treatment unit at Brooke Medical Center near San Antonio, Texas. He then went to Stanford University in Palo Alto, California, to undertake research in dermatology. In 1969 he discovered that if he kept skin in a nutrient solution for several weeks before grafting it, there was less likelihood of rejection. In fact, it was reported that he even succeeded in grafting white skin on a black patient.

Colleagues began to question the results of some of Summerlin's experiments, which they found impossible to replicate.

Reports of his success made Summerlin an instant celebrity in his field, and in 1973 he was invited to join the distinguished pathologist Dr. Robert Good, who had just been appointed director of the Sloan-Kettering Institute in New York City. Summerlin's research was of great importance, not only in regard to tissue rejection but also in the study of cancer.

Quite soon after Summerlin's arrival at Sloan-Kettering, colleagues began to question the results of some of his experiments, which they found impossible to replicate. He claimed to have transplanted adrenal glands in some of his laboratory animals and to have transferred human-eye corneas to rabbits. He claimed that the rabbits with one cloudy eye were showing signs of rejection; those with a clear eye represented a successful transplant. But fellow workers began to doubt whether the clear eye had ever received a corneal graft.

ANOTHER TOUCH OF BLACK INK

Part of Summerlin's research involved grafting skin from black mice to white mice, and on the morning of March 26, 1974, he had an appointment with Dr. Good to discuss the progress of his work. Taking some of his mice with him, he took the elevator and on the way noticed that the black patches on his white mice had faded. Taking out a black felt-tipped pen, he gently touched them up—and so destroyed his research career.

In fact, Dr. Good barely glanced at the mice. When he left the meeting, Summerlin carried them back to his laboratory and handed them to his senior assistant. The assistant immediately noticed that the patches had been darkened and quickly

confirmed it with a swab of alcohol. Word of this spread quickly and reached Dr. Good before the end of the morning. Summerlin was instantly suspended and subsequently dismissed. He retired to take up local medical practices in Louisiana and Arkansas.

One other revealing fact emerged in the aftermath of the affair. Summerlin had brought to Sloan-Kettering the only skin-grafted mouse ever to survive for more than six months; it was known as "Old Man." It turned out that Old Man was genetically related to the mouse from which the graft had come—making it far less likely that tissue rejection could have taken place and therefore invalidating much, if not all, of Summerlin's work.

Dr. Robert A. Good was Summerlin's supervisor at the Sloan-Kettering Institute, New York. On learning that Summerlin had colored skin grafts on laboratory mice, Dr. Good immediately suspended him.

INDEX

Captions to pictures are denoted by *italic* page numbers.

dyes 54, 116
Dynamizer *241*, 242–3

E

earth baths 238, *239*
Eaton, Robert *123*, 124
eBay 182
Edward IV 169
"Edward VI" 169
Eiffel Tower 205–6, *209*, 212
Elderly Man in a Cap
  (Rembrandt) *46*
electricity 237–8
Eliot, George 106
Elizabeth I *98*, 100
Emerson, Ralph Waldo 153
Emmaus 69–71
Endymion (Keats) 95
engraving banknote plates 21–2
Enigma program 217
*Enquiry into the Nature of
  Pamphlets* (Carter) 108
Erie Railroad *196*, 198
escudos *32*
ESDA (electronic static detection
  apparatus) 120–1
esparto 107
etchings 54–5
ether 238–41
Etruscan art *77*, 78
Europa in Gefahr 219
euros *9*, 12, 13, *23*
Eusebius of Caesarea *90*, 91
evolution 140, 247

F

F for Fake (movie) 83
Facsimiles (Simonides) 102
fairies *215*, 225–7, *229*
Fake? (exhibition) 48
Fake! (Irving) 83, 121, 122
Fake's Progress (Keating) 73
False Prince (movie) 185
fascism 245
FBI 61
Fifth Amendment 118
Fingal (Macpherson) 93
Fioravanti, Alberto 77
first editions 105–7
First Interstate Bancorp,
  LA 25
Fisk, James *196*
flax 222
Fleming, Ian 106
Flint Jack 139, 148–9, *150*
Florence 49, 57
fluorescence 62, 63
Flying (magazine) 109
Flynn, William 136
Fontenay, Fr. 92
Forman, H. Buxton 106–7
Formosa 91–2
Forsyth, Frederick 180
Fortune and Men's Eyes
  (Ganzel) 101

fossils 149–53
Foster, Joe 119
Fournier, François 29
Fox sisters 228
foxing 136
Fradin, Emile 146
Fragments of Ancient Poetry
  (Macpherson) 93
France 15, 33, 219
Franklin, Benjamin *27*, 108, 109,
  110, 237
Freemasons 216
Freer Gallery (Washington) 75
French Academy 102
Freppa, Giovanni 49
Freud, Sigmund 245
Frick Gallery (New York) 51
Function of the Orgasm
  (Reich) 245
Furguson, Arthur 209–12
furniture *55*

G

Gall, Franz Joesph 236–7
Gallerie Koller (Zurich) 61
Gallery Muse (Tokyo) 61
Galilei, Galileo *104*
Ganzel, Dewey 101
Gardner, Edward 225
Gauguin, Paul 59, 60–1
gender 155–60
genetics 249–50
George V 223
Géricault, Jean-Louis *52*
Germany 28–9, 218–25
Getty Museum 57
Ghiberti, Lorenzo 85
Ghirlandaio, Domenico 44
Giacometti, Alberto 87
giants 149–53
Gibbons, Stanley 28
Ginsburg, Christian 144
Giorgioni, Barbarelli 85
glass kilns 146–7
Gleizes, Albert 75
Glozel 146–7, *148*
Goering, Hermann 71, 128
Gokhman, Schapshelle 144
gold coins 10, 12–13, 33
gold standard 33
Good, Dr. Robert 250, 251
Gordon-Gordon, Lord 196–9
Gould, Jay *196*, 198, *199*
government bonds 205
government forgeries 217
Goya, Francisco 73
Graham, James 237–8, *239*
Grant, Ulysses S. 199
Grassi, Luigi 85
Graves, Philip 216
Greece 9
Greeley, Horace 196, *197*
Greppa, Giovanni 49
Griffiths, Frances *215*, 225–7

"grifter" 212
Grüner & Jahr 128, 129, 130
Guillotin, Dr. Joseph 237

H

Hain, Guy 56, 75
Hamilton, Lady Emma 238
handwriting 118–20
Harris, Martin 132
Harrison, Shirley 113
Harry Potter (Rowling) *106*
Hartt, Frederick 57–9
Harvard University *86*
Hathaway, Anne 98
Hauser, Kaspar *155*
Hebborn, Eric 52, 71–2, 78
Hebrew script 143–4
Heidemann, Gerd 127–8
Heminge, John 98, 99
Henry VII 169
Hermitage Museum (St.
  Petersburg) *50*
Hess, Rudolf 127, 128
Hewitt, John 142
Hieron II 11
Hill, Sir Roland 27
Himmler, Heinrich 222, 223
History of English Dramatic Poetry
  (Collier) 100
Hitler, Adolph *118*, 220
Hitler Diaries 126–31
The Hoax (Irving) 127
Hodges, Dr. Andrew G. 120
Hofmann, Mark 131–7
Holland 71
Holmes, Dr. Oliver Wendell 153
Holmes, Sherlock 225
Holy Blood and the Holy Grail
  (Lincoln) 229
Home, John 93
Homer 101, 144
Honegger, Arthur 58
horse racing 211
Hory, Elmyr De 54
Hoskins, Cyril Henry *178*
Howe, Ellic 218–19, 220
Hughes, Howard 118, 121–6
Hughes Tool Company *122*, 124
Hull, George 149–53
Humbert, Frédéric 199–202
Humbert, Gustave 199, 200
Humphry Clinker 92
Hunt, Robert 233
Hunter, Joseph 100
Hussey, George 28
hypnotism 237

I

identities 154–93
identity theft 180–2
Iliad (Homer) 101, 144
India 9
infertility 237–8
infrared 62
inheritances 199–202

inks 113, 115–16, 136–7
Innes, William 92
Insitute of Contemporary Art
  (London) 87
intaglio 20, *21*, 38
International Anthropological
  Congress 147, *148*
Internet 182
Intertel 125
Ioni, Ilicio Federico 87
Iran 26
Ireland, Samuel 98
Ireland, William Henry *89*, 98–100
Irving, Clifford 83, 118, 121–6
Irving, David 130
Irving, Edith 124, 125–6
Is Anna Anderson Anastasia?
  (movie) 175
Italy 13, *19*, 29–30, 49–51
Ivan "the Terrible" 170

J

Jack the Ripper 111–14
Jackson, Andrew 108
Japan 9, 219
Jerusalem 229
Jesus Christ *90*, 91, 104, 230–3
Jeune Fille à la Mandoline
  (Laurençin) 61
Jews 216
Joan, Pope 159
John Lydgate (Rowley) 95
John VIII, Pope 159
Johnson, Dr. Samuel 92, 94
Jory, Stephen 24–5
Jubilee Stamp 223
Julius Caesar 104
Julius II, Pope 64
junk mail 182

K

Kammerer, Paul *235*, 247–9
Katin, Brian 37–8
Keating, Tom *41*, 73–7, 78
Keats, John 95, 105
Keely, John Worrell 239–41
Keith, Sir Arthur 142
Kelly, Jane 77
Kertsa, Lawrence 125
Khrushchev, Nikita 249
Kipling, Rudyard 107
Klein, Joe 119
Know Your Money (movie) 16
Korea 9
Krüger, Bernhard *215*, 222, 223
Kujau, Konrad "Konni" 126–31

L

Ladies' Home Journal 124
Laflin, John 109
Lagrange, Francis 66–7
Lamanites 133
Lamarck, Jean Baptiste 247
Last Days of Hitler
  (Trevor-Roper) 130

PHOTOGRAPHY AND ILLUSTRATION CREDITS